Archaeology, Conservation and the City: Post-Conflict Redevelopment in London, Berlin and Beirut

Caroline A. Sandes

BAR International Series 2159
2010

Published in 2016 by
BAR Publishing, Oxford

BAR International Series 2159

Archaeology, Conservation and the City: Post-Conflict Redevelopment in London, Berlin and Beirut

ISBN 978 1 4073 0701 5

© C A Sandes and the Publisher 2010

The author's moral rights under the 1988 UK Copyright,
Designs and Patents Act are hereby expressly asserted.

All rights reserved. No part of this work may be copied, reproduced, stored,
sold, distributed, scanned, saved in any form of digital format or transmitted
in any form digitally, without the written permission of the Publisher.

BAR Publishing is the trading name of British Archaeological Reports (Oxford) Ltd.
British Archaeological Reports was first incorporated in 1974 to publish the BAR
Series, International and British. In 1992 Hadrian Books Ltd became part of the BAR
group. This volume was originally published by Archaeopress in conjunction with
British Archaeological Reports (Oxford) Ltd / Hadrian Books Ltd, the Series principal
publisher, in 2010. This present volume is published by BAR Publishing, 2016.

Printed in England

BAR titles are available from:

        BAR Publishing
        122 Banbury Rd, Oxford, OX2 7BP, UK
EMAIL info@barpublishing.com
PHONE +44 (0)1865 310431
FAX   +44 (0)1865 316916
        www.barpublishing.com

Table of Contents

- Table of Contents ... 1
- List of Illustrations ... 2
- Preface and Acknowledgments ... 4

Chapter One: Introduction ... 5
- I. Introduction ... 5
- II: Research Aims and Questions ... 7
  - The values of urban archaeological sites conserved for display ... 7
  - Conservation of archaeological sites within the modern urban context ... 7
  - Conservation and the post-war city ... 8
  - Presentation and use of fragmentary archaeological sites ... 8
- III: Research methods ... 8
- V: Definitions and Research Layout ... 9

Chapter Two: Archaeology, Conservation and the City ... 11
- I. Introduction ... 11
- II. The Urban Context ... 11
- III. Conservation and Archaeology ... 15
  - Conservation and archaeology prior to World War II ... 16
  - Conservation and archaeology after World War II ... 18
- IV. Discussion ... 29

Chapter Three: London after World War II ... 31
- I. Introduction ... 31
- II: The Urban Context ... 31
- III: Conservation and Archaeology ... 32
  - Conservation and archaeology prior to World War II ... 32
  - Conservation and archaeology after World War II ... 34
- IV: The Sites ... 35
  - The City Wall ... 36
  - Temple of Mithras ... 43
  - Ruined Churches ... 44
- V. Discussion ... 49

Chapter Four: Berlin since World War II ... 51
- I. Introduction ... 51
- II: The Urban Context ... 51
  - The Urban Context 1945 to 1989 ... 51
  - The Urban Context since 1989 ... 56
- III: Conservation and Archaeology ... 57
  - Conservation and archaeology prior to World War II ... 57
  - Conservation and archaeology after World War II ... 58
  - Conservation and archaeology since 1989 ... 63
- IV: The Sites ... 65
  - Town Wall Sites ... 66
  - Ruined Church sites ... 67
  - Anhalter Bahnhof ... 68
  - Topography of Terror ... 69
  - The Berlin Wall ... 71
  - The Stadtschloss ... 74
  - The Grand Hotel Esplanade ... 75
- V: Discussion ... 75

Chapter Five: Beirut after the 1975-1990 War ... 78
- I. Introduction ... 78
- II: The Urban Context ... 78
- III: Conservation and Archaeology ... 84
  - Conservation and archaeology prior to 1990 ... 84
  - Conservation and archaeology from 1990 ... 86
- IV: The Sites ... 91
  - The Roman Baths ... 92
  - The Arcaded Building ... 92
  - The Souks ... 92
  - The Ottoman Harbour Wall ... 95

The Ancient Tell and Glacis 95
The Petit Serail Site 96
The Zone des Eglises or 'Garden of Forgiveness' or Hadiqat as-Samah 97
V: Discussion 98
Chapter 6: Discussion 100
I. Introduction 100
II. Values of Urban Conserved for Display Archaeological Sites 100
III. Conservation of Archaeological Sites in the Modern Urban Context 103
IV. Conservation and the Post-War City 105
V. Presentation and Use of Fragmentary Archaeological Sites 108
VI. Conclusion 109
References Cited 112
Primary Sources 112
Secondary Sources 112

List of Illustrations
(All illustrations author's own unless otherwise credited)
Figure 1: City Wall, St Alphage's Churchyard, London 5
Figure 2: Garden of Forgiveness, Beirut, as a street litter bin 5
Figure 3: St Alphage's Tower, London, with buddleia and evidence of decay 6
Figure 4: Old Town Warsaw, 1945 (http://commons.wikimedia.org/wiki/File:Old_Town_Warsaw_waf-2012-1501-31(1945).jpg) 7
Figure 5: Section of the Berlin Wall near Potsdamer Platz in 2004, but now removed, despite the exhortation of 'Don't Destroy History' 10
Figure 6: Postern Tower foundations, Tower Hill, London 22
Figure 7: Gable of the Great Hall, Bishop of Winchester's Palace, Southwark 22
Figure 8: Bastion 12, Barbican Estate, Cripplegate (photograph by Richard Phillips) 33
Figure 9: City of London: sites mentioned in the text (map by Xander Veldheijzen, after the City of London Corporation) 36
Figure 10: City Wall, St Alphage's Churchyard (south-facing side) 37
Figure 11: Bastion 14; Bastion 13 and site of Barber-Surgeon's Hall in centre background. 38
Figure 12: West Gate of the Roman Fort (photograph by Sarah McCarthy) 38
Figure 13: London Wall Walk sign for the West Gate 40
Figure 14: Noble Street City Wall site with tower foundations looking north 40
Figure 15: Bay 53: City Wall in London Wall Underground Car Park (photograph by Richard Phillips) 40
Figure 16: City Wall, Tower Hill 41
Figure 17: City Wall, Coopers Row 41
Figure 18: Temple of Mithras 44
Figure 19: The surviving tower of St Alban's, Wood Street 44
Figure 20: St Mary Aldermanbury 45
Figure 21: St Dunstan-in-the-East 45
Figure 22: Greyfriars Christchurch 46
Figure 23: St Alphage's Tower 49
Figure 24: The Reichstag after the allied bombing of Berlin, 3 June 1945. http://commons.wikimedia.org/wiki/File:Reichstag_after_the_allied_bombing_of_Berlin.jpg 51
Figure: 25: The Palast der Republik with the Fernsehtrum (Television Tower) behind. http://commons.wikimedia.org/wiki/File:Bundesarchiv_Bild_183-R0423-0026,_Berlin,_Palast_der_Republik,_Fernsehturm.jpg 53
Figure 26: Reconstructed Nikolai Quarter, and the Nikolaikirche 53
Figure 27: Kaiser-Wilhelm Gedächtniskirche with Eiermann's church behind and campanile 54
Figure 28: Kulturforum: Hans Sharoun's Philharmonic (Reichstag visible in left of centre background; Sony Center (Potsdamer Platz) to right) 55
Figure 29: Potsdamer Platz (with traffic light) http://commons.wikimedia.org/wiki/File:Potsdamer_Platz_2,_Berlin_1900.png 57
Figure 30: Looking towards Potsdamer Platz from the Kulturforum (Sony Center on left) 57
Figure 31: The Stadtschloss, c.1900. http://commons.wikimedia.org/wiki/File:Berlin,_Mitte,_Schloss_%26_Schlossbr%C3%BCcke,_1901.jpg 59
Figure 32: Surviving capitals from the Royal Palace, Klosterkirche garden 59
Figure 33: Marienkirche and the Television Tower 59
Figure 34: Dismantling the GDR's Palace of the Republic, 2007 64

Figure 35 : Dismantling of the Palace of the Republic, 2007. The banner reads 'A Project of Prestige – East Germany Asserts its Legitimacy' 64
Figure 36: Central Berlin: sites mentioned in the text (map by Xander Veldheijzen) 65
Figure 37: Berlin medieval town wall and its 1963 plaque 66
Figure 38: Remains of the 18th century Customs Wall, Berlin; ivy-clad reconstruction in background 66
Figure 39: Sign for Customs Wall 67
Figure 40: Entrance to Klosterkirche, 2007 67
Figure 41: Front of the Anhalter Bahnhof, c.1910 (Photograph by Waldemar Titzenthaler ;
http://commons.wikimedia.org/wiki/File:Anhalter_Bahnhof_und_Askanischer_Platz.jpg). 68
Figure 42: Surviving portion of the Anhalter Bahnhof façade 69
Figure 43: Former Gestapo Headquarters, 1949 (Photograph by Heinz Funck
http://commons.wikimedia.org/wiki/File:Bundesarchiv_Bild_183-S85918,_Berlin,_Prinz-Albrecht-
Stra%C3%9Fe,_zerst%C3%B6rtes_Gestapo-Geb%C3%A4ude.jpg) 69
Figure 44: Basements, Topography of Terror (Berlin Wall above) 71
Figure 45: Topography of Terror (Berlin Wall above) 71
Figure 46: Berlin Wall along Niederkirchnerstrasse (bordering the Topography of Terror site) 72
Figure 47: Bernauer Strasse Wall monument 73
Figure 48: *Mauer* (east-facing Wall) in the Invaliden-Cemetery, painted in the original colour scheme 74
Figure 49: Excavated foundations of the Stadtschloss 75
Figure 50: Half of the Esplanade's Breakfast Room behind glass in the Sony Centre 75
Figure 51: War damaged building south of the BCD, in 2005 78
Figure 52: Martyrs Square 2007 looking south: City Center Building to left of centre; Mohamad Al Amine Mosque with Rafiq Hariri's grave (white tent) to right 83
Figure 53: Roman remains originally discovered near Place de l'Etoile in 1926-27 85
Figure 54: Mosque Al Omari 86
Figure 55: BEY 045 going (photograph by Tony Howe) 90
Figure 56: BEY 045 gone (photograph by Tony Howe) 90
Figure 57: Central Beirut: sites mentioned in the text (map by Xander Veldheijzen) 91
Figure 58: Roman Baths 92
Figure 59: Souks 2005 looking northeast; ribat in righthand middle ground 93
Figure 60: Souks site: Mamluk Ribat, 2004 94
Figure 61: Tell site looking north-northwest 95
Figure 62: Hellenistic tower foundations to east of Tell site 95
Figure 63: Citadel Square 96
Figure 64: Petit Serail site, Martyrs Square 96
Figure 65: Garden of Forgiveness in 2007 97

PREFACE AND ACKNOWLEDGMENTS

As may be evident from the title, this research is broad rather than deep in its sweep. Its aim is to place the conservation of urban archaeological sites into the wider context of the modern city and it therefore also incorporates a wide range of other disciplines concerning the city, particularly within the post-war situation, and how these may affect urban archaeology and its conservation for display. These include urban planning and development, a variety of histories, socio-cultural theories and trends, and politics. To cover such a canvas, some deeply complex arguments/ideas have been only lightly sketched, and there are many ideas that warrant further discussion and development, so that while conclusions are reached, this research is perhaps best approached as research in progress.

During the course of this research, I have depended on a great deal of people for their invaluable help and advice. Firstly I wish to thank Gustav Milne and Tim Williams (both Institute of Archaeology, University College London). I would also like to thank Professor Helga Seeden, Department of History and Archaeology, American University of Beirut, for not only having me to stay during the periods that I was in Beirut, but also for her generosity and her invaluable assistance in many ways. Also in Beirut, I wish to thank the following for making time to speak to me and providing me with much vital information and insight: Catherine Aubert (archaeologist, IFAPO-Beirut); Joanne Farchakh Bajjaly (journalist and archaeologist); Dr Hans Curvers (archaeologist, Solidere); Fabrizio Fuccelli (former Heritage Project manager, Solidere); Angus Gavin (Solidere's Urban Development Division Head); Professor Helen Sader (Dept of History and Archaeology, AUB); Dr Robert Saliba (architect and urban planner); and Assaad Seif (archaeologist, Directorate General of Antiquities). Also for help with Beirut, I am very grateful to Dr Dominic Perring (Institute of Archaeology, UCL), Dr John Schofield (Museum of London) and Reuben Thorpe.

I am also extremely grateful to Dr Ulrike Sommer for her comments and criticisms on the Berlin Chapter, and Professor Clive Orton (both Institute of Archaeology, UCL) for his comments on the whole text.

I wish also to thank the UCL Alumni Association for generously awarding me their maximum scholarship amount in 2005 and 2006; the London Archaeological Research Facility for a bursary in 2004; University of London Central Research Fund and the Institute of Archaeology for grants towards the cost of my fieldwork trip to Beirut in 2005.

Lastly, I would like to thank my family and friends for their support and encouragement.

Illustration acknowledgements:
I am very grateful to Xander Veldheijzen for producing the maps for London, Berlin and Beirut. The London map is based on a similar map at http://www.cityoflondon.gov.uk/Corporation/maps/.
Illustrations that have come from Wikimedia Commons are either clear of copyright or are published under the following licences:
Figure 26: Palast der Republik: from Wikimedia Commons, http://commons.wikimedia.org reproduced under licence: http://creativecommons.org/licenses/by-sa/3.0/de/deed.en
Figure 43: Former Gestapo Headquarters, 1949. Photograph by Heinz Funck. http://commons.wikimedia.org/wiki/File:Bundesarchiv_Bild_183-S85918,_Berlin,_Prinz-Albrecht-Stra%C3%9Fe,_zerst%C3%B6rtes_Gestapo-Geb%C3%A4ude.jpg. Reproduced under licence http://creativecommons.org/licenses/by-sa/3.0/de/deed.en.

Figure 1: City Wall, St Alphage's Churchyard, London

CHAPTER ONE

INTRODUCTION

*'A vagrant wanders empty ruins.
Suddenly he's wealthy.'*[1]

I. INTRODUCTION

Amongst the modern buildings, the skyscrapers, the railways, the historic buildings, the parks and gardens and the myriad other components that make up many cities throughout the world, are sometimes conserved small or minor archaeological sites and architectural ruins (figure 1). In the author's own travels, such sites have been discovered in towns in Britain, Ireland, France, Germany, Italy, Tunisia, Syria, Lebanon, Australia and many others in between. What most of these urban sites have in common is a general air of neglect (figures 2-3). They are often surrounded by an insensitive or inappropriate context, strewn with litter, daubed with graffiti or growing weeds. If they have a sign at all, then it is often either damaged or says very little, or both. For each of these sites, however, a deliberate decision was made to conserve them because they were considered to have some sort of value worth saving. Furthermore, as demonstrated in this monograph, such decisions were often the result of protracted arguments, between archaeologists and urban developers, before the site was finally conserved. Why, then, after all that deliberation and negotiation, are these sites often left in such a sorry state?

Figure 2: Garden of Forgiveness, Beirut, as a street litter bin

The roots of this issue are to be found within problems concerning the conservation of the built heritage generally. In 2000, the Getty Conservation Institute published a research report, *Values and Heritage Conservation* (Avrami et al 2000). It explains that, while there has been considerable advances in applying a more holistic approach to conservation of cultural heritage, the tendency is still to focus on the challenges of conservation of the physical fabric only (Avrami et al

---
[1] From 'Unfold your own myth' by Mowlana Jalaluddin Rumi (1207-1273) published in C. Barks with J. Moyne (trans) 1999. *The Essential Rumi*: 41. London: Penguin.

2000, 4-5). The physical aspect is, however, only one of three equally important aspects of conservation; the other two are management context, and cultural significance and social values (Avrami *et al* 2000, 4). The report highlights that conservation is a *multi*disciplinary endeavour (Avrami *et al* 2000, 3; italics original) and goes on to stress that conservation 'cannot unify or advance with any real innovation or vision' if the non-technical complexities of conservation, the role it plays in modern society, and the social, economic, political and cultural mechanisms through which conservation works, are not better understood and articulated (Avrami *et al* 2000, 6). These issues remain a concern, as evident in a subsequent report of 2002 (Mason and Avrami 2002, 15, 19).

This research is concerned with these issues of cultural significance and social values, and management context, as they specifically relate to the conservation and presentation of fragmentary archaeological sites conserved in the modern urban context. The term 'fragmentary' may appear superfluous – archaeological sites are by their very nature fragmentary – but it is used here to differentiate such sites from major monuments, such as the Acropolis of Athens or Colosseum of Rome. These 'fragmentary' sites comprise individual pieces of surviving historic masonry, such as sections of town wall, or collections of low architectural foundations and building remains, or individual ruined buildings such as ruined churches, as exemplified in figures 1-3.

Figure 3: St Alphage's Tower, London, with buddleia and evidence of decay

The modern urban context is essentially the modern city that these sites are a part of. It is one of fast-paced change and, usually, perpetual growth and development. The magnitude of such growth and development of cities worldwide is evident in a recent United Nations Population Fund *State of World Population Report* (UNFPA 2007): in 2008 over half of the world's population, 3.3 billion people, was living in cities, and by 2030 this is estimated to reach almost five billion (UNFPA 2007, 1). The majority of this growth will be in African and Asian cities, presumably including the many important historic cities of those continents, but clearly the pressure on urban space worldwide, already very high, will become increasingly intense. The wide ranging physical and social implications of this growth and development were highlighted at an exhibition held at the Tate Modern, London, in 2007 entitled *Global Cities* (Tate Modern 2007). While concern for the environment, the implications of climate change and the issues of urban sustainability, are rightly at the forefront of much urban discussion and research now, as demonstrated by the UN's Habitat programme and the many university-based urban research projects, concern for the historic urban landscape even as a whole is often entirely absent. Consequently, the need to identify the importance of conservation of the cultural built heritage, particularly of the smaller sites and monuments, within the urban context is now paramount.

Fragmentary archaeological sites are most often discovered and conserved within the process of urban redevelopment. Urban redevelopment, however, is one of the greatest threats to the historic urban landscape, especially to archaeological sites and strata. The massive growth of cities in the twentieth century is set to continue and thus can only increase this threat. Consequently, the principal aim of this research is to identify the values and uses of fragmentary archaeological sites that have been conserved for display in the past in order that clearer criteria can be developed to ensure a more secure place for such sites within the modern city in the future.

Alongside population growth, another major catalyst of urban change and rapid redevelopment is war. Since World War I, cities have increasingly become the centres of warfare and World War II caused a record level of destruction of them (figure 4). As is evident in the case studies for this research, the devastation caused by war in London, Berlin and Beirut includes amongst its tragedies damage to historic buildings and exposure of archaeological sites, all of which were dealt with while attending to the crucial needs of rebuilding. In a city traumatised by war, however, the period of post-war redevelopment is often one of great socio-political and cultural sensitivities. The city must be rebuilt and organised to function again; socially, survivors must deal with a range of physical and emotional difficulties – for example lost loved ones, destroyed homes, trauma and other negative emotions. In fact it is the loss of relationships, dignity, trust, confidence and faith in others that can be the most detrimental to overall reconstruction in the long-term (Barakat 2005, 10). The physical remains of the past, both the distant and the immediate, and what they may be seen to represent, are therefore considered from a variety of often strong, sometimes conflicting points of view: questions of identity and continuity, the need to remember, the wish to forget. Within this context, there is a much wider need and extent of rebuilding meaning a greater exposure of archaeological strata that simultaneously represents an opportunity for research and a major threat to the survival not only of archaeological sites but also damaged historic buildings. Consequently not only are the dynamics of redevelopment more evident and concentrated, but so too are the arguments and reasoning for the conservation or destruction of sites and buildings.

Figure 4: Old Town Warsaw, 1945

Comparisons and contrasts are drawn for London, Berlin and Beirut and their respective post-war reconstruction to illustrate these themes. London was a victorious and comparatively socio-politically unified city at the end of World War II that has since completed its rebuilding, albeit only within the last decade. Berlin was a defeated and occupied city after World War II that was subsequently divided until 1990, when it has had to go through a complicated unification process and is now in what may be considered a second phase of post-war redevelopment. Beirut was also divided and was one of the main centres of fighting during Lebanon's long but inconclusive war between 1975 and 1990. Post-war redevelopment in Beirut is very much still in progress. Taken together, these three cities cover the period between World War II and today, and their post-war redevelopment and treatment of archaeology within that context provides a broad and contrasting range of the social, political, cultural and academic concerns of conservation.

II: RESEARCH AIMS AND QUESTIONS

The aim of this research is two-fold: firstly it aims to examine the wider historical context of urban archaeological conservation in the post-war situation, and secondly to identify more clearly the reasons and values behind the conservation of archaeological sites within the modern city. From this a clear criteria may be drawn up as to why such sites should or should not be conserved, and how they may best be considered and used in order that they may play an active and valuable role within the city. It is important to have such criteria relating to the valuing and decision-making regarding the conservation of sites so that the reasons for keeping such sites are more comprehensible to non-archaeologists, especially to the urban development professions, so that the sites' values may be better represented in their presentation.

In order to identify the values of fragmentary archaeological sites and related conservation criteria, this research is considered under four main themes. Each one considers a number of questions that are subsequently addressed using the case studies of London, Berlin and Beirut.

The values of urban archaeological sites conserved for display

1. *What kinds of site are conserved?* It is evident from sites visited, both in the past and as part of the research for this monograph, that how these sites are conserved and presented varies greatly, even within individual cities, giving the impression that sites are conserved in an ad hoc or extemporized site-by-site fashion. Can, therefore, a closer examination reveal any patterns of reasoning or particular tendencies (other than 'because they are old') that are inherent to sites that are subsequently conserved for display?

2. *Why were these sites conserved: what were the principle reasons for their conservation?* Other than any fundamental or inherent value that may be identified, are there more specific reasons and values that are considered when the decision was being made to conserve a site, and what were they?

3. *Who is involved or who influences the decisions of whether a site should be conserved?* Who decided on whether a site should or should not be conserved, and was this decision based on their own particular values or on a broader range? What other groups may have influenced a decision and was it for the same reasons as, for example, those of the archaeologists?

4. *Who were these sites being conserved for, and how do different groups value these sites?* Traditionally, the answer to the first part of this question is 'the public', but not every member of the public is interested in archaeological sites, so what particular sections of the public were those sites actually being conserved for? Is it possible to identify them and the values they may place on archaeological sites more specifically?

Conservation of archaeological sites within the modern urban context

1. *How does the process of conserving fragmentary archaeological sites for display fit in with the process of urban redevelopment?* Since World War II, there has been a change in how cities are planned and redeveloped, as epitomized by the change from modernism to postmodernism. How has this affected the way the built heritage, including archaeology, is regarded and handled within urban redevelopment?

2. *Is there a dichotomy in terms of values and appreciation between archaeology and urban development?* Conservation of archaeological sites and urban development appear diametrically opposed – what are the reasons for

this and can this opposition be lessened in anyway?
3. *Do urban development professions recognise any values in conserved archaeological sites?* The assumption is that urban development professions often place no value whatsoever on the remains of the past but is this really the case, and if not, what values do they recognize and how do they use them? How reflective are these values of their own interests as opposed to those of the site in question and archaeology in general? How influential are these developer interests and values in affecting the way sites are conserved?

Conservation and the post-war city
1. *Were provisions made for archaeological research and conservation of sites in post-war rebuilding plans?* The destruction of World War II was in many cases the stimulant for the inclusion of urban archaeology as part of the process of urban development as we know it today, but was archaeology factored into post-war urban reconstruction, and if not, should it be and at what point in the process?
2. *What are the particular problems that affect the built heritage, including archaeology, in the post-war period?* What are the fluctuating socio-political issues that may affect the built heritage and how it is treated? How do these change as the temporal distance grows between the end of the war and today? How do these affect the conservation of sites?
3. *What socio-cultural role can the built heritage, specifically conserved archaeological sites, play in the post-war urban context?* Rebuilding a city is more than just physical reconstruction, it is also about reconstructing social and cultural relationships and re-establishing a sense of continuity, identity and place, while also dealing with the traumas of the war. Does archaeology, particularly the conserving and display of archaeological sites, have any positive role to play in these situations?

Presentation and use of fragmentary archaeological sites
1. *Was the presentation of such sites effected by the predominant values that the site was conserved for?* Sites are often badly maintained and have poor or no signage, making it hard for all but the very knowledgeable to appreciate them. Is this a reflection of which values were considered most important? Were those values thought about in the wider context of public appreciation, i.e. in terms of social value?
2. *What makes a site 'successful'?* Which of the sites examined for this research appear to offer the most to the greatest number of people and why?
3. *What uses can be identified for such sites?* Fragmentary archaeological sites are rarely considered to have any active uses, other than as a conserver of scientific material and a supposed display of cultural values, but could they in fact have some active uses in their own right if properly conserved and managed?

The accumulation of the knowledge and insights provided by the examination of such issues through the case studies allows the identification of definite and comprehensible values of fragmentary archaeological sites within the modern urban city and the development of criteria that will help insure that sites are conserved for long-term demonstrable reasons and more widely appreciated values.

III: RESEARCH METHODS

Due to the multi-disciplinary nature of this research and the on-going nature of, for example, redevelopment in Beirut, a variety of qualitative research methods were employed. These included desk-based research of urban planning and development history and theories; of the history, practice and theories of archaeology and conservation as they relate to the subject matter of this research; and also in a number of other subjects including history and cultural studies. Although not referred to in the bibliography, the research also included reading contemporary literature in order to gain a wider insight into the situations in Berlin and Beirut; for example Peter Schneider's *The Wall Jumper* about divided Berlin and Hoda Barakat's *The Tiller of Waters* about post-war Beirut.

In relation to the sites themselves, fieldwork was carried out in London, Berlin and Beirut; the author lives in London; Berlin was visited in March 2004, Beirut in April 2005, and both cities were visited again in 2007. Sites and potential sites were identified from the literature including excavation reports, maps and guidebooks, though it should be noted that another feature of these fragmentary sites is that their presence or exact location is often ill-recorded. If such a site was found, then the name and type, its present state and immediate context and the extent and quality of its signage, if any, were recorded. The site was also photographed. The selection of sites detailed in the research is not exhaustive but designed to provide examples of the widest range of types and values.

Each of the three cities involved some additional research methods. In London, while there are publications on the archaeological excavations carried out by Professor Grimes in the post-war period, there is little on the subsequent conservation of the sites. It was thus necessary to carry out archive research both in the National Archives, Kew, and in the London Metropolitan Archives. Many of the sites included from the City of London had material on them in Ministry of Works files from the period that are now open to the public.

Berlin's sites were the best detailed in published sources. Berlin and its recovery has been the subject of many books and papers, as referred to in that chapter. The international nature of Berlin also meant that there was sufficient material available in English, including detailed publications on a number of key sites, for example the highly informative survey and guide book, of all the surviving elements of the Berlin Wall (Klausmeier and Schmidt 2004). Various crucial aspects of the post-cold war redevelopment such as that of Potsdamer Platz and the dismantling of the Palast are closely followed on the website of the Senate Department of Urban Development in Berlin.

The post-war redevelopment of Beirut is very much an ongoing process, inevitably complicated by more recent events such as Rafiq Hariri's assassination in 2005, the July War in 2006 and ongoing internal political instability. Although there has also been a great deal published about Beirut, the fact that the work is continually changing necessitated interviewing many of those involved (see Acknowledgements), and subsequent judicious and sensitive use of this material regarding the relationship between the redevelopment, the archaeology and the related politics.

V: DEFINITIONS AND RESEARCH LAYOUT

Before proceeding further, a word on definitions. In reference to 'postmodernism', there are a number of ways of spelling/constructing this term, but for the sake of standardisation, this monograph uses the above construction throughout. The term 'heritage' is used as a collective noun – for example the term 'cultural built heritage' is used to include historic buildings as well as archaeological sites. This research does not overly divide up the cultural built heritage – i.e. between historic buildings and archaeological sites. The principle reason for this is that, when it comes to conservation, little distinction is made between the two, as seen in, for example, in Bernard Feilden's (2003) *Conservation of Historic Buildings*. This is reflected in the fact that conservation of the built heritage has long been the preserve of architects rather that archaeologists. Angus Gavin, Solidere's Urban Development Division Head in Beirut explained that, when it came to the designing of Beirut's heritage trail, he made little distinction between archaeological sites and historic buildings and that they were all considered in much the same way (A. Gavin pers. comm.).

There are six chapters including this chapter and Chapter Two which comprises a general historical and theoretical background of the urban context, and the practices of archaeology and conservation, along with a literature review. Chapter Two is followed by individual chapters on London, Berlin and Beirut. The case study chapters are each divided up into sections comprising the urban context, conservation and archaeology before and after the respective wars, the sites including how each site came to be conserved, and then a discussion. The final chapter is Chapter Six. This chapter draws together all the ideas and discoveries of Chapter Two and the case studies for the main discussion and analysis. It highlights the wide range of issues encountered in the cities concerned, demonstrating both similarities and differences of urban development and conservation of archaeological sites from post-World War II London, through post-World War II and then post-Cold War Berlin to post-war Beirut. This chapter identifies the values of fragmentary archaeological sites and a set of criteria to consider when deciding to conserve such sites.

An omnipresent feature of this research is, not surprisingly, the perpetual change not only of the cities themselves as buildings are constructed or demolished, but also with the sites. In many cases they have simply become more weathered and weed-covered, or signs have become more faded or dropped off, though on occasion one or two boards have actually been replaced. This change is somewhat dramatically demonstrated by a listed section of Berlin Wall (figure 5) that was standing at the corner of Potsdamer Platz and Stresemannstrasse in 2004. By 2007 it had been removed.

Figure 5: Section of the Berlin Wall near Potsdamer Platz in 2004, but removed in 2007, despite its exhortation

CHAPTER TWO

ARCHAEOLOGY, CONSERVATION AND THE CITY

I. INTRODUCTION

This chapter considers the modern urban context with reference to the history of development of the city since the late nineteenth century, along with an examination of the principal cultural movements of modernism and postmodernism that have dominated urban development and the attitude to the historic urban landscape in modern times. This is followed by a review of the literature and theories to date on the conservation of urban archaeology, including reference to various writings on ruins.

II. THE URBAN CONTEXT

The city is a much-studied phenomenon as is evident in, for example, Reader's (2004) *Cities* or Rykwert's (2000) *The Seduction of Place*. Prominent thinkers and designers have also given it much thought, for example Mumford in his books *The Culture of Cities* (1940) and *The City in History* (1961), Hall's *Cities of Tomorrow* (2002) and Sennett in his many writings, for example *The Conscience of the Eye* (1992). The urban context is not, of course, just a physical entity but a multi-faceted socio-cultural, political and often violent environment that is subject to cycles of growth and decline, and thrives on generations of design and redesign, building and rebuilding. The driving forces for this growth and development are multifarious, but in modern times these have been principally, at least in the West, modernism and capitalism. Despite many urban centres being ancient in origin and continuing to be places of intensive settlement, there has been little mention in writings about modern urban planning and design of archaeology or conservation or the issues that these may cause for urban redevelopment. There are some exceptions to this, notably a reader in urban design, *Designing Cities* (Cuthbert 2003) includes a paper by Ashworth, 'Conservation as Preservation or as Heritage: two paradigms and two answers', that was originally published in the journal *Built Environment* in 1997.

The major feature of the development of modern cities up to 1939 was their phenomenal growth that began in the nineteenth century as a consequence of the Industrial Revolution. Industry had developed rapidly, there were new inventions in machinery, engineering, transport and communication, and it was the era of imperialism. The world thus became a smaller place. At the same time, populations grew and there was mass migrations both from the countryside to the city and from the 'old' world to the new, particularly to the USA. Whereas in 1875 there were, worldwide, just five industrial cities with populations greater than one million, by 1925 there were thirty-one. Europe's population alone had grown dramatically from 356 million in 1880 to 487 million in 1920, and European cities had grown likewise, for example Vienna's population had trebled to more than 2 million by 1910, Paris had gone from 2.25 million to 4.8 million and London had gained an extra 3.5 million (Reader 2004, 160-162). Similar growth was seen in North America, with New York growing from 1.9 million in 1887 to nearly 8 million in 1925, making it one of the world's largest cities along with London and, by 1933, Berlin (Reader 2004, 161, 284).

In the early part of the twentieth century there were also socio-cultural changes. One of the main examples was the change in the way goods were produced and how people were employed to produce these goods, a change often referred to as 'Fordism' after the American car manufacturer, Henry Ford. These changes included the introduction of the production-line or conveyor-belt method of production along with the eight-hour working day. People now did specific jobs at specific points and were no longer responsible for a product from beginning to end. This meant a devaluing of traditional skills and crafts and a separation of products from those who produced them. It also meant an increase in the type and amount of cheaper goods available. A kind of 'fetishism of commodities' developed that gave material goods their own intrinsic identity (Thomas 2004, 208). Cultural objects were also caught up in this increased commodification and consumption.

This was also a period of broad philosophical development as examined in, for example, Thomas's (2004) book *Archaeology and Modernity*, and as epitomised in the concepts that came to make up 'modernism', which began developing in the second half of the nineteenth century. Modernism in urban planning and architecture was based on a desire to solve the problems – 'the evils' – of the nineteenth century city caused by rapid industrialisation and population growth (Hall 2002, 7). What started out as a belief that architecture could play an improving role in social conditions, as contemplated by the likes of John Ruskin, William Morris and Augustus Welby Pugin, formed the basis of the linking of urban planning to utopian thought (Gold 1997, 21). These ideas are best seen in the 1933 Athens Charter[2], compiled in 1940 by architects Le Corbusier and José Luis Sert of the *Congrès Internationaux d'Architecture Moderne* (CIAM) IV conference held in 1933 (Gold 1997, 66). The conclusions that were drawn from this meeting were grouped under four functional headings: dwelling, leisure, work and circulation. The dwelling section was concerned with problems of sanitation, pollution, crowding and the availability of open space, proposing what is probably the best known of modernist urban planning principles – the construction of high buildings built away from the traffic and industry, widely spaced and with plenty of surrounding open and green space. Under leisure there was further concentration on the

---

[2] There are *two* Athens Charters referred to in this research – the *1931* Athens Charter deals with architectural conservation; the *1933* Athens Charter is concerned with the practices of Modern Architecture (though it does refer to conservation briefly).

importance of green space with leisure facilities, particularly in the poorest areas of the city. These green spaces were to be protected but could include schools and community facilities. The section on 'work' was particularly concerned with actually getting to work – journeys from home to work even then were taking on average an hour in Berlin and an hour and half in London because of rush-hour congestion. Furthermore, business districts had problems expanding without damaging residential areas, so their recommendations were to reduce the distances between home and work but to put barriers of open space between industrial and residential areas. These problems led to consideration of circulation, under which section some of the legacies of the past were considered to be the main impediments to the efficient running of the city, and the aims were to improve transport circulation and networks, and, again to use green space to separate housing from major routeways (Gold 1997, 69).

The 1933 Athens Charter did give some consideration to the special problems of historic areas of cities. In the short section discussing the need to conserve historic buildings, it was suggested that such conservation was only appropriate if the buildings truly represented the past, did not constitute a health hazard, and did not either stand in the way of developing the transport system or affect the organic growth of the city (Gold 1997, 70). The last point suggests that, rather than seeing historic buildings as representing the organic growth of cities over time, they were generally considered by modernist urban planners as a hindrance to present and future growth. Modernism specifically enshrined a break with the past. Essentially modernists had a general horror of the haphazard structure that most cities had developed over time; there was a desire for brightness and open spaces, and a belief in 'large-scale, metropolitan-wide, technologically rational and efficient urban *plans*, backed by absolutely no-frills architecture' (Harvey 1990, 66; italics original). The aim was a 'new urban order'; 'mistakes of the past' – essentially any aspect of the existing city that was not approved of – should not stand in the way of developing this new order (Gold 1997, 22). This desire to break with the past is seen, for example, in the writings of the Mumford (1940, 434, 446) who declared that the city was in danger of becoming a burial ground 'with its mass of dead buildings' and went on to suggest that if the city was to avoid becoming a 'confused rubbish heap' then it must not be forced to serve the purposes of a museum. Le Corbusier, one of the most famous of the modernist architects of the time and author of the influential *The City of Tomorrow* published in 1929, was in favour of a complete overhaul of cities, as was demonstrated by his plans for central Paris, that would have transformed it into an expanse of tower blocks, as the only way to turn them into 'healthy organisms' again (Esher 1981, 32).

Patrick Abercrombie, responsible in part for both the county and regional plans for London and for plans for a number of other British towns and cities, identified Le Corbusier's principles as de-congesting the city centres; augmenting their density; increasing the means of getting about; and increasing parks and open spaces. Le Corbusier's way of doing this was to build tall correctly orientated slab-like buildings which would allow for maximum light while freeing up the ground level for parks and gardens and, of course, roads (Esher 1981, 32; Abercrombie 1959, 117). Abercrombie did, however, in his *Town and Country Planning*, first published in 1933, question Le Corbusier's ideas for central Paris:

> 'If one might criticize a living and brilliant practitioner, M. Le Corbusier's theoretic basis of the modern city takes on a very different complexion when, with all its squareness unmollified, it is dropped on to about 1,000 acres of Central Paris, which are to be wiped out at one stroke. A few old features like the Place Vendôme, the Madeleine, the Opera and the Palais Royale are left lying in the midst discordantly and disconsolately, "like lumps of marl on a barren moor, encumbering what it is not in their power to fertilize". If the whole of Paris might be scrapped and something entirely new substituted there would be less objection – the survey then would limit itself to physical characteristics of the site – there would be no background of human endeavour which, however antiquated, cannot be ignored' (Abercrombie 1959, 131-132).

There appears then to be some tacit understanding that not all the urban past should be wiped out but what was considered worth keeping tended to be highly selective. A rare exception to this general view of the past was one of the fathers of modern urban planning, the polymath Patrick Geddes, who argued that urban planning should start with an all encompassing survey of the landscape, its resources and human responses to it, and that 'we must excavate the layers of our city downwards, into its earlier past – the dim yet heroic cities over and upon which it has been built; and thence we must read them upwards, visualizing them as we go' (Geddes 1925 quoted in Hall 2002, 147; 148-149). Geddes seems to have been alone, and ahead of his time, in this view. Modernism is generally blamed for destroying the traditional city along with its older neighbourhood culture (Jameson 1992, 2; Clarke 2003, 30).

Modernism in the post-war period became an orthodoxy within late-capitalist society and a particular kind of modernist aesthetic became absorbed into the established ideology, particularly in the USA (Jencks 1992, 12; Harvey 1990, 37). Modernism had, therefore, come to represent a certain elitism, a desire to maintain the separation between the 'high' and the 'low' to ensure protection from the onslaught of mass culture (Jencks 1992, 18). The connection of modernism to industrialisation within architecture was in more-or-less direct opposition to modernism within other arts. Architecture had promoted industrialisation while, for example, failing to have any appreciation for the local or existing urban fabric. As has been explained, it was a case of "bring in the bulldozers. Tear it all down" (Hall quoted in Porter 2000, 438). The often disastrous results of this combination of industrialisation, modernism and a perpetual drive of the two towards new technology and increasing efficiency is perhaps best seen in the endless soulless blocks of housing estates, of which Pruitt-Igoe, St Louis, USA, completed in 1956 but ignobly condemned and blown-up by the authorities in 1972, is just a single but more infamous example of many.

Modernism is also held responsible for radically changing 'the urban landscape of twentieth century capitalism' (Clarke 2003, 29). The alignment of capitalism with modernist urban planning is argued by many, not least by Harvey in *The Condition of Postmodernity* (Harvey 1990, 10ff), where he suggests that both modernist urban planning and capitalism evolve around the Nietzschian notions of 'creative destruction' and 'destructive creation', a concept that was dramatically expanded by what may be considered the greatest event in capitalism's history of creative destruction, World War II (Harvey 1990, 17, 18). The overlap of capitalism with modernism in the concept of creative destruction is most obvious in property development and investment. In cities, buildings occupy space but if the space becomes more valuable than the building, then the building is preventing the realization of that value; consequently it is required that the building be demolished and the space be more profitably occupied. This, naturally, is not generally conducive to conservation, as Peter Larkham points out in the first chapter of his book, *Conservation and the City* (Larkham 1996, 3), and as was evident in post-war London and Berlin. The destruction of the existing urban fabric also led to a growing belief that modernist planning was far from being for the social good. The reaction against modernist urban planning and architecture can be seen in the scathing and highly influential book *The Death and Life of Great American Cities* by Jane Jacobs (1961) in which she roundly condemned the modernist development of cities. She pointed out that the so-called modernist social housing had caused worse problems than the slums that they had been built to replace and had, amongst other things, reduced city centres to places where only those with no where else to go hung around. She also criticised urban planners such as Le Corbusier of not rebuilding cities since 1945 but sacking them (Harvey 1990, 71, 72).

Despite all the modernist beliefs of urban planning, there was in reality little official urban planning theory until the 1960s; urban planners had long worked from their own inherent beliefs and knowledge rather than from any sort of theoretical background and thus imposed a kind of 'top-down' planning (Hall 2002, 355). By the late 1960s-early 1970s urban planners were increasingly seen as working for no one's good but their own and being accused of being un-democratic (Esher 1981, 77; Sandercock 1998, 170). There was then growing public discontent with the destruction wrought by modernist planners and with the functional aestheticism of modernism – those endless slab-like tower blocks and high rise buildings that formed part of an increasingly mundane urban environment. Furthermore it was evident that the social beliefs of modernist planning had not been realistic – as demonstrated by the growing social problems of those high-rises, and of cities in general at this time. This rejection of modernism is clearly exemplified in the clashes that occurred over the initial redevelopment plans for Covent Garden in London that included tearing most of it down and putting a motorway through it. The leader of the official planning team for this subsequently aborted redevelopment suggested that in about 1968 there was 'a national nervous breakdown', that virtually overnight change and large scale redevelopment became 'a bad thing' and suddenly everything was worth saving (Hall 2002, 287). Modernism seemed to have run its course and had nothing more to offer, urban-dwellers began resisting both the destruction of neighbourhoods and, in the suburbs, demanding that urban growth be contained; in essence 'the production of space became impeded by a sensitivity to *place*' (Clarke 2003, 35; italics original).

The late 1960s-early 1970s is a period marked by a social sea-change right across North America and Western Europe, an incredible period worldwide that 'defies a short description' (Clarke 2003, 35). There were, for example, the Civil Rights Movement in the USA and Northern Ireland, the Vietnam war and the anti-war demonstrations that accompanied that, and there were student riots in both the USA and Europe. There seems to have been a rejection of much of the current ideologies by the generation that had grown up since World War II, and it is a highly interesting period in the already fascinating though traumatic history of the twentieth century. The post-war boom period came to an end and there was a series of economic slumps, and in 1973 an oil crisis. The economic crises of the 1970s were not confined to the 'developed' countries, but a world-wide phenomenon and continued on through the 1980s, interspersed by periods of growth, and were particularly felt in the poorer regions of the world such as West Asia (including Lebanon), Africa and Latin America (Hobsbawm 1994, 402). In the USA and in western Europe, where something approaching full employment had been reached in the post-war period, by the 1970s and 1980s, unemployment began to soar and the urban fabric of the inner cities began breaking down, as seen, for instance, in Britain with the Brixton riots of the 1980s (Collins 1994, 97). There was a rapid decline of heavy industry and manufacturing, and the employment they had provided, in the cities of Britain and the USA. The need to regenerate the resulting industrial wastelands and waterfronts, mostly as part of anti-poverty measures, was already recognised in the 1960s in the USA. The idea was to create some sort of service-sector role for the city centre as a way of finding a new economic base for it, and to encourage visitors. Two of the earliest examples of this were the regeneration of the Boston Waterfront and the Inner Harbour, Baltimore. These were large-scale redevelopments that combined private and government funds, led by radical business elites (Hall 2002, 384). Baltimore's Inner Harbour revitalisation led by the developer James Rouse, and that of the Boston

Waterfront, marked something of a new departure: firstly they were large schemes, 250 acres in Baltimore for example, secondly they incorporated a mixed-use policy of recreation, culture, shopping and mixed-income housing, and thirdly they were based on the then new concept of 'adaptive re-use': restoring and recycling of old buildings for new uses (Hall 2002, 384). The redevelopment of Covent Garden was along similar lines, and they are all, as Hall puts it, 'unashamedly tourist-based'; Baltimore by the late 1990s was attracting 22 million visitors a year of which seven million were tourists (Hall 2002, 386). The Baltimore Inner Harbour redevelopment was one of the main sources of inspiration for the post-civil war redevelopment of Beirut's central district (Gavin and Maluf 1996, 66; see Beirut chapter). What is evident from this period is that cities came to be seen not so much as 'machines for living', as they were by modernists, but as 'machines for wealth creation', and the traditional enmity between the planner and the developer changed as the former joined forces, or was subjugated, by the latter (Hall 2002, 379).

This period of the late 1960s-early 1970s has been nominally identified as the beginning of the postmodern period. The notion of a 'postmodern condition' is something that has now been incorporated into the studies and interpretations of virtually everything of the period since the late 1960s, from architecture to cinema and literature, as seen in, for example, Jameson's 1992 book *Postmodernism or, The Cultural Logic of Late Capitalism*. Other major critiques of postmodernism include Harvey's (1990) *The Condition of Postmodernity*, and *The Post-Modern Reader* edited by Jencks (1992). Whether postmodernism is a complete break with modernism or whether it is simply a periodization within modernism is endlessly debated and an argument that shall not be entered into here. What is evident is there was some kind of socio-cultural change at this time, as is suggested by the events mentioned above.

Postmodernism has been seen as either a reaction to or a resistance of the apparent elitism as perpetuated by modernism (Jencks 1992, 18), particularly seen in the emerging feminism of the 1960s on, but also against the elitism of culture. There is a now a need to appeal to a broad range of tastes, and postmodernism may be generally defined by a pluralism – a gathering together of a 'rainbow coalition of changing interests' (Jencks 1992, 15, 24). Jencks identifies the 'Post-Modern Movement' within architecture and urbanisation as a wider social protest against modernisation and against the destruction of local culture 'by the combined forces of rationalisation, bureaucracy, large-scale development, and, ... the modern International style' (Jencks 1992, 26). Harvey identifies postmodernism within architecture and urban design as signifying a break with the modernist ideals of large-scale planning and unadorned architecture, suggesting that instead postmodernism cultivates 'a conception of the urban fabric as necessarily fragmented, a "palimpsest" of past forms superimposed upon each other, and a "collage" of current uses, many of which may be ephemeral' (Harvey 1990, 66). In other words, where modernism required a break from the past and control over the urban environment as a totality, postmodernism acknowledges the presence of the past and that it cannot be eradicated. What has happened, however, is an increasing tendency towards the superficial. Inam (2002) in an award winning paper writes that one of the ongoing problems of urban design is that there is,

> 'a focus on the superficial aesthetics and the picturesque aspects of cities (instead of what role aesthetics play, say, in community development processes), an over-emphasis on the architect as urban designer and an obsession with design (instead of a more profound interdisciplinary approach that addresses fundamental causes), an understanding of urban design primarily as a finished product (instead of an ongoing long-term process intertwined with social and political mechanisms) and a pedagogical process that is comfortably rooted in architecture and design (rather than in the rich experiences, processes and evolution of cities)' (Inam 2002, 37).

The questioning of how cities are designed and developed also involves how such changes are financed, particularly after the financial crises from the late 1960s onwards. These aspects are examined in a paper, 'The Economic Currency of Architectural Aesthetics' by Clarke (2003, 28) who argues that there has been a profound transition in advanced capitalism and in the production and control of space that is reflected in the change of architectural philosophy from modernism to postmodernism. A major sector of capitalist accumulation was the speculative land and property development that dominated the development and construction industry, the idea being to gain land rents and to build profitably, quickly and cheaply (Harvey 1990, 70). As mentioned above there was something of an urban crisis as modernism faltered and this was compounded by an economic crisis, but crisis is a significant mode of transition for capitalism (Clarke 2003, 35). Such practices as land speculation were abruptly stopped, property markets collapsed and the reduction of capital going into the creation of physical and social infrastructure slowed just at the time when the efficiency and productivity of such investments was crucial; there was pressure to try and rescue investments without devaluing physical assets or destroying the services offered, and to rationalize the entire urban process to make it more efficient and cost-effective (Harvey in Clarke 2003, 36). Urban areas had to adapt from having a 'demand-side heritage' to a new 'supply-side world' (Clarke 2003, 36), with four current practices evolving. Cities now compete for the location of new industry; seek to improve urban life-style and prestige thus generating greater consumption, as seen for example, in the redevelopment projects in Baltimore and Boston; attempt to attract government and corporate headquarters, as perhaps seen in the London Docklands development; or fourth, continue a 'Keynesian' programme of expenditure on redistribution which develops opportunities for regional and urban competition (Clarke 2003, 26-37). The consequences of cities following these paths has led to greater competition at all levels from intra-city upwards. Gone is the modernist master plan to be replaced by portions of cities being developed, leading to great disparity and fragmentation (Clarke 2003, 37). In the West, there has been a movement away from manufacturing towards the service industries. Business is increasingly dominated by multi-national conglomerate corporations who work at a global level. These changes have also led to changes in society and divisions into 'complex class fractions', which are then reproduced in space through property relations mediated by the design professions and conditioned and reflected by the built environment (Knox 2003, 357). It is a period of late capitalism that has been identified as one of 'flexible accumulation' (Harvey in Clarke 2003, 37). Postmodernism provides a structural role of aesthetic innovation and experimentation that supports flexible accumulation, but it also subsumes it (Clarke 2003, 37, 38). This can, however, result in a kind of depthlessness where it is the image that is important, and hence the enhancement of 'symbolic capitalism' – 'the collection of luxury goods attesting to the taste and distinction of the owner' (Clarke 2003, 38). The idea of symbolic capitalism may be apparent in architecture, which Inam (2002, 3) argues is reflected in some of the problems of current urban design.

Changes, as represented in those from modernism to postmodernism (and now perhaps to post-postmodernism), are reflected in conservation of the historic urban landscape. Whereas the decline of modernism and its need to break with the past may seem to be a positive change, the end of long-term planning amongst other aspects, seem to be detrimental to one of the basic aims of urban conservation, which is to ensure the permanent survival of a site. Postmodernism may claim to embrace history but what results may simply be gentrification – a usurping of the place and history of others – and a concern with ornament and style. Clarke (2003, 38) further points out that creative destruction is also integral to the pursuit of symbolic capital, and that this is evident even in the restoration or preservation of a building – it is reconstituted but destroyed as a cultural and historic symbol (for example the Grand Hotel Esplanade, Berlin – see Berlin chapter). Façadism being a most obvious example of this. As Jencks (1992, 23) suggests, the past is either consulted and lovingly received, or plundered and ridiculed. The postmodern urban context is about image and the mobilisation of this image; about being able to convert the symbolic capital into money capital. It is also about the spectacle; 'Disneyland becomes an urban strategy', and the past gets appropriated into this creation of symbolic capital (Clarke 2003, 39, 41). At the same time, the acceptance of fragmentation, chaos and the ephemeral has given the impression that postmodernism, more specifically the postmodern city, is the result of some random set of processes, but in fact it is not. The increasing view of the city as a 'machine for wealth creation' has meant, it has been argued, careful and concerted plans that have led to what may be considered the 'post-justice city', where social housing and welfare has been dramatically reduced, policing has been reconfigured to reinforce marginalization, and urban designs that are promoted are the ones that remove residents considered to be undesirable - the human equivalent of blight (Cuthbert 2003, 5). In other words the aim has been 'to establish a program of public space regulation that does not rely on the universalizing tendencies of either law or rights' (Mitchell quoted in Cuthbert 2003, 5).

That this rather nightmarish scenario is indeed what is happening to cities, or at least parts of cities, is evident in how both central Berlin, principally the Potsdamer Platz, and Beirut's central district, have been redeveloped after the reunification of Germany and the end of Lebanon's civil war respectively. From the point of view of this research, the disregard for universal laws and rights may also contribute to a disregard for the values of the past and its protection in urban redevelopment. Development has been recognised as one of the biggest threats to archaeology (Palumbo 2002, 4). In fact, if anything, the threats to urban archaeology and to the proper conservation of sites and historic buildings seem greater now than they ever were, as much from gentrification as from demolition, even in countries that have specific and enforceable laws to protect the built heritage including the archaeology, as will be discussed below.

III. CONSERVATION AND ARCHAEOLOGY

The development of conservation and archaeology will be examined in detail as relevant to each of the case studies within their respective chapters. Following here is a synopsis of conservation history and developments generally, combined with a review of the literature specifically relating to urban conservation and archaeology, along with an examination of the development of values behind such practices.

Conservation is a multi-disciplinary practice involving many subjects, including the environment, art and architecture, and, of course archaeology. In fact, the practice of archaeology has some of its roots in an age-old desire to save elements of culture as embodied in art and architecture. The practice of architectural conservation has, consequently, a long and involved history, as is demonstrated in Jokilehto's (1999) *A History of Architectural Conservation*. Historically, the conservation of archaeological sites has tended to be subsumed within the field of architectural conservation, or at least not specifically distinguished from it. This is understandable on some levels – the various considerations that must be examined such as what to remove, what to restore, how to deal with various physical problems, are much the same. On other levels, however, principally that in terms of values – why is the site being conserved, who is it being conserved for, what purpose is it to serve, how is it to be presented and managed; what to do about its immediate context – approaches may be radically different between those adopted for an historic building and for an archaeological site, particularly if the latter is of a more fragmentary nature.

In order to identify and clarify the specific nature of conservation of archaeological sites in modern urban contexts, it is necessary to examine both the history of conservation and its development in terms of values to date.

Conservation and archaeology prior to World War II

Jokilehto (1999) takes the subject matter of architectural conservation in its broadest sense, and traces its history from at least the first century BC and Vitruvius's *Architectura*, up until the present. He includes archaeological sites and monuments in so far as they are part of the architectural heritage. Interest in protecting ancient sites and monuments is recorded at least as early as Roman times when in AD 458 the Roman emperors Leo and Majorian ordered that 'all the buildings that have been founded by the ancients as temples and other monuments, and that were constructed for the public use or pleasure, shall not be destroyed by any person', on penalty of a fine of fifty pounds of gold (quoted in Jokilehto 1999, 5). In medieval times, the value of past works of architecture and art were valued as evidence of the past and as tools for education and discussion for, amongst others, artists and historians. This was an aspect of them much promoted by Petrarch in the fourteenth century as he also saw the political significance in the 'relics of past grandeur of ancient Rome'. Furthermore, the beginnings of modern archaeological consciousness may be seen in attempts at this time to relate literary history with actual sites, and in the development of interest in antiquity collections for study as well as an indicator of social status (Jokilehto 1999, 16). Jokilehto (1999) also explains the development of the aesthetic interest in ruins, beginning as early as the fifteenth century when visitors were drawn to Rome to visit the remains there, that culminated in the aesthetic tastes of eighteenth-century England for the landscape garden and the appreciation of the picturesque of ruined medieval religious buildings and castles. It is also during the eighteenth century that Johann Joachim Winckelmann, who is considered as one of the founders of modern archaeology and art history, established the concept of the value of the original and the authentic being over and above that of the copy (Jokilehto 1999, 47). The idea of conserving sites *in situ* came with some of the earliest systematic approaches, as opposed to treasure-hunting, to archaeology, as developed by La Vega in his excavations at the urban centres of Pompeii and Herculaneum beginning in 1765. It was here he proposed a number of interesting ideas such as preserving frescos *in situ* for the public to see, and because he considered the value of these paintings to lie in their relationship to their surrounding environment (Jokilehto 1999, 59).

So, by the end of the eighteenth century, some of the values that have developed into some of the principles underlying modern conservation practice were nominally in place. These included some aesthetic appreciation for old buildings and ruined monuments; the understanding of the value of the original over the copy; and the beginnings of the concept that the original may be best served by keeping it *in situ*. The understanding of the political aspects of sites and monuments and in their conservation appears also to have its roots in this time.

The nineteenth century, in Britain, is characterised firstly by the desire to 'restore', and then by the reaction against this in the form of the anti-restoration movement and the founding of the Society of Protection of Ancient Buildings by William Morris and others. Ashworth and Tunbridge (1990) in their book *The Tourist-Historic City*, have a chapter on the development of urban conservation, suggesting that due to the 'spatial discrepancy' between the northern European interest in classical monuments, as exemplified by the Grand Tours of earlier centuries, and the predominantly southern European distribution of such monuments, there was an early internationalisation of both the conservation movement and of historic-city tourism (Ashworth and Tunbridge 1990, 9). The nineteenth century was one of radical change in terms of industrialisation and urbanisation, and although modernism inspired to break with the past, there was, towards the end of the century a growth in interest in both museums and in historic preservation. There was the development of a nostalgic romanticism for the apparently rapidly disappearing 'rustic idyll', as demonstrated by the setting up of the National Trust in Britain in 1895 and the establishment of the National Parks movement in the USA, Canada and Australia around the same time (Ashworth and Tunbridge 1990, 9). Conservation of monuments at this time was part of an interest in preserving the countryside in general, but it must be noted that, at this stage, the idea of specific urban conservation in living cities was unheard of (Esher 1981, 72). Perhaps the most interesting aspect of this growth in the nineteenth century in the protection of monuments is that, according to Ashworth and Tunbridge, it was a fairly uniform international development. The nineteenth century saw attempts at government-sponsored inventories – for example in France, Belgium and Netherlands (Ashworth and Tunbridge 1990, 10) and then, eventually, laws to provide some sort of protection – for example Britain's 1882 Ancient Monuments Act, France's 1913 Law on Historic Monuments, which included a compulsory purchase option, and Belgium's 1931 Act to protect landscapes and monuments. These, however, were reliant on local support to be effective and consequently developers often got round them (Ashworth and Tunbridge 1990, 11). Thus, leading up to World War II, there was some sort of legislation to protect monuments and historic buildings in most European countries, and in North America, but the legislation tended to be predominantly rural-orientated, added to which the enthusiasm and means of implementing it appears to have been universally lacking (Ashworth and Tunbridge 1990, 11). The practice of archaeology in the living cities of Europe was in a similar situation; up to the outbreak of the second world war excavating in the middle of a busy active city was virtually unheard of. In fact it was the destruction wrought by the bombing of that war which, due to the extensive rebuilding, led to the development of urban archaeology as we know it today (Gerrard 2003, 95).

In the development of the interest, albeit mostly spurred on by what Ashworth and Tunbridge (1990, 9) describe as a 'passionate minority' (the 'elitism' of culture as part of modernism is perhaps also reflected in this) in saving monuments and historic buildings from destruction, there also developed various philosophies behind such practices, and in the whole concept of what monuments and ruins may signify. In a comprehensive collection, *Historical and Philosophical Issues in the Conservation of Cultural Heritage* (Stanley-Price *et al* 1996), published by the Getty Conservation Institute is Alois Riegl's (1996) 1903 paper, 'The Modern Cult of Monuments: its essence and its development', which examines some of the values behind the monument and its preservation. Riegl does not separate artistic from historic monuments but discusses them together and gives all-encompassing definitions of both a work of art and an historical monument: 'a work of art is any tangible, visible, or audible work of man of artistic value; a historical monument with any of the same properties will possess a historical value' (Riegl 1996, 69). He goes on to suggest that every monument of art is an historical monument and vice versa. He identifies historical value as applying to all things that 'once were and no longer', but also includes everything that 'once was but can never be again'. He goes on to point out that although every historical event is irreplaceable, it is impossible to take them all into consideration as they multiple infinitely at any given moment and that one has no choice but to limit attention primarily and exclusively to such evidence that seems to represent particularly notable stages in the development of a particular branch of human activity. To demonstrate this he suggests how one might regard a torn-off scrap of paper with writing on it (an example that perhaps has direct comparisons with the more fragmentary archaeological site): this fragment of paper might hold various pieces of important information, such as the type and quality of paper used, the script the hand-writing demonstrates and so forth, but since there are likely to be other more richer and detailed sources that would give the same information, there would be an inclination to disregard this scrap of paper. But, should this piece of paper be the only surviving evidence of a particular creation, it would be necessary to keep it and consider it 'an utterly indispensable monument of art' (Riegl 1996, 70). He further explains that art encountered as in this example is of interest specifically from a historical point of view – it is an 'irreplaceable and inextricable link in a chain of development' of art history; its value is historical not artistic and consequently, the distinction between 'monuments of art' and 'historical monuments' is wrong because the former are included in the latter and merge with them (Riegl 1996, 71). He goes on, however, to say that value is not applied equally to all works of art and then only increases with age or as something becomes scarce but that there is also a purely artistic value. This has been based on an aesthetic said to be objective but never clearly defined, though there is also an artistic value based on contemporary artistic values. This is even less clearly defined and changes from moment to moment, suggesting to Riegl that artistic value of a monument is no longer commemorative but contemporary. In other words, the artistic value of a monument is a present-day value and not really anything to do with its historic value. Riegl also argues for the distinction between age value and historic value as each requires a different process. The former, appreciable by more-or-less everyone instantly is a kind of artistic or emotional value; it requires that the monument be left to follow the natural cycle of decay and should not be restored or preserved. The latter, historic value, is, he suggests a more intellectual value with a greater scientific leaning. It consequently means the monument is seen as an original document which must be preserved for future restoration and art-historical research reasons.

Riegl also discusses the 'use value' of monuments and suggests that one of the attributes of the use value of a monument is the interaction of people with the monument; he further argues that no-one would feel comfortable with the ruins of a house or church suddenly destroyed as people would be used to them being places of activity and life, and to leave them in their ruined state could only leave the impression of some violent destruction (Riegl 1996, 79). This is an interesting thought when one considers the wide-scale violent destruction of World War II and the apparently urgent need to remove ruins, particularly seen in West Berlin. It also points towards some of the reasoning behind keeping ruins as war memorials, something that will also be examined in later chapters.

A second, somewhat complementary paper to Riegl's is Georg Simmel's 1911 paper, 'The Ruin' (Simmel 1959). Here he concentrates on the duality between the ruin and nature, and on the artistic attributes of this combination of decaying architecture and reclaiming nature. He argues that the significance of the ruin rests on the contrast between the work of humans and the effect of nature, and that the fascination of a ruin is that the work of the former can appear a product of the latter (Simmel 1959, 260, 261). He also discusses the aesthetic appeal of the ruin (reflecting Riegl's age value), how the development of patina adds a 'mysterious harmony', and argues that the aesthetic value is found in the way a ruin 'combines the disharmony, the eternal becoming of the soul struggling against itself, with the satisfaction of form, the firm limitedness, of the work of art' (Simmel 1959, 262, 265). As with Riegl, this was a paper written before the destruction of two world wars, in particular World War II that left most of Europe with a density of ruins and level of destruction never quite experienced before. Simmel is thus able to suggest that the 'ruin strikes us so often as tragic – but not as sad – because destruction here is not something senselessly coming from the outside but rather the realization of a tendency inherent in the deepest layer of existence of the destroyed', and goes on later to suggest that ruins suggest a unity of existence and give an impression of peace because the conflicts between the metaphysical upward striving and downward pulling, which architecture tends to represent, are at one. His final thought is that the peacefulness of a ruin may be also ascribed to its character as past: that although life has departed, it once contained a wealth of life and this gives it a presence. The ruin, therefore, 'creates the present form of a past life, not according to the contents or remnants of that life, but according to its past as such', and that it 'fuses the contrast of present and past in to one united form, on the whole span of physical and spiritual vision in the unity of aesthetic enjoyment, which, after all, is always rooted in a deeper than merely aesthetic unity' (Simmel 1959, 265, 266).

Simmel's paper compares with Riegl's in that it reinforces something of the age value that Riegl discusses. What Simmel is highlighting is not so much any historic value but the aesthetic and artistic values of the ruin. Christopher Woodward's much later book, *In Ruins*, first published in 2001, extols the same values – artistic and aesthetic rather than historic or academic. In fact he complains that archaeologists have been responsible for destroying these artistic and aesthetic values of the Colosseum in Rome, and pointing out that no artist or writer has been inspired by it since, except for Hitler (Woodward 2001, 24, 27). This is perhaps the definable difference between a 'ruin' and an 'archaeological site' or 'historic monument'. A ruin demonstrates Riegl's age value; its duality of nature highlights these aesthetic values, and that according to Riegl, such value is destroyed by any form of preservation (the heavy-handed nature of conservation practices in the nineteenth century should, however, be taken into account here). Once a ruin is conserved, it ceases to be part of this cycle of nature and becomes, for all intents and purposes, frozen in time. Indeed this is the primary aim of modern conservation – to insure the survival of the object concerned for as long as possible (Berducou 1996, 250). A ruin once conserved then, ceases to be a ruin with predominantly age values and instead becomes an archaeological site or historic monument with predominantly historic values. It is, therefore, not so surprising that age values and the corresponding aesthetic values have become subjugated by historic and the corresponding academic values. The last true expressions within the urban context of the former values, which have their roots in the Romantic period and eighteenth century aesthetic tastes of the picturesque, are perhaps to be found in the ruined churches conserved as war memorials after World War II in Britain; what Woodward (2001, 212) describes as 'the last great fling of the British Picturesque' (see London chapter). The only concession made to such values in the city nowadays is to be found in the archaeological site conserved within a park or small garden, as seen in, for example, figure 1, but even this is being lost due to an increasing tendency to conserve such remains within buildings.

Conservation and archaeology after World War II

The extent of devastation caused by the fighting of World War II was unlike anything seen before. The development of aerial bombing and the concentration of fighting in urban centres left many towns and cities in ruins – horrific images of Dresden and Coventry remain legendary, as do those of Hiroshima and Nagasaki. In fact the damage was such as to spur the drawing up of the 1954 *Convention for the Protection of Cultural Property in the Event of Armed Conflict*, the Hague Convention, which was agreed upon by a majority of the world's countries then in existence and issued by UNESCO. It was subsequently followed up with a Second Protocol in 1999. This, however, was not concerned with the post-war situation and it is evident that there was as much destruction of the built heritage in the process of post-war rebuilding as there was during the war itself. This was for a number of reasons – the need to rebuild quickly and the desire to be rid of so many ruins; the problems of dealing with buildings that had become tainted by association with, for example, the Nazis; and the whole underpinning of modernism to break with the past while rebuilding in such a way as to eliminate the blight caused by pre-war urban problems. One of the other main problems, particularly in the case of archaeology, was lack of interest. The excavation of archaeological sites in living cities was a rare practice – archaeology was first and foremost a research and rural discipline and there was little interest in what lay under the pavements of many British and European cities, as exemplified in Coventry (Rylatt 1977, 7) and indeed in Berlin. The whole concept of developer-led rescue excavation that accompanies urban redevelopment was only in its infancy, as will be discussed in the London chapter. More specifically, how to deal with the cultural built heritage including archaeology in post-war situations was something entirely uncontemplated in 1945. This has, however, begun to change, as demonstrated by the publication of *Cultural Heritage in Postwar Recovery* (Stanley-Price 2007) by ICCROM. There are a number of earlier publications that deal with some of issues of archaeological sites and war – for instance *Archaeology under Fire: nationalism, politics and heritage in the Eastern Mediterranean and Middle East*, edited by Meskell (1998), *Destruction and Conservation of Cultural Property* edited by Layton, Stone and Thomas (2001) and a BBC published book *Under Fire: people, places and treasure in Afghanistan, Iraq and Israel* (Cruickshank and Vincent 2003). Alongside these is Kohl and Fawcett's *Nationalism, Politics and the Practice of Archaeology* (1995), which examines the effects of politics on archaeology. In relation to the specific post-war situation, UNESCO do now have strategies for safeguarding the cultural heritage which are based on four components: safeguarding of symbolically significant monuments, emphasis on socio-economic aspects of culture which includes the development of skills of local inhabitants so they can look after the sites themselves; integration of different parts of the population to bring them together to work on cultural projects; and recreation of cultural identity of the people or country concerned (Manhart 2006). The emphasis is, however, on the 'symbolically significant monuments', rather than either the cultural built heritage or archaeology in general. For the most part protection of historic buildings and archaeological strata remain reliant on the enforcement of whatever laws the country had in place prior to war breaking out. The specific detailing of how best to protect and manage the built heritage including archaeology in the immediate post-war period is very much undeveloped, as stressed at a lecture given by the director of the Post-War Recovery and Development Unit, York (Barakat 2006), and even now is still only in its infancy.

The specific situation regarding urban conservation and archaeology, including legislation, in the immediate post-World War II period will be examined in detail in both the London and Berlin chapters. As for the actual legislation protecting historic buildings and archaeological sites and monuments in Europe, there were no major changes until the 1960s-1970s, when remarkably similar types of legislation were put in place throughout Europe (Ashworth and Tunbridge 1990, 12). The main difference rested on whether it was administered from a central authority, as in France, a regional authority, as in West Germany, Belgium, Austria and Switzerland, or from a local basis, as in Britain. For the most part, these new laws consolidated and continued previous laws, and inventories were maintained but were often enlarged or reorganised. The main new features were the shift in emphasis from single buildings to ensembles and, most importantly perhaps, the development, at least in theory, of conservation as a general part of urban planning rather than a reaction to special cases. Another major development, from the point of view of this research, was the broadening of monument definitions and the inclusion of smaller, less spectacular or newer examples (Ashworth and Tunbridge 1990, 14). Ashworth and Tunbridge stress that one of the main points of interest is that the legislation happened at all, as it involved accepting a major role for the collective sector and, in particular, for national governments, with the development of a single framework for inventorising, protecting, maintaining and rehabilitating monuments, especially in cities which often had long traditions of local rather than national concerns (Ashworth and Tunbridge 1990, 13). Furthermore it was something that appeared internationally, for example throughout both West and East Europe, North America and even China, regardless of political traditions, and all within just over a decade (Ashworth and Tunbridge 1990, 13), possibly reflecting something of the social change in the attitude to the destruction caused by modernism, as detailed earlier. That is not, however, to say that everything dramatically improved in terms of the protection of the built heritage. In some countries the legislation remained ineffective, as was the case in, for example, France and Denmark (Larkham 1996, 42). From the early 1960s the rate of destruction in Britain actually became worse – necessitating, for example public enquires to save buildings in the 1960s (Earl 1996, 72), while the destruction of urban archaeological layers and the necessary rescue excavations as a result of development increasingly became the *status quo*. In 1971, fear for the archaeological record as a whole led to the establishment of 'Rescue', the Trust for British Archaeology (Jones 1984, 51), and this was followed by a number of influential publications – *The Erosion of History* (Heighway 1972) and *The Future of London's Past* (Biddle *et al* 1973). During this time, government funding for archaeology in Britain, especially London, was minimal, particularly when compared to other European countries (Jones 1984, 50, 56; Haynes *et al* 2000).

The ineffectiveness of national legislation protecting sites and monuments to keep up with destructive tendencies of modernist post-war rebuilding is perhaps reflected in the plethora of international documentation relating to all things connected with protecting, conserving and appreciating the cultural heritage that have come from organisations such as UNESCO and ICOMOS since World War II. One of the earliest and most influential charters is, though, the pre-war *Athens Charter for the Restoration of Historic Monuments*, which was adopted at the first International Congress of Architects and Technicians in Athens in 1931. This document provided the basis upon which later conservation theories and practices have been built, including to 'abandon restorations in toto', the recognition of the importance of regular maintenance, the introduction of the concept of protecting the areas around historic sites, and that 'excavated sites which are not subject to immediate restoration should be reburied for protection'. It formed the basis for the 1964 *International Charter for the Conservation and Restoration of Monuments and Sites*, more commonly known as the Venice Charter, which was also the result of another International Congress of Architects and Technicians. The preamble to this charter notes that 'People are becoming more and more conscious of the unity of human values and regard ancient monuments as a common heritage', and stresses the importance of being able to hand this common heritage on to future generations. It stresses the importance of 'making use of [monuments] for some socially useful purpose', and that any restoration must preserve and reveal its historic and aesthetic values. The charter states in Article 15, in relation to excavations, that 'ruins must be maintained and measures necessary for the permanent conservation and protection of architectural features and of objects discovered must be taken', and continues, 'every means must be taken to facilitate the understanding of the monument and to reveal it without ever distorting its meaning.' Crucially, Article 1 of the Venice Charter recognises the importance of not just rural but also urban settings of monuments, and insists that its recommendations apply not just to 'great works of art but also to more modest works of the past which have acquired cultural significance with the passing of time'.

Many of the concerns of the Venice Charter were reflected in the 1975 *European Charter of Architectural Heritage,* adopted by the Committee of Ministers of the Council of Europe (Appleyard 1979, 294-296). This charter, a response to the destruction of historic architecture in the process of development, stresses the significance of not only major monuments but also lesser ones, of the importance of their surroundings and how 'the past as embodied in the architectural heritage provides the sort of environment indispensable for a balanced and complete life'. The destruction caused by indiscriminate redevelopment has not, however, just been a problem in Europe; in 1976 UNESCO issued the *Recommendation concerning the safeguarding and contemporary role of historic areas*, the result of a conference held in Nairobi and in essence concerned with the rate of destruction in the developing world but with relevance to the developed world. In 1987, ICOMOS produced the *Charter for the Conservation of Historic Towns and Urban Areas* (the Washington Charter) which continued in much the same vein. It is concerned with the historic city as a whole, recognising that 'all urban communities, whether they have developed gradually over time or have been created deliberately, are an expression of the diversity of societies throughout history'. It expresses concern over the fact that many historic urban areas are being adversely effected by industrialization and the development that it entailed. It advocates careful conservation and aims 'to encourage the preservation of those cultural properties, however modest in scale, that constitute the memory of mankind (sic)' (ICOMOS 1987, preamble).

This recognition of the importance of historic urban areas and the need to conserve them grew in tandem with other important changes in attitude as to what constitutes cultural heritage, and the different attitudes different peoples of the world hold in relation to what and why things are important to them. This is reflected in, for instance the *Nara Document on Authenticity* (1994), and the *Charter for the Conservation of Places of Cultural Significance* (Burra Charter, 1996). Other documents issued by ICOMOS include the *Charter for the Protection and Management of the Archaeological Heritage* (1990) and the *International Cultural Tourism Charter: managing tourism at places of heritage significance* (1999). While these types of international documents do represent the changes in attitude towards sites and monuments since World War II and the development of the concepts of the built heritage and its wider contexts, for the most part their primary focus is on historical architecture and by extension the larger archaeological sites. There have been, however, some such documents more specifically concerned with archaeology. An early charter is the 1956 UNESCO *Recommendation on International Principles Applicable to Archaeological Excavations*. It is principally aimed at research excavation but it does stress, in Item 21, the importance of providing for 'guarding, maintenance and restoration of the site together with the conservation, during and on completion of [the excavator's] work, of objects and monuments uncovered'. In its preamble it stresses a crucial but, it would seem, constantly overlooked opinion that 'that the surest guarantee for the preservation of monuments and works of the past rests in the respect and affection felt for them by the peoples themselves' (UNESCO 1956).

A later document following on from the 1956 UNESCO *Recommendation* was that issued by the twelfth Session of ICCROM General Assembly of May 1983, in Rome. It dealt specifically with the conservation of archaeological sites and acknowledges that 'archaeological finds from excavations may far exceed the existing possibilities for conservation, and that these researches undertaken may ignore or be in contradiction with the basic needs of conservation – a situation which can lead to serious damage to the historical and cultural heritage of each country and, consequently, of mankind (sic)'. It further highlights the negative consequences of the lack of publication, and recommends that Member States 'take the necessary measures to prevent archaeological sites being opened up – except in special circumstances – without due consideration being given to the necessary requirements of conservation' (Stanley-Price 1995, ix), something which perhaps resonates in the increasing tendency to rebury urban archaeological sites, as seen with two preservation *in situ* conferences (Nixon n.d. [1998]; Nixon 2004).

One of the more comprehensive documents that deals specifically with urban archaeology and development issues is the Council of Europe's 1992 *European Convention on the Protection of the Archaeological Heritage* (the Valletta Convention); it has also been used to provided the framework for the work in Beirut (H. Curver pers. comm.; see Beirut chapter). In its preamble it acknowledges that,

> 'the European archaeological heritage, which provides evidence of ancient history, is seriously threatened with deterioration because of the *increasing number of major planning schemes*, natural risks, clandestine or unscientific excavations and *insufficient public awareness*' (emphasis added).

It states in Article 1 that its aim is to protect the archaeological heritage as 'a source of the European collective memory and as an instrument for historical and scientific study', while Article 4 exhorts each state to take measures to protect and make provision for the archaeological heritage including 'for the conservation and maintenance of the archaeological heritage, preferably *in situ*'. The most relevant section is that of Article 5, which deals specifically with the integrated conservation of archaeological heritage, and is included here in full:
Each Party undertakes:
i. to seek to reconcile and combine the respective requirements of archaeology and development plans by ensuring that archaeologists participate:
   a. in planning policies designed to ensure well-balanced strategies for the protection, conservation and enhancement of sites of archaeological interest;
   b. in the various stages of development schemes;
ii. to ensure that archaeologists, town and regional planners systematically consult one another in order to permit:
   a. the modification of development plans likely to have adverse effects on the archaeological heritage;

b. the allocation of sufficient time and resources for an appropriate scientific study to be made of the site and for its findings to be published;

iii. to ensure that environmental impact assessments and the resulting decisions involve full consideration of archaeological sites and their settings;

iv. to make provision, when elements of the archaeological heritage have been found during development work, for their conservation *in situ* when feasible;

v. to ensure that the opening of archaeological sites to the public, especially any structural arrangements necessary for the reception of large numbers of visitors, does not adversely affect the archaeological and scientific character of such sites and their surroundings.

Another crucial matter that the Valletta Convention highlights is the one of public awareness and its promotion. Article 9 claims that each Party undertakes:

i. to conduct educational actions with a view to rousing and developing an awareness in public opinion of the value of the archaeological heritage for understanding the past and of the threats to this heritage;

ii. to promote public access to important elements of its archaeological heritage, especially sites, and encourage the display to the public of suitable selections of archaeological objects.

Everything needed to protect archaeological sites during development, from ensuring their *in situ* preservation to allowing sufficient resources for their 'preservation by record', and to encourage public interest is theoretically provided by the Valetta Convention. The unfortunate thing is that, despite this convention and indeed all these documents and declarations that have been discussed, agreed upon and published since the end of World War II, none of them have any legal standing. Thus proper treatment of urban archaeology is reliant not only on the enforcement of such relevant legal protection as there is but on the professional behaviour, interest and understanding of all parties concerned. Generating and co-ordinating these attributes is a significant challenge to the practice of urban archaeology and conservation. A paper that examines the issues of conserving cultural heritage of any sort in cities is 'Preserving the historic urban fabric in a context of fast-paced change' (Serageldin 2000). Serageldin (2000, 58) concludes that the challenge for conservation specialists, within the context of rapid urban change, 'is to devise methods by which cultural heritage can be interpreted, valued and valorized in the light of emerging trends, new perceptions, growing diversity, and divergent attitudes'. In a later Getty Institute report published in 2002, the issue of values was again raised. It was argued that while conservation was happy with the 'how', the profession was only just beginning to examine the 'what' and 'why' questions, and was also still failing to translate its own issues and beliefs in such a way as to make them understandable in relation to the beliefs of the broader public (Mason and Avrami 2002, 15, 19).

Before the 'what' and 'why' questions and the issue of values are discussed, however, it is necessary to examine briefly the 'how' in terms of the development of practical conservation of urban archaeological sites. In the immediate post-war period, archaeology, despite the increase in urban and rescue excavations, was carried out in much the same fashion as previously, as will be shown in the London and Berlin chapters. Archaeology was not immune to the social changes in the 1960s-1970s and there was much change in the archaeology of the Western world, principally in the field of theory. Thomas (2004), in his book *Archaeology and Modernity*, traces the development of archaeology in tandem with the development of modern Western thought and examines these changes in archaeological theory; 'Modernity has created a world from which meaning has been exercised … Archaeology addresses itself to a world of bare material things, which are quite separate from the realm of meaning and value, which lies inside the mind (Thomas 2004, 233-234). In the 1960s substantial new theories were developed, the first of which was processual or 'New Archaeology'. The basis of New Archaeology was a belief in objective science; the aim was to make archaeology more scientific and to apply similar rigorous testing to archaeological data. The only problem was that it was realised that it is not possible to test theories in the past, only in the present, and some way of linking the static archaeological record with the dynamics of past society had to be established, hence the development of Middle Range Theory. The problem, however, is that people neither now or in antiquity live their lives disengaged from the material world around them and everything is imbued with meaning – it is not something that can be added later, once the analytical study of the record has been done (Thomas 2004, 234), though this process did suit rescue archaeology as will be examined below. A critique of processual archaeology, namely postprocessual archaeology, developed, which Hodder (1999, 5) briefly describes as interpretive and self-reflexive, and places emphasis on the individual, agency, historical context and meaning. It has come to include a whole range of perspectives including Marxist and Feminist archaeologies. Postprocessual archaeology, by its very nature, encourages a much more diverse field of archaeology, and generally calls for discussion with other relevant disciplines (Smith 1994, 301). As with the end of modernism, this has seen the end of grand narratives combined with increased multivocality, along with a greater choice of theoretical position (Hodder 1999, 5). Johnson (1999, 166) argues that although postprocessual thought does equate with some of the thinking of postmodernism, namely the loss of confidence in science, the attack on essentialism, the stress on diversity of readings and a lack of fixity of meanings, it does not derive from postmodernism but parallels its development. He suggests that postmodernism has led to the breaking down of barriers between disciplines, a questioning of the notion of a single 'archaeological method', and the suggestion that there is a need for archaeology to engage outside the traditional boundaries of archaeology and science (Johnson 1999, 166). This has encouraged the development of such sub-disciplines as heritage management and public archaeology, and has also encouraged recognition in the more recent interest in alternative means of expression in archaeology and the use of performance and art, for example as a way of examining past experiences that cannot be reached by standard academic discourse. Thomas also points out that 'Contrary to modernist dogma, investigations that have been shorn of aesthetics, rhetoric and poetics are impoverished rather than more secure in their conclusions, for they arrive at patterns of understanding which exclude significant dimensions of human existence' (Thomas 2004, 235). The same may be said of the conservation for display of archaeological remains; one of the issues of the highly scientific nature of archaeology as it has developed since the 1960s is that it has translated, I would argue, into the over-emphasis of scientific values at the expense of other values such as aesthetics in the practice of the conservation of the more fragmentary urban archaeological sites, as demonstrated by, for example, the conservation and display of two sites in London, the remains of the Postern Tower (figure 6) and the Great Hall of the Bishop of Winchester's Palace (figure 7), both excavated and conserved in the late 1970s-early 1980s.

is concerned almost exclusively with the larger rural site already exposed, rather than with newly discovered site during the process of excavation. He does, however, provide a definition of a ruin as a 'roofless shell [which] may stand to roof height or exist only as foundation (or even merely as an archaeological fossil in the subsoil), but it is clearly sharply distinguished from a roofed structure which provides shelter and is in some sense usable' (Thompson 1981, 9). He also highlights the importance of being able to understand a ruin, along with some of its values, though he also recognises the aesthetic attraction of ruins,

> 'The pleasure of a ruin is to stimulate our imagination and reconstruct in our mind's eye the structure in its original state. The better we understand the ruin (common sense or, if necessary, archaeology), the better the imaginative reconstruction. If it requires ivy and moonlight or the occasional fall of a stone to stimulate excitement, then this is probably a form of self-dramatisation and a different, more theatrical, experience. The boundary between the two is blurred, and the Romantic tends to flit from one side to another' (Thompson 1981, 17).

Figure 6: Postern Tower foundations, Tower Hill, London

While, then, there were theoretical developments and changes of practice within archaeology, there was little in terms of specific theoretical development regarding the conservation of urban archaeological remains. As was pointed out by Mason and Avrami (2002, 14), the profession of conservation is still developing and the more theoretical side, particularly in terms of values, is still at a comparatively early stage of this development. The majority of publications that deal specifically with the conservation of archaeological sites have had a tendency to deal with the essential matter of practicalities and with those of rural sites. In 1981, M.W. Thompson published *Ruins: their preservation and display*. Most of the book deals with the practical issues of conserving ruins, such as restoration and access for the public, but he

Figure 7: Gable of the Great Hall, Bishop of Winchester's Palace, Southwark

A volume that deals more specifically with the conservation of archaeology as a process of excavation is Nicholas Stanley-Price's (1995) *Conservation on Archaeological Excavations*, first published in 1984. This has a number of detailed papers on the practicalities of conservation during all stages of the excavation. The importance of planning for any conservation eventualities before the excavation starts is emphasised (Stanley-Price 1995, 1). A second paper also highlights this need for comprehensive planning before, during and after excavation, and that these plans should have short and long-term objectives that can be updated and developed as work progresses (Stubbs 1995, 74). Stubbs (1995, 74) also suggests that after excavation an objective and comprehensive evaluation of the site should be made, along with assessing the problems and potential of the site; some key questions 'might' also be asked, such as 'should the site be presented at all?' and 'to what level should one intervene in preserving a site and its structure?'. Furthermore the preliminary objectives for conserving, presenting and maintaining the site, along with a budget, should be agreed upon as early as possible so that such things can be borne in mind when excavation is going on (Stubbs 1995, 74). A more recent book on the subject is *Conservation of Ruins*, edited by John Ashurst (2007). This book does have a short, somewhat theoretical introduction written by Ashurst, entitled 'Introduction – continuity and truth', which makes reference to some of the issues of conserving ruins, such as authenticity and the lack of appreciation of the level of information that may be gleaned from them, and also to the more poignant memorial ruins, such as those of the French village of Oradour-sur-Glane where the SS massacred the entire village's population. There is a short chapter on conservation concepts by Jokilehto (2007, 1-9). Apart from these two, however, the overall content is overwhelmingly practical with, as ever, little consideration given either to the broader reasons behind conservation or to the issues concerning the conservation of urban archaeological sites.

There are, however, a number of papers that deal with specific aspects of conserving archaeological sites within the urban context, which reflect the development of the methods that have evolved to deal with such sites. These shall be reviewed presently but firstly the methods that have evolved: there are three, possibly four, ways of dealing with urban archaeological remains, none of which are mutually exclusive and which may all be applied on the same site: excavation and preservation by record; preservation *in situ* (i.e. reburial); and excavation and conservation for display. Within the last option is a possible fourth that is the currently evolving method of 'enhancement of urban subsoil archaeological remains', as put forward by the European Commission-sponsored APPEAR project (APPEAR 2007).

The first, 'preservation by record', is relatively self-evident: the site is fully excavated, all archaeological material is recorded and removed, and the ideal end result is a comprehensive report that includes the history and development of the site, details of the uncovered stratigraphy; analysis of all organic remains; specialist reports on the artefacts, and a discussion on what was found and what it all means. Ideally there should, for more important sites, also be some sort of 'popular' publication that is available to the wider public. Unfortunately, it is fair to say that the record in most countries of the publication of excavated archaeological sites in any form, let alone in a form accessible to the general public, has been at best insufficient, at worst truly atrocious. There are a number of reasons for this, not least the dramatic jump in the number of excavations since World War II as part of the process of urban redevelopment. The theoretical developments of archaeology in the 1960s, particularly of the processual school, provided for the collection of archaeological data as a separate stage to the research and interpretation of it, which would be done at a later stage of what was considered a linear process (Thomas 2004, 76). This philosophy perfectly complemented 'preservation by record', particularly in the 1960s and 1970s in Britain where the resources could not keep up with the amount of rescue excavation that was taking place as it allowed for the archiving of excavated material and site records on the basis that the report could be written up at a later date (Thomas 2004, 76). Ensuring enough funds for the post-excavation work remains, however, a constant problem, an issue further complicated by the tendency for urban excavations to be highly complex. The importance, and indeed the duty of the excavator, to ensure a complete and comprehensive report is something that has been stressed for many a decade now, not least in official documentation as mentioned previously. Archaeology is fundamentally about the discovery and dissemination of knowledge about everybody's past, and consequently archaeologists have a duty to provide for the widest possible audience. While excavation and 'preservation by record' will allow for the fullest knowledge of an archaeological site, it remains something of a euphemism for many excavated sites.

At the opposite end of the spectrum to preservation by record is 'preservation *in situ*'. This is where the site is either not excavated or only partly so and left as it is, though with the addition of anything needed to ensure its long-term survival, and reburied. This was a concept first expressed in the Athens Charter but it has become an increasingly favoured option in relation to urban redevelopment archaeology. Two conferences have been held in London to discuss the procedure, one in 1996 (Corfield *et al* n.d. [1998]), the other in 2001 (Nixon 2004). The first set of proceedings, *Preserving Archaeological Remains in situ: proceedings of the conference of 1st-3rd April 1996* (Corfield *et al* n.d. [1998]), is almost entirely concerned with the practical issues of preserving archaeological remains *in situ* in a variety of situations. One paper that deals specifically with the urban contexts is 'Practically preserved: observations on the impact of construction on urban archaeological deposits' (Nixon n.d. [1998]). Nixon examines the effects of such construction techniques as piling on archaeological remains (Nixon n.d. [1998], 41, 45), but she concludes that as yet no criteria existed for preservation *in situ*, and that an assessment framework within which preservation criteria could be identified should be developed, to include such crucial areas as ground and soil conditions, the nature of the proposed development, various economic and environmental constraints, significance, and various issues surrounding the future of the site (Nixon n.d. [1998], 45-46).

A second paper of interest is that on archaeology and development by Huw Moseley, Planning Partner of Jones Lang Wootton, in which he examines the issue of archaeology within urban development in London, centring around that crucial issue for developers – risk (Moseley n.d. [1998], 47). He points out that even a combination of excavation and preservation *in situ* can cost twice as much as just excavation and preservation by record, mentioning one case where preservation *in situ* in central London cost over £7000 per cubic metre of archaeology (Moseley n.d. [1998], 49). He emphasises, however, that the key issue is not the quantum costs but the ability to assess the costs in advance so as to be able to decide whether to embark on the development or not; suddenly having to lose a basement and pay for bridging is a cost that can run into millions (Moseley n.d. [1998], 49). He suggests that there are some important questions that no-one should be afraid to ask when it comes to deciding whether to conserve or not, principally 'Do you really know what you are saving – and is it really that important?'. He further asks what is the public benefit of preservation *in situ* (i.e. reburial). He also suggests that it is no longer good enough merely to assemble a team of experts, but that it is necessary to select people 'who can think laterally and understand cross-discipline issues' (Moseley n.d. [1998], 50).

In relation to the whole issue of preservation *in situ*, Henry Cleere (n.d. [1998]) in his 'Closing Remarks', makes several valid points that in fact remain to be discussed. Firstly he notes a comment from Tim Darvill that raised the very important issue that 'archaeological preservation is predicted on a fallacy: namely that a stable state exists.' In other words archaeologists are prone to ignore that our work interferes with the natural process of decay, which, Cleere suggests, is an 'important philosophical, even metaphysical aspect' of archaeologists' work that has received little attention (Cleere n.d. [1998], 188). This is something reflected in Christopher Woodward's insinuation that archaeologists ruin historic sites by upsetting their natural aesthetic qualities (Woodward 2001, 24, 27). Cleere also chides Nixon for placing 'significance' at number six of her recommendations, saying it should be a prime concern, and then goes on to note that there is a tendency to assume that preservation *in situ* is a good thing, which is something that also requires discussion (Cleere n.d. [1998], 188).

The proceedings from the second conference, held in London in 2001 (Nixon 2004), suggest a more professional approach to preservation *in situ* and more successful cooperation between archaeologists, engineers and developers, as demonstrated in the collection of papers under the heading of 'Design and decision on five development sites in London' (Hughes *et al* 2004). One paper that deals with some of the practicalities of archaeology and urban regeneration in Gloucester concludes that there is a need for 'bespoke solutions' if regeneration of historic cities is to proceed successfully alongside archaeological preservation; that the concept of 'forensic engineering' should be developed early on, and that the design solution should be developed 'as much from the archaeology upwards as from the building downwards'. The authors also add that the design of suitable foundations should be such that it can be used elsewhere (Pugh-Smith *et al* 2004, 149). Although the papers of this second set of proceedings are wider-reaching and suggest much development in the whole practice of *in situ* preservation, it shares with its predecessor the overwhelming focus on practicalities with again little attention given to any theoretical concepts.

The third method of urban archaeological conservation, and the one this research is primarily concerned with, is conservation for display of archaeological sites. This practice can be sub-divided between those sites conserved in the open air and those conserved within buildings. The tendency to keep them in the open air was usually favoured up until the post-war period, but the practice of incorporating them within the building being constructed on the site has become the preferred course of action. This is partly a reflection of the increasing market value corresponding with the decreasing availability of space in cities. The change in preference from the former to the latter is again something that has happened without any apparent theoretical or philosophical thought, though it may also reflect the changes in archaeological theory which allow for a greater diversity in how a site may be interpreted and displayed. The lack of a specific philosophy and, indeed any apparent long-term consideration, however, is something of an issue particularly as the site concerned is then usually incorporated within private property not only completely surrounded by an entirely modern and insensitive context but often with restrictions on public access to the extent that it may be completely out of bounds. Thus the concept of 'conservation for display' also becomes something of an euphemism. Furthermore, what happens to the site when, in the continuing 'creative destruction' of capitalism, it is decided to demolish the building?

One of the few papers that deals specifically with some of the issues concerned with such *in situ* conservation is that by Haas (1999) entitled 'The presentation of research in and under existing buildings', in which he examines the case for keeping open and presenting evidence of former building phases. He asks a number of pertinent questions and ultimately suggests that there is one requirement only, which is 'to search in every case… for the answer that shows respect for the historical remains revealed by excavation' (Haas 1999, 81). Another rare paper that deals specifically with the conservation for display of urban archaeology is by Baugher and DiZerega Wall (1997) entitled 'Ancient and modern united: archaeological exhibitions in urban plazas'. This paper details three case studies of incorporating archaeological exhibitions into the modern spaces of the Wall Street district of New York City. Although this mostly looks at exhibitions of artefacts, this is a useful paper as it examines, amongst other issues, how the results of excavations were conserved and presented, how the commercial enterprises concerned were involved, what the practical problems were and how successful or not the exhibitions ultimately were. The authors conclude that this is a good way of disseminating information about a city's urban archaeology to the public, and that the sites helped enhance the public's awareness of this rich archaeological heritage (Baugher and DiZerega Wall 1997, 114, 129).

A paper that does look at the whole issue of conservation either via preservation *in situ* or for display in urban settings is Cumberpatch's (1995-96) 'Archaeology in the Beirut Central District: some notes and observations'. His argument is in favour of 'preservation by record', arguing that preservation *in situ* (both of unexcavated/reburied sites and of those for display) is essentially fetishistic as it gives greater intrinsic significant to some elements, specifically architectural elements, rather than to others, specifically the details of the stratigraphic sequence and the information contained therein. In other words, by insisting on preserving material *in situ* instead of excavating it in totality, greater importance is given to structure than to historical and archaeological context of those structures (Cumberpatch 1995-96, 160). He further argues that conservation for display is essentially conservative and antiquarian, and tends to rely on pre-determined assumptions about what to conserve (Cumberpatch 1995-96, 160). He further expounds on his arguments in a second paper, 'Approaches to the Archaeology of Beirut' (Cumberpatch 1998). He argues that preservation *in situ* (including conservation for display) and preservation by record represent two different approaches to the possibility of knowledge of the past. Preservation *in situ*, he points out, is essentially concerned with structures, usually stone-built, and 'an encounter with the monumentality of a past society'. In other words, there is a tendency to focus on the hard archaeology of specific periods at the expense of the strata that lie beneath or behind them. He argues that it is antiquarian to focus on conservation of particular material elements which come to represent the presence of the past in the present and to highlight certain types of technical achievement, 'which we recognise, through our own experience and sets of values, as being of particular significance' (Cumberpatch 1998, 19). The use of pre-existing assumptions about cultural significance to designate what is worth preserving inevitably restricts investigation of earlier periods sealed under the archaeological structures in question, which he argues, places greater value on the preservation of particular items of immediate visual impact than on the significance of the stratigraphic record and the contextual aspects of the site as a whole (Cumberpatch 1998, 19). Preservation by record, on the other hand, is a contextual approach that places greater value on the interrelationships of everything from the smallest artefact fragment to the largest structural remain along with the environmental context. The distinction between the contextual approach and the antiquarian approach 'lies in the investigative nature of the encounter with the past and the attempt to identify and interpret a broad range of phenomena through the acknowledgement of the essential difference and 'otherness' of the past and past societies' (Cumberpatch 1998, 19).

As noted above, preservation by record does in theory provide the greatest knowledge of a site, and it is acknowledged that to leave anything *in situ* inevitably means that the archaeological layers below the remains in question will not be accessible. But it is worth noting several things here. Firstly, in relation to full excavation and preservation by record: in living urban contexts, the provision of enough financial and temporal resources to excavate thoroughly and to the highest possible standards, is not always forthcoming, particularly if something unexpected comes up. There is also the issue of funding for post-excavation, something in the context of urban development is also often under-resourced, along with issues of where to store the archive. Furthermore there is the very serious problem of the comprehensive report that is the key component of 'preservation by record', not being produced for a variety of reasons (though this is perhaps less of a problem now that it was, particularly with an increasing ability to publish via the internet). So, in an ideal world, excavation and preservation by record is indeed the best way of both learning about a site and preserving this knowledge and in making this knowledge available in the most accessible or widely available form, but it is hardly necessary to stress that it is far from being an ideal world. Consequently if sufficient resources, particularly in terms of post-excavation storage and research and for publication of a full report are not likely to be forthcoming, to not excavate and/or to rebury and preserve the site *in situ*, is arguably the best method, at this time, of ensuring the long-term survival of the potential knowledge of the site in question.

It is agreed that conservation for display is a highly selective process that inevitably focuses on masonry remains, mostly for practical reasons – masonry survives best and is easiest to conserve of any structural remains. Furthermore, in this part of the world, these remains are most usually Roman or medieval and consequently that creates a bias of representation towards these periods. Nevertheless, the retention of material *in situ* for display does at least allow the public to have their own 'encounter with the past'. These arguments will, however, be returned to in the Discussion chapter.

The most recent development in conservation for display of urban archaeological remains is the APPEAR – Accessibility project, which is described as 'sustainable preservation and enhancement of urban subsoil archaeological remains'. It was funded by European Commission Community Research: Energy, Environment and Sustainable Development (APPEAR 2007). A number of position papers, research reports and guidelines were produced, and there are also the proceedings of a conference held in Brussels in 2005, *Urban Pasts and Urban Futures: bringing urban archaeology to life, enhancing urban archaeological remains* (APPEAR 2007). The two-day conference brought together professionals from all over Europe and beyond. The majority of the case studies dealt with sites that were conserved within buildings or under shelters, and there was much discussion about a variety of issues including how one may integrate a site conserved inside with its urban context outside. The APPEAR project was the first comprehensive international project to tackle the whole issue of conservation of archaeological sites for display in urban contexts. It focussed, however, on 'covered sites' and certainly at the conference there was heavy bias towards sites conserved inside (APPEAR 2005, 3).

The first position paper (Teller and Warnotte 2003) stated that,

> 'The term "accessibility project", refers to all actions which, together with the progress of the research, aim to conserve, integrate, enhance and exploit urban subsoil archaeological remains in a sustainable way so as to make them available to the population. The act of displaying the remains, that is making them visible, attractive and understandable in a manner compatible with their preservation and their usefulness to research, is the meaning that should be given to "accessibility"' (Teller and Warnotte 2003, 5).

The main concern of the APPEAR project was 'enhancement' of archaeological sites. It never quite defines what it means by enhancement, except to say that 'enhancement is in itself a fairly vague concept which encompasses a number of different and sometimes incompatible ideas, ranging from the purely economic to the most insubstantial symbolism' (Teller and Warnotte 2003, 1). The position paper goes on to explain that due to experiments with a number of case studies, such as the Cathedral of St-Pierre in Geneva and the new access to the Grand Louvre Museum in Paris, a 'number of previously firmly held archaeological doctrines, such as the place of hyporesearch, the limitations of restoration and the conflict between heritage and contemporary creativity' have been called into question (Teller and Warnotte 2003, 2). The paper also discusses the value of archaeological sites, explaining that while they maintain aesthetic, cultural and symbolic values, they have lost their original function and thus any reuse values, but that, above all, they have a scientific value in terms of archaeological research (Teller and Warnotte 2003, 2).

The whole issue of values is a complicated and a still developing concept in conservation, particularly urban conservation. Conservation is primarily about keeping something, and we tend only to keep things if we place some kind of value on them. As UNESCO states in the preamble to their 1956 *Recommendation* and as Article 9 of the Valetta Convention emphasises, the best way to ensure protection of the archaeological heritage, and, of course, the historic environment generally, lies in public interest and understanding. In order for the public to have interest and understanding they have to be able to place value on a site. They can only really do this if they have some kind of initial interest or knowledge or attraction to it. The initial value, one that is most probably appreciable by the widest range of people, comes from the aesthetic or artistic value that Riegl first defined in his 1903 paper, but what are the other values of, in particular, fragmentary archaeological sites conserved in urban contexts, and how are they defined? A paper by Zancheti and Jokilehto (1997) entitled 'Values and urban conservation planning: some reflections on principles and definitions', defines a value as 'the quality of a thing that makes it useful or desirable', and what actually makes something valuable as 'the relative and social attribution of qualities to things'; in other words values do not exist independently but are dependent on what people assign to things, and are, therefore, in a state of constant change and re-appraisal. In order to survive, values must, they argue, be presented to society at all times (Zancheti and Jokilehto 1997, 40-41). They suggest that there are both socio-economic values which include financial and political values and a cultural value of the built environment that is identified through a symbolic system of reference based on age, history and aesthetics (Zancheti and Jokilehto 1997, 41). One of the clearest statements of what the values involved in the built heritage are is to be found in Feilden's (2003) *Conservation of Historic Buildings*, first published in 1992. His argument is simply that conservation 'must preserve and if possible enhance the messages and values of cultural property', and he identifies three main groups of such values, which are emotional, cultural and use (Feilden 2003, 3, 6). The emotional values comprise wonder, identity, continuity, spiritual and symbolic values. The cultural values are those of documentary; historic; archaeological, age and scarcity; aesthetic and symbolic; architectural; townscape, landscape and ecological; technological and scientific. Use values include functional, economic, social, educational, political and ethnic (Feilden 2003, 6). In relation to use value, it is worth stressing that the conservation of archaeological sites and historic buildings also has the potential to encourage tolerance between communities, as demonstrated by work done in Northern Ireland (Hamlin 2000), though use values are not always benign and the cultural heritage also has the potential to cause or represent division. Naturally many of these values are relevant to archaeological sites, but with smaller, more fragmentary sites such as those often found in urban centres, it is somewhat more of a challenge to appreciate them, particularly the use values. Consequently to identify and preserve such values in order to hand them on to future generations, which is, as Clark suggests in her book, *Informed Conservation: understanding historic buildings and their landscapes for conservation*, is the main reason for conserving something in the first place (Clark 2001, 12), becomes a greater challenge; a challenge that very often is not met.

The concept of values and of cultural significance is not new – it is something included in the 1964 Venice Charter. It is, however, something that has been expanded on in the *Australia ICOMOS Charter for the Conservation of Places of Cultural Significance* (the Burra Charter, 1996), partly because of Australia's specific interests concerning the Aboriginal heritage. This charter marks a movement away from just the physical fabric to the actual place of the monument, defining place as meaning the 'site, area, building or other work, group of buildings or other works together with pertinent contents and surroundings'. It also defines cultural significance as meaning 'aesthetic, historic, scientific or social value for past, present or future generations'. The importance of values and all that concerns them in relation to the archaeological heritage and in the conservation planning process has been discussed in a number of publications. These include Kate Clark's (2004) paper ,'Between a rock and a hard decision: the role of archaeology in the conservation planning process', in the proceedings of the second preservation *in situ* conference (Nixon 2004), and Mason and Avrami's (2002) paper, 'Heritage values and challenges of conservation planning' published in the Getty Institute's report, *Management Planning for Archaeological Sites* (Teutonico and Palumbo 2002). The key issue for successful conservation is planning. This should not only be about practical issues, but should consider as an equal priority the identifying of what, why and for who something is being conserved. The valuing process cannot be separated from the decision making about the site as it is intrinsic, if not always initially recognised, to the process. It is only since the 1980s, however, that the assessment of values has been recognised in policy documents as a discrete part of the conservation process, and consequently there has been an increase in the tendency to incorporate values more efficiently into the decision-making of conservation (Mason and Avrami 2002, 18). Firstly values can be divided into two essential groups – those subjective qualities that include context-bound values such as the emotional, cultural and use values, and objective qualities which are effectively age and size (Mason and Avrami 2002, 16). This identification of objective and subjective values is important because the objective values provide something of a fundamental or unchanging point on which the other values may be built, because subjective values have a tendency to change. This is particularly the case in the post-war situation where priorities and values can or have to change dramatically; for example the need for housing over preserving a site; the problems of sites and buildings suddenly being considered politically tainted and so forth.

The other problem with subjective values, however, is that they are mostly intangible and therefore extremely difficult to assess or measure. The one value that may potentially be measured is the economic one, as demonstrated in Navrud and Ready's (2002) book, *Valuing Cultural Heritage: applying environmental valuation techniques to historic buildings, monuments and artifacts*. They equate cultural heritage with the environment which is considered by economists as a public good. Economists define a public good as a good that must have two specific characteristics: it must be "non-excludible" – i.e. it should not be feasible to exclude people from enjoying it – and it must be "non-rival" in consumption – i.e. more than one person should be able to enjoy the good at the same time without diminishing anyone else's enjoyment of that good (Navrud and Ready 2002a, 3, 4). The degree of excludability varies with cultural heritage – while enjoying the historic part of an old city is not usually an excludible activity, visiting a museum or a site that charges an entrance fee may be. The excludability aspect is of particular importance because economic theory argues that private, profit-driven markets will not provide enough non-excludible goods as private providers tend not provide anything that does not make a profit. In other words the private sector would only provide or protect the cultural heritage goods that had a high market demand. The other more subtle problem of relying on private provision of an excludible good is that, for example, the aesthetic value of an old building may be of far greater value to the town it is situated in than to the owner, particularly if they gain no financial benefit from it, and so they may be less inclined to provide for its conservation (Navrud and Ready 2002a, 4). The second characteristic of non-rivalry is an equally important aspect to cultural heritage in allowing for the greatest number of people to enjoy it, but some sites have colossal visitor numbers and hence some become 'congestible' public goods as too many people will cause damage. The most obvious way of limiting this is to charge an entrance fee, which has the advantage of generating some income but also, in theory, 'it assures the limited number of entry slots go to those who place the highest value on the experience' (Navrud and Ready 2002a, 5), though this does rather disingenuously equate ability to pay with ability to appreciate. What underlies both non-excludability and non-rivalry, is that such goods do not have a market or generate a profit. Consequently, the private sector cannot be trusted to provide enough cultural heritage and so it is up to government and not-for-profit organisations, but as Navrud and Ready point out, the availability of resources for cultural heritage is naturally limited and so decisions about what to keep and what not to have to be made. The theory of public goods states that 'the correct amount of a public good is determined by comparing the marginal cost of providing more of the good with the marginal social benefit of providing more of the good'; in other words the cost of protecting a site has to be compared to the resulting social benefits. The 'socially-optimal' number of sites is the number where the additional cost of protecting one more site is equal to the additional benefit of protecting one more site – the cost-benefit ratio for the last site considered should be equal to one (Navrud and Ready 2002a, 5). The book goes on to analyse how some of these benefits may be assessed, including using such concepts as 'willingness to pay', and the use of various non-market valuation techniques such as the Hedonic Pricing Technique, which, basically, is a pricing method that examines situations where the purchase of a market good, for example a property, includes the opportunity to enjoy a given level of a non-market good, for example the local park or, perhaps, an historic building, and how this affects the price of the market-good, thus giving some idea of the value of the non-market good (Navrud and Ready 2002b, 12). Navrud and Ready (2002b, 12) note that while this technique is used to value environmental goods, it has not been used for cultural heritage goods. It is, however, quite possibly something that could be done to ascertain the economic value of archaeological sites conserved for display in urban centres, bearing in mind that it inevitably comes down to who is doing the valuing and what their priorities are.

In the concept of valuing based on the concept of the 'public good', it is the social benefit that is considered foremost. Ultimately the identifying of all values comes from the 'stakeholders' – anyone who has an interest in, in this case, an archaeological site and its conservation, and ideally equal weight should be given to everyone's various concerns and ideas until some sort of balance is achievable between them. Mason and Avrami (2002, 22) suggest that the net must be cast more widely to try and ensure some sort of social equity and to allow for the 'soft' voices – i.e. those usually unheard such as the poor, minorities and so forth – to be heard. This is absolutely right but in reality the tendency is that some stakeholders are more influential than others, and these are not usually the locals who have to live with the site in question but more often whoever is holding the purse-strings, which in the case of urban redevelopment is most often the person or company financing the redevelopment. Most usually, though there are exceptions, developers place no value on having a conserved archaeological site in the middle of their development, and even where sites are legally protected, the successful, i.e. sustainable, conservation and management of such a site rests a good deal on the goodwill and interest of not just the development company but the succession of owners and/or tenants of the site that will follow. It is for this reason that not only is it absolutely crucial that some way of identifying and promoting the values of conserved for display archaeological sites be developed but that archaeologists and conservation specialists must be able to answer clearly those questions, to paraphrase those asked by Moseley (nd [1998], 50) mentioned above, 'Do you really know what you are saving and why – is it really that important, and to who, and what is the public benefit?'

In relation to the broader issues of the conservation of archaeological sites there have been several developments, mainly the development of two sub-disciplines, one being site management, and the other, public archaeology. In relation to the former is the *Charter of Krakow* (2000), which was produced by the joint ICOMOS and ICAHM committee on Archaeological Heritage Management. The Krakow Charter focuses on key issues such as the responsibility of the community for their own heritage and appreciates the presence of social, cultural and aesthetic values. It also highlights that while cultural tourism is important it must also be considered a risk to cultural heritage. Alongside the development of the various international documents and the defining of values/meaning or reasons for saving historic architecture, there is a vast quantity of literature now in print that deals with the conservation of the built environment and its management from a variety of angles. A brief sample may include *Cultural Resource Management in Contemporary Society: perspectives on managing and presenting the past* (McMahamon and Hatton 2000), which considers the place of cultural resource management within modern society, and has a number of interesting papers including Hamlin's (2000) paper on archaeological sites in Northern Ireland, another on the threat to conservation in Africa (Folorunso 2000), and a third paper entitled 'Conflict between preservation and development in Japan' (Okamura 2000). An interesting collection is that edited by Jameson (1997), entitled *Presenting Archaeology to the Public: digging for truths*. It is orientated towards the USA and museum studies but does have some papers on sites on the role of the public in archaeology. A third collection, edited by Krumbein *et al* (1994) is *Durability and Change: the science, responsibility, and cost of sustaining cultural heritage* and contains both practical and theoretical papers including a thought-provoking paper entitled 'Should we take it all so seriously? Culture, conservation, and meaning in the contemporary world' that discusses the implications of contemporary cultural criticism for arguments about conserving cultural heritage (Cosgrove 1994, 259ff). A rare exception that deals with both historic architecture and urban archaeology is a collection of papers entitled *Conservation and Change in Historic Towns* (Dennison 1999), which is the proceedings of a conference held in Scotland in 1996. The papers examine many aspects of conservation in the historic town, though mostly in Scotland but also including a number of other European cities. A paper on Dublin mentions the conserving of the remains of two medieval wall-towers, of which one, St Isolde's Tower, may be viewed by the public (Clarke 1999, 154).

What is evident in recent times is the increased awareness of the public and their entitlement to access to the past. An early paper is that by Philippe Planel (1994), called 'Privacy and community through medieval material culture', published in Stone and Molyneaux's (1994) *The Presented Past: heritage, museums and education*. Planel's paper deals with the question of presenting medieval remains to modern children. He suggests the aim of a site visit should be 'to enrich present lives by examining past lives' and that the real question is 'how can we use material remains to fulfil these aims?' (Planel 1994, 208). He is primarily referring to castles and other such larger archaeological remains, but his aim and his question are relevant to all sites and monuments conserved for display to the public. In a useful paper by Nick Merriman, entitled 'Archaeology, heritage and interpretation' (2002), the whole development of 'public archaeology' is summarized. As Merriman suggests, although archaeology always has had a public dimension, it is really only in the last ten to fifteen years that the whole concept of 'public archaeology' – of the acknowledgement by the archaeological profession of public interest in archaeology – has been developed (Merriman 2002, 541). This volume includes a paper on presenting archaeological sites to the public in which it is pointed out that there has been a gradual change from a positivist approach, where the public were essentially told what to see, to a more open rationale of helping the public to understand what archaeology is all about and what archaeologists do and why (Copeland 2004, 133). Copeland argues for a 'constructivist' approach based on the belief that 'individuals are constantly constructing and reconstructing meaning as they react with the world, negotiating thought, feelings and actions'. In other words an individual visiting a site will bring their memories, interests and experiences with them and react to what they see based on a combination of these, and will take up the information that they consider as most significant to them. In terms of presentation, however, this aspect has been, for the most part, ignored. The visitor has often been considered as some homogeneous blank. Copeland further points out that little work has been done on visitor experience designed to understand what visitors' perspectives are, but he mentions a research project on visitor experience carried out retrospectively on a group of students in Indiana. They were asked what they thought were the benefits of the visit. The attribute considered most important was the past or the past and culture of the site, but also valued were: activities engaged in, such as walking around the site; having a companion with them; site personnel; the information learned; the built environment; the natural setting of the site. They also mentioned the knowledge gained, the personal experience including 'the social benefits of significant interactions with companions and aesthetic experiences gained through the natural setting', and it was concluded that the student visitors 'think of heritage sites as a mosaic of different aspects' (Masberg and Silverman 1996 in Copeland 2004, 139-140).

IV. DISCUSSION

In the period up to the outbreak of World War II, many European cities saw unprecedented change and growth, much of it in historic cities with layouts and street systems unsuitable for industrialisation, the development of motor transport, and indeed for housing the vast numbers of people who flocked to cities in search of work. The consequences included traffic gridlock, pollution, frightful overcrowding and slums. The development of modernist urban planning was for the most part founded on a desire to improve cities for the benefit of all; in other words to provide more suitable housing, plenty of green spaces and to encourage zoning – the separation of, for example, housing and industry, and pedestrians from the traffic. The problem was that no city could simply be wiped away and rebuilt. Until the devastations of the second world war redevelopment was piecemeal and much of this idealistic planning remained in theory only. In terms of conservation and archaeology, these, in Europe, were principally rural activities and concern was for the most part with larger-scale Roman or prehistoric sites and monuments. The predominant value of 'ruins' was considered to be aesthetic.

The destruction of World War II gave modernist planners opportunities to start putting their city planning ideals into practice. It also gave archaeologists opportunities to investigate the archaeology of many of Europe's historic cities, though in reality urban rescue archaeology was very much in its infancy and not something that most archaeologists were interested in, nor had the resources for. Added to which one of modernism's basic tenets is to break with the past, which meant conservation of the built environment, apart from particularly important buildings, was simply not considered by them. That is not to say, however, that all bomb-damaged cities were rebuilt under modernist planners. In Southampton, for example, radical modernist plans were rejected by the town's traders and politicians, and a plan was put forward that was, for the most part, the work of the borough engineer, F.L. Wooldridge. He saw that much of the remaining old town could in fact be utilised and without interfering too much with the surviving historical fabric (Hasegawa 1992, 61). The City of London did retain much of its historic street layout and property boundaries, and in some cities of West Germany, such as Münster, Freiburg, and Nuremberg, efforts were made to retain the surviving historic architecture (see Berlin Chapter).

Destruction of the historic urban environment, including archaeological sites, became steadily worse in London, and indeed it would seem elsewhere as indicated both by the increased legislation in many countries in the 1960s-1970s to protect the built heritage and the growing concern expressed in various international documentation produced by UNESCO, ICOMOS and other such organisations. The late 1960s-early 1970s is an important period in the history of the twentieth century as there was a broad-based socio-cultural change that swept through North America and Europe, generated mostly, it would seem, by the generation that grew up since the war. These changes are reflected in many ways, but the birth of the 'postmodern condition' stems from this time, the change of attitude towards the historic built environment, and indeed the changes within archaeological theory are the most relevant ones to this research. Postmodernism, in theory, embraced the past but in reality increasingly appropriated it for present-day aesthetical reasons, and the notion of 'creative destruction', originally a force that joined modernism to capitalism, is still very much part of present-day urban redevelopment. The practice of urban rescue or developer-led archaeology is now a common part of urban redevelopment, and a number of ways of dealing with preserving or conserving the archaeology within this situation have been developed, principally 'preservation by record', 'preservation *in situ*' (i.e. reburial) and conservation for display. The second option is increasingly used, and the third option has seen an increasing tendency to conserve sites within the new building being constructed, rather than outside. Furthermore since the 1960s, the more academic or scientific values have come to dominate the conservation of sites, simultaneously overshadowing the aesthetic values, which are arguably the more popular values. There has been little thought given to the reasoning behind the whole practice of either preservation *in situ* or conservation for display of fragmentary archaeological sites in urban contexts, as urban development-led archaeology appears to be still considered something of a poor relation in the field of academic archaeology and the tendency is still to concentrate on the larger, more prominent sites.

The problem with the lack of a theoretical framework is that it is not always apparent, particularly outside the profession of archaeology, why sites have been conserved for display in the past, nor why certain sites are conserved now. This has led to poor management, inadequate or no signage and to many developers not appreciating what is important about a site, or indeed about archaeology in general. Development remains one the biggest threats to archaeology (Palumbo 2002, 4). Furthermore as cities continue to grow rapidly, it is crucial that we understand why we conserve some sites and why we should not conserve others, who we are conserving them for, and how we are going to ensure that they remain valued and accessible in the long-term.

The following chapters examine these issues through consideration of the urban context and conservation of archaeological sites in London between 1945 and c.1965 (chapter 3); East and West Berlin between 1945 and 1989 and then Berlin from 1990 to 2007 (chapter 4); and Beirut from 1990 to 2007, though concerned primarily with the post-war period of the 1975-1990 War (chapter 5). The post-war situation highlights the effects that the urban redevelopment and socio-political biases have on the level of conservation of archaeological sites for display.

CHAPTER THREE

LONDON AFTER WORLD WAR II

I. INTRODUCTION

London had prepared for intensive air bombardment well before World War II actually broke out. In fact it would seem that, as Hebbert (1998, 62) suggests, unlike almost anything else in London's history, the Blitz was foreseen and planned for. Heavy bombardment began in 1941 and continued sporadically until 1945. Swathes of the metropolis were reduced to roofless ruins and rubble, particularly parts of East London, and in the City[3] from St Paul's north up to Cripplegate. For quite some time prior to the war, however, there had been much discussion about redeveloping the city and some believed that the Blitz had not destroyed enough (Hebbert 1998, 63).

In relation to the damage suffered by the built heritage, one of the most enduring images is of the dome of St Paul's Cathedral emerging out of the dark smoke of the Blitz: the cathedral survived with comparatively minor damage despite all around being laid flat. Many other historic buildings were not so fortunate; for example the Tower of London was caught by a bomb in 1940 and St Bride's Church was completely gutted as were a number of other churches; Westminster Abbey was hit, and the House of Commons destroyed. The destruction, however, was a benefit to archaeology. In the case of London, as with other British cities such as Southampton, Bristol and Coventry, war damage resulted in the discovery and exposure of archaeological sites and deposits. Medieval and urban archaeology in living cities, both still very much in their infancies prior to World War II, became from this point onwards irreversibly established as major elements of general archaeological practice and as part of the process of urban redevelopment in Britain.

This chapter considers the conservation of archaeological sites in the period from 1945 to c.1965 in the City of London (see figure 9 for map). The City comprises London's historic centre, where the Romans first established their fort and later walled town. It was deserted during the Anglo-Saxon period but with the increasing Viking raids, the old Roman walled town was revived and the walls re-built during the medieval period. It was within the City that the Great Fire of 1666 broke out, after which it had to be substantially rebuilt, along with many of its churches, to the designs of Sir Christopher Wren.

The first section of the chapter examines the socio-cultural and political context of post-war London alongside the planning and redevelopment beliefs expounded and put into practice. Following this is the section on the conservation policies and practice. Then, those archaeological sites conserved for display will be assessed and, through detailed analysis of contemporary records, an attempt is made to reconstruct the value judgements that underpinned the conservation process.

II: THE URBAN CONTEXT

London, as with a number of other urban centres such as Southampton and Coventry, suffered extensive damage during the Blitz between August 1940 and May 1941, and continuing bombing raids until the end of World War II. In fact, London's largest loss was in property with almost half of the housing stock and some nine million square feet in office space being destroyed. Within the City, the damage covered about a third, just over half of the acreage that had been destroyed by the Great Fire of 1666, and to the east and south districts including Stepney, Poplar and Bermondsey were devastated (Porter 2000, 416). Londoners, on the whole, rose to the challenge both during the war and afterwards, and there was much discussion about rebuilding, represented by publications ranging from the official *County of London Plan 1943* prepared for the London County Council by Forshaw and Abercrombie (1943) to Purdom's (1946) *How Should We Rebuild London*.

Concerns regarding the rebuilding of British cities, as with cities throughout Europe, were an issue even before the war. There had been large population growths throughout the preceding century. In 1841 the population of Britain was just over 18.5 million, which included 1.9 million living in London. By c.1939, the country's population was an estimated 46.5 million, of which 6.25 million lived in London (Ashworth 1959, 7; 9; Porter 2000, 421). Much of this population growth had congregated in urban centres, though many such cities, particularly those which had retained their medieval street layout, were ill-designed to accommodate such expansion, leading inevitably to over-crowding, slums, chronic traffic congestion, and piecemeal and insensitive redevelopment.

The replanning of London was something of a divided affair, not least because the City and the county were dealt with separately, and what arose was a division between the conservatism of the City of London Corporation (the Corporation) and the fashionable 'clean-sweep' planning notions being propounded for the rest of the metropolis (Hebbert 1998, 70). There were three separate plans – a County plan (1943), a Regional plan (1944) and a City plan (1946) – and there were three principle concerns regarding London's rebuilding – housing, restraining growth, and transport. London was felt to be becoming unwieldy – slums, congestion, little control over what was being built where, and many of the areas that had not been blitzed were badly run down. In the 1930s, the aim had been slum clearance and to move everyone out to new towns and suburbs, and after the war, this idea persisted, combined with restraining London to within its green belt. The 1943 *County of London Plan* identified eight areas as being particularly

---

[3] In relation to London, where the term 'the City' with a capital C is used, this refers to the borough of that name; where the term 'the city' with a small c is used, this refers to London as a whole.

badly damaged and defined them as Reconstruction Areas: Stepney-Poplar, Bermondsey, South Bank, Elephant and Castle, Bunhill Fields and, in the City, Barbican (Cripplegate), St Paul's Precinct and the Tower of London (Johnson-Marshall 1966, 178). The *Town and Country Planning Act* of 1947 allowed for the compulsory purchase of property within these areas so that where was particularly badly blitzed or blighted could be acquired for wide-scale reconstruction. The Corporation, the Planning Authority until the 1947 Act came into being, had defined three such areas within the City, as listed above (Johnson-Marshall 1966, 178). Unlike for the rest of the metropolis, the concern within the City was, initially, to retain and accommodate rather than replace: 'at the present time the opinion of the authors of the plan is that the seventeenth-century scale should be preserved and that St Paul's Cathedral – the noblest building in the City – should remain architecturally, as in other ways, its chief building' (Holden and Holford 1951, 45-46). The plans for the City did however include the compulsory purchase of property within the Cripplegate area for the development of the ultra-modern Barbican complex.

The apparently positive attitude to the City's historic buildings contrasted somewhat with one of the basic tenets of modernism, which was a break with the past, and with the plans for the rest of London. In Abercrombie and Forshaw's plan of 1943, historically and architecturally interesting buildings get two small paragraphs devoted to them under the chapter heading of 'Focus Points', where they acknowledge that London possesses many such buildings that 'give to the metropolis its external character and interest, and reveal its evolution and traditions', but that such buildings should be dealt with on an individual basis where necessary (Forshaw and Abercrombie 1943, 140). One option put forward elsewhere in the report was that historic buildings could be moved if they were in the way (Forshaw and Abercrombie 1943, 59-60). As with development plans generally, there is no mention of archaeological remains. In 1943, this oversight may be forgiven – urban archaeology within a living city and medieval archaeology as a whole were both very much novel concepts. Secondly, in relation to historic sites and buildings, this was a period well before the development of the concept of the historic environment; in general, historic sites and buildings were considered in isolation, rather than as part of a larger whole. As has been noted (Esher 1981, 72), there had long been interest in protecting the countryside, and its sites and monuments, but the idea of protecting the urban environment had not yet come into play. This is evident, for example, in Abercrombie's (1959) *Town and County Planning*, where he has a whole section entitled 'Country planning and preservation' that includes a chapter on rural preservation and 'disfiguration', but there is no mention within his section on town planning on urban preservation or disfiguration, though he does praise an example of rebuilding in south London by the London County Council that 'shows modern ideas brought into exact harmony with traditional needs and feelings' (Abercrombie 1959, 131-132). This lack of thought regarding urban preservation was symptomatic of the belief that new was good and would unquestionably be better than what had been before; this attitude was expressed in, for example, Le Corbusier's pre-war plan for Paris and perpetuated by his followers (Esher 1981, 72). These ideas combined with the general assumption that wide-scale clearance and redevelopment was the best option continued until the late 1960s (Hall 2002, 245). On the other hand, a general conservatism seemed to dominate the plans for the rebuilding of the City, but there were exceptions. One area that saw radical, modernist redevelopment was Cripplegate. This northwest corner of the City had been subjected to some of the worst bombing of the war. It was decided to rebuild completely the area as the Barbican Estate – a huge complex, comprising residential accommodation, an arts centre, a school and the Museum of London, with the modernist requisites of tall towers, open spaces and walkways. It was initially designed in part to accommodate the workers, such as cleaners, security personnel etc. that would be needed by the City offices. The modernist tendencies of wanting to break with the past, while maintaining select pieces of it, will be demonstrated below. In the period that followed World War II, it was the modernist ideals and concerns of the pre-war period – slum clearance, reducing congestion and providing for more open spaces – that continued as the driving principles behind post-war redevelopment. It was within these whole-scale modernist planning ideals and the pressing post-war concerns that archaeology and conservation had to find its place.

III: CONSERVATION AND ARCHAEOLOGY

Conservation and archaeology prior to World War II

The practice of conservation in Europe stemmed from a very early art-historic interest in ancient Classical monuments. In England, because there was little by way of major Roman remains, it was the ruins of the medieval monasteries resulting from Henry VIII's rapacious dissolution that became the focal point (Woodward 2001, 96; 111). By the eighteenth century, this interest had metamorphosed into the English aesthetic theories of the Picturesque and a fashion amongst the upper classes for ruins in their landscaped gardens. This is the main catalyst for some of the earliest preservation in England, and is the reason for the survival of, for example, the ruins of Fountains Abbey – now a UNESCO World Heritage site (Jokilehto 1999, 51). This interest in antiquities was also demonstrated by the popularity of prints and engravings of monuments not just in rural settings but also those depicting urban scenes, such as those published between 1747 and 1906 in *Vetusta Monumenta* (Peltz 1999, 13).

The growth of interest in antiquities amongst the wider population was a slower process that began towards the end of the eighteenth century. This is attributed to several reasons such as greater education and the development of Romanticism (Hunter 1996, 4). England and France fought various wars against each other between 1793 and 1815, severely curtailing travel to the continent. As a result attention was turned to the English landscape and its architectural and natural heritage. The nineteenth century saw the growth of nationalism and a corresponding development of the concept of 'national' antiquities and their association with national identity (Hunter 1996, 5). The growth in appreciation of historic monuments is demonstrated, for example, by visitors to the Tower of London, which was opened to the public in 1828; by the 1850s it was drawing c.200,000 visitors per year (Hunter 1996, 5). The Industrial Revolution of the late eighteenth and nineteenth centuries led to Britain undergoing fundamental social and physical changes that included considerable dislocation. There was much destruction wrought on the countryside, including its monuments, from mining and the development of industry. In urban centres, there were huge population growths and change, and throughout this period historic buildings and archaeological monuments were under perpetual threat.

Despite the developing interest in archaeological and historical monuments and the growing threat to their survival, there was no legislation in place to protect them; for the most part protection was voluntary and the rights of private property was sacrosanct. After a long hard battle, the Ancient Monuments Protection Act finally came into being in 1882 (Champion 1996, 38). This allowed the State to take sites into guardianship, though only with the agreement of the owner, but historic buildings and medieval ruins were excluded (Champion 1996, 39). The general perception of an archaeological monument was that it was prehistoric and mostly of stone; a perception which remained, unfortunately, at the root of subsequent legislation (Champion 1996, 38). Added to which there was the general concept of archaeology and preservation generally being a rural and not an urban concern, for while William Morris founded the Society for the Protection of Ancient Buildings in 1877 and the National Trust was founded in 1895, little was done to protect the historic urban environment and its sites and architecture (Esher 1981, 72).

After the 1882 Act, a number of others followed that improved State protection and extended the definition of what was considered a monument. The Ancient Monuments Act 1931, tried to address the issue of context of monuments. It introduced the concept of the preservation scheme 'for the purpose of preserving the amenities of any ancient monument' by where a scheme could be prepared for 'any area comprising or adjacent to the site of the monument' (Ancient Monuments Act 1931, 1). In relation to these preservation schemes in urban areas, it merely states that 'If it appears to the Commissioners that a town planning scheme approved after the commencement of this Act under the Town Planning Act, 1925, has the effect of preserving to the satisfaction of the Commissioners the amenities of an ancient monument, the Commissioners may defray, either in whole or in part, such part of the expenses incurred by any local authority in connexion with the scheme' (Ancient Monuments Act 1931, 3). It does not, however, mention any policy to deal with those that were not satisfactorily preserved. One of the other things the Act did was to extend the powers of the Commissioners in relation to maintenance of ancient monuments in their care, including 'power to do all such things as may be necessary for the maintenance of the monument and for the exercise of proper control and management' (Ancient Monuments Act 1931, 4). The Act goes on to amend various aspects of preservation orders, of the listing of ancient monuments and of regulations regarding public access. It also defines the terms monument and ancient monument: the term 'monument' refers to 'any building, structure, or other work, whether above or below the surface of the land, other than an ecclesiastical building for the time being used for ecclesiastical purposes, and any cave or excavation', whereas the term 'ancient monument' encompassed any monument in the Schedule to the Ancient Monuments Act, 1882, any monument 'for the time being specified in a list published under section twelve of the principal Act' and 'any other monument or group of monuments and any part or remains of a monument or group of monuments which is in the opinion of the Commissioners of a like character, or of which the preservation is, in the opinion of the Commissioners, a matter of public interest by reason of the historic, architectural, traditional, artistic or archæological interest attaching thereto:' (Ancient Monuments Act 1931, 10-11).

The legal protection of most archaeological sites and historic buildings was, therefore, theoretically in place prior to World War II, but it depended considerably on the co-operation of the property owner, and was much more relevant to rural sites; protection of urban sites was minimal, and non-existent for below-ground sites. In reality protection of any archaeological site proved difficult to implement (as is exemplified by the destruction wrought on Coventry's historical fabric mentioned later), and development continued to take its toll on the built heritage up to the outbreak of the second world war (Champion 1996, 50).

Figure 8: Bastion 12, Barbican Estate, Cripplegate

In relation to the practice of archaeology itself, prior to World War II, it continued to be a predominantly rural or foreign activity. There is also some debate as to what type of, and how much, theoretical discussion was involved with the practice of archaeology prior to 1939 or even up to the 1960s (Johnson 1999, 15). As has been mentioned previously, both urban archaeology in a living city and medieval archaeology were in their infancy in Britain. Terry (1905) excavated and had restored a extramural tower (Bastion 12[4]; figure 8) in the Cripplegate area towards the end of the nineteenth century, but the first excavation for specifically archaeological reasons in London had been carried out in 1914 under the supervision of Frank Lambert of the Guildhall Museum. The archaeology concerned was some Roman features under the General Post Office on St Martin-le-Grand. Apart from this example, however, all development within London both before and after the first world war was carried out without either concern for or attention paid to archaeological strata. Between 1928 and 1937 things were improved somewhat by an initiative of the Society of Antiquaries of London who employed observers to record whatever archaeological material came up on building sites (Sheldon and Haynes 2000, 3). A similar situation existed in Coventry where development to replace some of the medieval street system with new, wider streets in the 1930s led to the destruction of thirteenth-century houses and some of Coventry's oldest streets such as Palmer Lane and Ironmonger Row, with no record of what was destroyed (Rylatt 1977, 23). At the inaugural meeting of the Coventry Archaeological Research Society in 1934, this destruction was discussed but they still persisted in providing funding and support for excavations at the Roman, Saxon and medieval sites at Baginton, some three miles south of Coventry, while providing nothing to support archaeological work within Coventry itself (Rylatt 1977, 23).

Conservation and archaeology after World War II

Many of England's historic towns and cities suffered considerable damage from wartime bombing; in Canterbury rescue excavations began even before the war ended. With the end of the war came the extensive replanning and rebuilding of many of these urban centres under the directions of the Town and Country Act of 1947. This Act gave little consideration to archaeology but at the last minute, a requirement to compile lists of buildings worthy of preservation was inserted. This incorporation of the preservation of historic buildings into a planning act was considered something of an 'intellectual seismic shift' (Hall 2002, 245). It did not, however, cause any fundamental change in attitude. In 1953 the Council for British Archaeology (CBA) felt it necessary to issue a note on the preservation of historic buildings as dealt with by the Act as they felt that not enough use was being made of the 'new and extensive powers' within it to protect such properties (CBA 1953, 1). Also in that year the *Historic Buildings and Ancient Monuments Act* 1953 came into effect. It also was mostly concerned with historic buildings, though it did allow for owners to be prosecuted for damaging scheduled sites and revised the system for issuing preservation and guardianship orders (Champion 1996, 52). The CBA (1954) then felt it necessary to produce a *Memorandum on the Ancient Monuments Acts* summarising the main points of the 1913, 1931 and 1953 Acts, not because of the destruction of archaeological deposits and historic buildings in towns and cities that was happening during this time, but because of 'the destruction of a certain scheduled earthwork in the West Country which came to light recently after a long interval of time', which led them to consider 'ways and means' of strengthening the position (CBA 1954, 1). The last point of the Ancient Monuments Acts they summarize is in relation to what may be destroyed: 'it may seem to the Ministry that in all circumstances preservation of the ancient monument for all time would be unreasonable, e.g. unduly repressive', and goes on to say that an adequate record should be made prior to the ancient monument's destruction, which in the case of an earthwork or similar, would involve a 'scientific excavation' but 'where the monument is a building or a ruin the case can sometimes be met by the provision of an adequate survey (drawn or photographic) and a description for publication' (CBA 1954, 2-3). This 'preservation by record', it would seem, left little actual protection for archaeological sites and their recording in urban contexts.

The attitude towards historic buildings in London in relation to planning thus ranged from the belief that redevelopment should 'thread its way between the sites and buildings which everyone wants to preserve' (Holden and Holford 1951, 54) to moving them if they were in the way of development (Forshaw and Abercrombie 1944, 59). Of those historic buildings that were deemed worth preserving, the primary concern was their restoration. Churches were given careful consideration, and their settings were taken into account, with provision to improve them where it was required. Although St Paul's Cathedral managed to escape with all but minor damage, many of London's churches were not so fortunate: seventeen were destroyed and seven more were damaged, though of the total, only seven were considered beyond rebuilding (Milne 1997, 2). Of the many other historic buildings that sustained bombing, the Tower of London suffered some damage, though most of it to later rather than earlier buildings (Parnell 1993, 114), as did some of the buildings of Westminster; conservation work had to be carried out on the medieval Jewel Tower and some excavations in the vicinity resulted in the fourteenth century moat being re-opened (Green 1976, 59). The Guildhall sustained a direct hit on the night of the 29th December 1940, leaving it with only its outer walls, tracery, porch and crypt (Waller 2004, 9), but while the Guildhall remained a ruin, in 1946 the Corporation gave £5,000 to help restore St Paul's Cathedral (The Times 1960, 6).

---

[4] The term 'bastion' and their numbers were allocated to the extramural towers of the City wall by Grimes during the RMLEC excavations of the sites in the 1940s-1950s.

Initially, however, no provision was made for the archaeology of London even though it was acknowledged that 'the whole area [the City] might be said to be an historic monument' and that 'unlike the case of Rome or Pompeii' archaeologists had not had the chance to excavate Roman or medieval London (Holden and Holford 1951, 53). So although, for the most part, the opportunity for wide-scale archaeological research provided by this damage was lost (Milne 2002, 1), partly due to a lack of expertise and financing but also because, as Rylatt (1977, 7) said of Coventry, 'the inclination was lacking', it was the extensive bomb damage that was, indirectly, to be a principle cause for the growth of the practice of urban and medieval archaeology as we know it today (Gerrard 2003, 95). The damage suffered by London for example, especially in the City, led to various archaeological features – in particular sections of the City wall – coming to light which could not be ignored, and sparked the enthusiasm of a number of people, as shall be detailed later. The Society of Antiquaries set up the Roman and Mediæval London Excavation Council (RMLEC) in 1947 under the directorship of Professor W.F. Grimes, and the government via the Ministry of Works (MoW) provided significant funding to them (£26,300 in total). Their excavations were among the first major campaigns of urban archaeology in a living city (Gerrard 2003, 95).

When Grimes and the RMLEC began work on the Cripplegate sites in the late 1940s, the legal source of protection for archaeological sites was then the Ancient Monuments Act 1931, followed later by that of 1953, both of which were very much concerned with historic buildings, and archaeological sites in a rural context. At an international level the Athens Charter of 1931 was the main guiding document, followed later by the 1956 UNESCO *Recommendation on International Principles Applicable to Archaeological Excavations* (New Delhi 1956). It is debatable how relevant these international charters and recommendations were to archaeologists struggling to work in cities such as London in the post-war period, where resources, funding and even trained personnel were limited, and where often sites were blocked by rubble until the last minute, or rebuilding had already begun. In relation to archaeological theory, as with urban planning, there was no major change until the 1960s and the development of 'New Archaeology'. The developments in archaeology in the post-war period mirror those of urban planning to some extent – the appeal of science, the notions of process and the concepts of middle range theories. Both practices attempted to make use of the new systems theories (the main early application of which had been to weapons systems), which ultimately failed in terms of urban planning (Hall 2002, 360, 365) and caused considerable debate amongst archaeologists (Johnson 1999, 66ff). But the RMLEC ended its intensive City programme in 1962 and as the 1960s progressed, archaeology, along with the built heritage generally was under greater and greater threat from urban redevelopment. The idea of 'preservation by record' come to the fore as even if a site was physically destroyed, it could still be reconstructed on paper, provided that an adequate record of the associated sequence and related artefacts had been made. In parallel with this was the development of the concept that archaeological methodology is a series of abstract or objective skills and therefore once a site was recorded and the material archived, anybody, not necessarily the excavator, could write it up. Initially, at least, the preservation by record maxim proved a somewhat convenient and relatively cost-effective solution to the problem of archaeological sites threatened by major urban redevelopment schemes (Thomas 2004, 76).

IV: THE SITES

There are sixteen sites conserved in the post-war period of 1945 to c.1965 in the City of London that shall be examined here (figure 9). They comprise City wall sites, including the West Gate; the Temple of Mithras; and the medieval tower of St Alphage's. These sites are either Roman or medieval, or both in the case of the City wall. There are also three other sites referred to; these are the ruined churches of St Dunstan-in-the-East, Greyfriars Christchurch and St Mary Aldermanbury. These were originally medieval churches subsequently rebuilt by Christopher Wren after the Great Fire of 1666 but were severely damaged by bombing during the Blitz, not repaired or demolished but had their ruins conserved.

There were a number of organisations involved in the conservation of sites within the City in the post war period. These included the Ancient Monuments Board within the Ministry of Works; the RMLEC responsible for the majority of the archaeological excavations carried out in the City under the directorship of Grimes, together with a host of other bodies such as the City Engineer and the City Planning Office within the Corporation, the Ministry for Housing and Local Government, various developers and their architects and surveyors, the public, and on several occasions, Parliament.

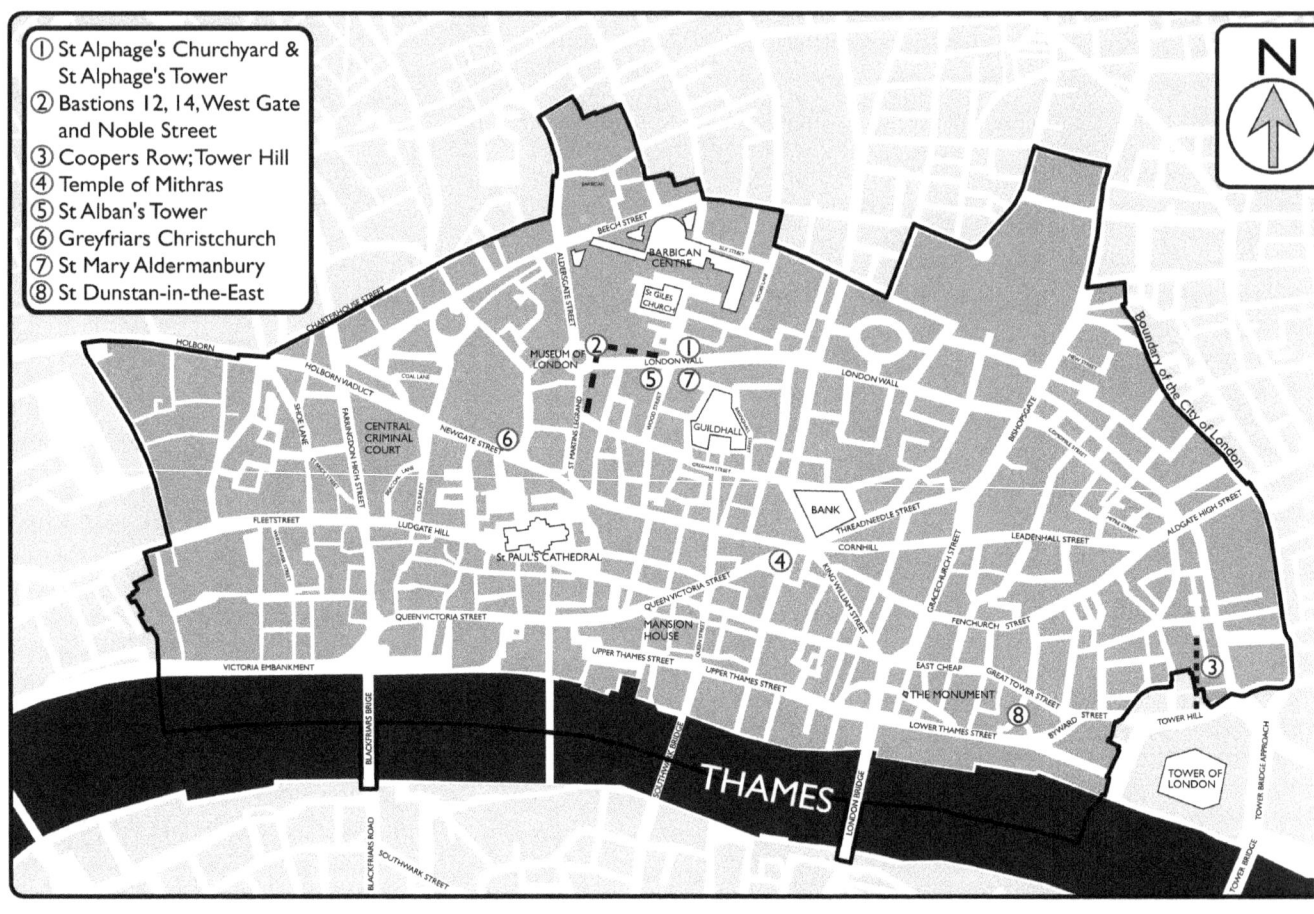

Figure 9: City of London: sites mentioned in the text

The City Wall

The town wall of the City of London was originally a Roman construction built between AD 190 and 220, and was extended to include the fort at Cripplegate (Milne 1995, 77). The preservation of the wall was not an issue that suddenly arose during the war, but something that had been considered important from at least the late nineteenth century. The Society of Antiquaries conducted an excavation in the early 1900s on the site for the then new General Post Office off Giltspur Street and found, as had been expected, remains of a bastion there. It was conserved within the basement, paid for from the sum voted for the building of the GPO (MoW file Work 14:1721), and it attracted many visitors up until the war, when it was closed. (It remains in the basement but of what is now the Merrill Lynch Financial Centre and may be seen by appointment.) During World War II, however, the destruction caused by the Blitz led ironically to the re-appearance of a number of stretches of the City wall; remaining pieces had survived subsumed within later buildings that were subsequently destroyed by the bombing. At least two influential people took note of this and developed ideas to save as many of these fragments as possible – they were the then Chief Inspector of the Ancient Monuments Board (CIAM), B.H. St John O'Neil, and the then City Engineer, Francis Forty. As will be seen, the conservation of the surviving City wall fragments was generally considered favourably by the Corporation; an attitude that was in marked contrast to their almost always negative attitude towards other archaeological sites.

The two main sections of the City Wall that will be dealt with here in detail are those conserved after World War II, along with parts of the Roman fort, at Cripplegate/the Barbican, and two sections at Tower Hill.

Cripplegate

There are eight individual City Wall sites in the Cripplegate area, and they include surviving pieces of the earlier Roman fort, which was incorporated into the later town wall. The fort formed the north-west corner of the walled Roman and then medieval city, and it was in this area that Grimes and the RMLEC began their post-war excavations. As the City wall stands today in Cripplegate, it is mostly within the Barbican complex and, going from east to west and then south, it comprises the sections in the London Wall underground car park and in St Alphage's Churchyard; a not entirely continuous stretch, which incorporates five bastions and the West Gate and a corner tower of the Roman Fort, that runs from the Barbican gardens opposite St Giles' Church, and then past the Barber-Surgeons' Hall and the Museum of London, under Route 11 and along Noble Street.

Figure 10: City Wall, St Alphage's Churchyard (south-facing side)

St Alphage's Churchyard (figures 1 and 10): The first site to be conserved after World War II was the section of City wall of St Alphage's Churchyard that incorporated the twelfth-century remains of the first parish church of St Alphage (Forty 1955; Milne 2002, 101). Although the Corporation did not actually own the St Alphage churchyard section of the wall, they were prepared to pay for its conservation, and were, as Forty (1955, 5) noted, 'entirely in sympathy with the principle involved'. Expenditure was approved for it and work, carried out by Ministry of Works staff, began in the early 1950s. Grimes expressed the idea, at a RMLEC meeting, that this section of wall might be cleared in time for the Festival of Britain in 1951. Whether this was achieved is unclear but work on the first phase of the conservation was completed by late 1952, at a cost of £2653 (MoW file Work 14:2043). Both the sum of money paid for this conservation by the Corporation and their sympathy towards the project are worth noting, particularly when it is compared to the level of their support, or rather lack of it, given to other archaeological sites within the City and, in particular, to the RMLEC. The Corporation contributed a paltry £550 to the RMLEC funds – a sum far below the £26,300 from the government via the Ministry of Works, and even below donations from the Bank of England (£2750), an anonymous donor within the London County Council (£2000), the Church of St Bride, Fleet Street (£1050) and Lloyd's Bank Ltd (£950) (Grimes 1968, 245). This lack of support from the Corporation went as far as the Lord Mayor even declining to sign a letter of appeal for funding in 1954, for no reason that could be ascertained (MoW file Work 14:2034).

The principle involved in conserving the section of City wall in St Alphage's Churchyard was expressed by Forty in the introduction to his report:

> 'The enemy bombing of London which started in 1940 presented an opportunity to expose, preserve and keep visible in the future, lengths of the ancient Town Wall of London which, for centuries, had been hidden from view... It was now possible to envisage the creation of small Public Open Spaces so as permanently to give access to such lengths of the Wall as might be exposed, in order that these historic fragments of the City's ancient fabric should be visible in perpetuity for future generations of Londoners and countless visitors to the City' (Forty 1955, 5).

There is a sense from both Forty's report and from the Ministry of Works files that the conservation of the City wall, as exemplified by the attention given to the section in St Alphage's churchyard, was very much a personal project of Forty and O'Neil. O'Neil at an early stage proposed 'to argue for as long as we can in favour of the complete clearance of this part [Cripplegate] of the wall...' (MoW file Work 14: 1235). On the completion of the first phase of the conservation of the section in St Alphage's Churchyard in 1952, Forty wrote to O'Neil expressing the hope to get the authority to begin work on the open space around the wall. It was going to have to be temporary at first, but Forty continued in his letter that he hoped,

> 'for a good permanent open space layout here with the development of office buildings planned may be erected in the vicinity are proceeding. This may, of course, be some time, thus a first stage of what you and I so often talked of in the difficult war years has been satisfactorily realised and we can feel reasonably happy that future generations interested in the history of our city will bless those who have been concerned in getting this done.'(Forty 4/12/52; MoW file Work 14:2043).

Further to the creation of this open space, there was interest expressed in its presentation, as demonstrated by the Minutes from various meetings of the Improvements and Town Planning Committee within the Corporation. A Special Sub-Committee meeting of the 12th February 1954 recommended that the City Engineer authorise the construction of a small outdoor model of the wall, showing its original construction and subsequent alterations, to be placed in the proposed garden. It was further suggested that a pamphlet based on Forty's preservation report might be published (Corporation of London 1954, 73). The reason why this particular stretch of wall was singled out for such attention is unclear – it is possible that initially the Corporation did not foresee having to preserve anything else, or perhaps it was symbolic, or perhaps it was simply the enthusiasm of Forty and O'Neil that carried it through? It did, though, fit very much into the modernist requirement of green space, and indeed, today, the Corporation's sign, 'Welcome to St Alphage's Garden' implies that it is the garden rather than the monument that remains as the primary importance. By the mid 1950s there were at least a dozen other sites clamouring for such attention – more stretches of the City wall, the Roman Fort, the Temple of Mithras – about which the Corporation were less than enthusiastic.

Figure 11: Bastion 14; Bastion 13 and site of Barber-Surgeon's Hall in centre background.

The Northwest corner sites: The inaugural excavations of the RMLEC were conducted in what was the northwest corner of the Roman and medieval City, and part of St Giles' Without churchyard. The presence of the wall in this area was known about prior to World War II; the Royal Commission Survey had listed Bastion 12 (figure 8), as existing and worth preserving in the 1920s, although it recorded that what became known as Bastion 14 had disappeared (RCHM 1928, xi). Bastion 14 (figure 11) reappeared with the demolition of a warehouse of which it was part. The conservation of the City wall and its bastions north of and including Bastion 14 were relatively uncontroversial. Sections of the City wall were scheduled in 1951, and a Ministry of Works memo of 1956 noted 'that it has always been in our minds that the reasonably complete remains, in this area [Barbican complex] should be preserved and displayed to the public. Given in their present dilapidated condition they are an impressive relic of the fortifications of the City, and properly treated would be one of the sights of that historic area' (MoW file: Work 14:2044).

Despite the almost automatic decision to preserve the wall in this area, other than the excavations no further work was done. There was a small campaign to get conservation work done on them in 1956 comprising of a letter to *The Times*, a letter to Duncan Sandys, Minister of Housing and Local Government, and a question in Parliament that asked Sandys to what extent the pieces of the City wall excavated since the war were to be preserved in the rebuilding of the City. His response was 'In accordance with the London Development Plan the principal remains of the Roman Wall now exposed are to be preserved in open settings' (MoW file Work 14:2044; 14: 2042). In reality the City wall sites had to wait on the Barbican development. Meanwhile, the preservation of the West Gate of the Roman Fort, discovered by the RMLEC in 1947 came to be in danger of demolition due it lying in the path of the new multi-laned highway, Route 11.

Figure 12: West Gate of the Roman Fort

The discovery of the West Gate of the Roman Fort (figures 12-13), and subsequently a corner tower of the fort further south on Noble Street, was an exciting discovery in terms of understanding the early history of London, as is evident from Grimes' report to the RMLEC (Grimes in Forty 1955, 36). Its discovery was considered to be of great importance both in itself and for what it had disclosed about the Roman period of the City, along with explaining the 'curious' angle in the course of the City wall at that point. Its discovery was considered of far greater importance than that of the Temple of Mithras as expressed in a memo of 1956 (MoW file: Work 14: 2592). Despite, though, its archaeological and historical importance, the conservation of the West Gate of the Roman fort was by no means certain. It lay right in the way of the proposed new Route 11 beneath which it was planned to put an underground car park. Grimes, with the support of the Ancient Monuments Board, wanted the Corporation to conserve it (MoW file Work 14:2042). In a letter to Baillie Reynolds (O'Neil's successor as CIAM), in November 1956, he pointed out that the situation was 'quite different to the Walbrook [Temple of Mithras] one; this gate could be preserved *in situ*, and it is a unique feature in London, with more than one implication for the City's past' (emphasis original). Although Forty, the City Engineer, was in favour, he pointed out to Grimes in a letter on the 15th November 1956, that the conservation of the West Gate would be difficult, because of the necessary ramp access to the proposed subway and car park, and expensive not least because of the 'sterilisation' of at least nine car parking spaces 'to each a potential capital value exceeding one thousand pounds may be allocated'. At an Ancient

Monuments Board meeting in December 1956, Grimes had to report that the Corporation 'had not been favourable' to the conservation of the fort for financial reasons (MoW file Work 14:2044).

There appears though to have been a change of heart, because when on 12th February 1957 a question was asked in Parliament by Mr E. Fletcher of Hugh Molson, the Minister of Works, about what steps he was taking to ensure the conservation of the Roman fort, he replied 'I am glad to say that the Corporation of the City of London, which owns the wall at this point, has already arranged for the preservation of the remains of the West Gate of the Cripplegate fort, and for access for inspection.' Fletcher goes on to reply 'whilst thanking the Minister for that welcome reply…, may I say that the decision will be particularly welcome, because this gateway is the most outstanding structural symbol of London's strategic significance in the first centuries of her existence.' There was a further question from Anthony Greenwood of whether access to the site would be permanent, to which Molson replied 'Yes, sir, it will be. It will be in an underground room, under Route 11, and there will be access for the public.' (MoW file Work 14: 2044). It is apparent from the files that the practicalities of admitting the public to the site once it was enclosed were never considered, though in one memo in the previous file it was considered it would be accessible to 'accredited persons', from which one would infer that the general public were not, in reality, to have ready access to the site (MoW file Work 14: 2044).

There was slight consternation at the West Gate being conserved underground, and within the Ministry of Works, there is a memo asking whether or not they should push for the site to be preserved in the open air. It is noted that the Corporation would probably simply say the funds would not be available and, as Baillie Reynolds pointed out in a following memo, he had no problem with the site being preserved underground as it 'will make the preservation of the site infinitely easier if it is not exposed to the elements' (MoW file Work 14: 2044). Grimes supplied the plan, and the site was duly conserved *in situ* in a chamber in the underground car park at the Corporation's expense.

Problems materialised, however, when the ramp down to the underground car park from Route 11 was being put in, in May 1958. This ramp enters the underground car park just beside Bastion 14 and the West Gate. On the 7th May 1958, Lord Mottistone contacted Baillie Reynolds to say that the developers were destroying the City wall at this point. Bastion 14 and the short section of wall to the south of it had been scheduled in 1951; the interesting feature about this particular stretch of wall was that although the parts of the lower courses had been replaced by modern brickwork, the upper part retained its medieval stonework. Baillie Reynolds and Grimes inspected the site only to discover that this piece of wall had gone. A report by Curnow, an inspector for the Ancient Monuments Board, of the 8th May noted that damage had been done by the putting in of a ramp to the car park which included the removal of a brick buttress and of the bank that was a particular feature of the City wall. He goes onto to say, though, that the damage of the previous days should not be exaggerated 'for the high upstanding portion of the scheduled wall to the south of the Bastion, visible in the photographs taken in 1941 disappeared at least one year ago and perhaps more. I can so far find no trace of when it actually did go.' (MoW file Work 14:2044). Grimes was surprised to see that that section of the wall had gone but as he had not been working on the site recently, he was none-the-wiser as to when this stretch of the City wall disappeared. In a note in the file, Grimes goes onto to say that 'frankly I do not see how we can find out unless Mr Forty knows and will 'own up' to having let it be destroyed without statutory notice'. Forty was quick to respond to such allegations and in a report by him of the 13th May, he pointed out that the Corporation had had to change their plans to ensure the preservation and accessibility of the West Gate of the fort and that all the costs, both constructional and implied, had been borne by them. Furthermore the structural design of the road supports had had to be amended and the access ramp completely redesigned, and that it was necessary that the ramp side wall cut across the line of an abutting modern brick wall, 'that is to say, on the line of the Town Wall', and that its removal had been necessary. He went out to say that 'the contractors … demolished the whole of this modern brick wall, part of which bore isolated medieval stone work at a higher level. They also demolished the modern brick wall abutting the south end of Bastion 14 and in doing so a few small stones may have been dislodged.' He continued that it had been an error on behalf of the contractor that the piece adjoining the bastion had been destroyed as that had not been the intention, and mentioned that a length of 'Roman work' of the Roman City wall at the east end of the under ground car park was to be preserved by the Corporation – work that would be carried out subject to advice from the Ministry of Works [this piece now takes up Bay 53 in London Wall underground car park, figure 15]. Forty finished his report with 'It will be understood therefore to be particularly galling to me in the present circumstances that there should have been an unauthorised interference by the Contractor giving rise to this very regrettable condition' (MoW file Work 14: 2044).

In light of Forty's perpetual support for archaeology and its preservation within the City during this period, it would seem likely that the demolition of this section of the City wall was, at least formally, unauthorised. The issue, however, was raised in Parliament on the 24th June 1958, with assurances being sought from Molson, Minister of Works, by Fletcher that such destruction of the 'Roman Wall' would not happen again (MoW file Work 14: 2044).

Figure 13: London Wall Walk sign for the West Gate

The stretch of the City wall that continues along Noble Street and includes part of the foundations of another bastion, along with those of a corner turret of the Roman fort, was part of the initial excavations in this area in 1947 (Grimes 1968, 17) (figure 14). At a meeting of the Improvements and Town Planning Committee of the Corporation in 1955, Forty suggested that the preliminary layout of Noble Street, which combined a pedestrian way with an open space on the east side of the street, be changed so that the pedestrian way and open space was on the west side and so would ensure the preservation of these remains of the City wall (CoL 1955, 387), which was agreed to but nothing was done until c.1965 when a new building was being designed for the area. Initially all the pieces of City wall at Cripplegate were to be treated as one unit, but by 1965, Grimes complained that this no longer seemed to be the case (MoW file Work 14: 2042). Furthermore, any enthusiasm the Corporation did have for preserving the City wall at this point seem to have waned as their plans were sent back by the Ministry of Public Buildings and Works (the former Ministry of Works) because the Corporation had failed to carry out proper consultations (MoW file Work 14: 2042).

In recent years conservation work has been finally completed on Noble Street and this stretch of City wall was re-opened to view in 2004, and since then has been provided with new signage. It also has a sign that dates from the 1980s that is associated with the London Wall Walk (Chapman *et al* 1985) put in place at that time. The London Wall Walk was a heritage trail between the Tower of London and the Museum of London that followed the route of part of the historic city wall with a series of signs (see for example figure 13); there was a booklet to accompany it, which is now out of print (Chapman *et al* 1985). Many of the signs have also deteriorated, but there are plans to renew the walk. All the sites mentioned in this section have London Wall Walk signs, though the one for the section in St Alphage's Churchyard is badly damaged. Bastion 14 has an additional sign on the walkway overlooking it which also dates from the 1980s, but needs replacing. The Bastion is also viewable from a specially placed window in the Museum of London, which towers rather unsympathetically over the site. All these sites are, however, generally well-maintained and accessible. The exceptions are the West Gate which remains locked in a basement, though a regular and popular tour from the Museum once a month takes people to visit it, and the small section in bay 53 (figure 15), which, while accessible, is technically on the private property of the Corporation's car park. The latter site has an original sign dating from the 1950s that is almost a museum piece in its own right.

Figure 14: Noble Street City Wall site with tower foundations looking north

Figure 15: Bay 53: City Wall in London Wall Underground Car Park

Tower Hill

On the east side of the City, at Tower Hill, there are two large stretches of City wall conserved – one beside the present Underground station and the other in what is now the courtyard of a large modern building off Coopers Row. Both are substantial sections and both were listed by the RCHM inventory as 'structural relics' worthy of preservation (RCHM 1928, xii), though both were surrounded to a greater or lesser degree by buildings. The first (figure 16), near Tower Hill Underground station, suffered some damage during the air raid of the 29th December 1940. O'Neil and Forty discussed this stretch of wall, and a report by O'Neil of the 14th January 1941, stresses,

> 'The value of the permanent clearance of this site to indicate how the town wall joined the castle [Tower of London] does not need emphasis for us, and, as you will notice from my letter to Mr Forty, I have already begun to educate the City [Corporation] in this matter. At any rate we should be successful in saving this piece of wall from any demolition gang.' (MoW file Work 14:1804).

The Tower Hill Improvement Trust, even before the war had been keen to have the City wall conserved and displayed. In 1939, for example, they transferred a section of the City wall on the properties of numbers 19 and 20 Tower Hill to the Office of Works; a letter to the Inland Revenue from the Ministry of Works notes that 'The land taken over is to be preserved for use as a public open space. The public are admitted to the land free' (MoW file Work 14:1088). The idea was to open up this section of the City wall down to its Roman levels, which was feasible for the west side, but the east side was on Crown Lands. The Crown was less sympathetic, renewing a long lease to a bottling factory and permitting the presence of an 'aesthetically obnoxious' corrugated iron shed against the wall itself (MoW file Work 14:1804). None-the-less the Ministry of Works approached the bottling company, but they received a less than supportive letter from Haynes and Carpenter Chartered Architects on the 17th September 1952 complaining that if the City wall was to be exposed and opened to the public on their client's property, their clients would loss their existing cellars, would be unable to carry on with their business, and that if the principle was taken to its extreme, would render the whole of the City into a park dotted with ancient structures (MoW file Work 14:1804).

Today it remains on display under the guardianship of English Heritage, the eventual successor of the Ancient Monuments Board of the Ministry of Works.

Figure 16: City Wall, Tower Hill

One of the most interesting surviving pieces of the City wall is that at Coopers Row (figure 17) – it is a model example of co-operation and of the successful conservation of an urban site – on the outside of the Ministry of Works file (Work 14:2041), it is noted that it is a precedent. When the demolition of No. 6, The Crescent, Minories, in 1938 revealed a section of the City wall, the decision was taken to conserve it. A letter from the Ministry of Works to the Tower Hill Improvement Trust of the 6th January 1939 explained that 'This portion of the ancient Roman Wall will in due course be one of the sites of London, and I'm sure that the Trust will share our view that it is of the utmost importance that its masonry should be properly treated' (MoW file Work 14:1087). In a 1946 report O'Neil noted that, other than the section at Tower Hill mentioned above, this was the only place where it was possible to show more of the City wall, where it stood to full height and that it included almost the only known example of a small window opening (MoW file Work 14:3120).

Figure 17: City Wall, Coopers Row

In early 1960, planning permission was sought to redevelop the area, including the properties of 8-10 Coopers Row and part of 10-11 The Crescent, Minories, and, of course the City wall that ran between them. Because of this, and because of the fact that the proposed building was to be twelve storeys and therefore visible from the Tower of London, it was decided to hold a public inquiry. The proposed development would incorporate the remains of the Roman wall but demolish the wall above that, so destroying the medieval levels, down to the present-day ground level. The result of the inquiry was that the Corporation would agree to the application provided that, amongst eight other conditions, 'the whole of the remains of the Roman London Wall must be preserved in a proper setting as may be agreed with the Corporation'. London County Council (LCC) also agreed to the application provided four conditions were met, including condition 5 [of the City Corporation's conditions] being extended to include the preservation of the medieval and Edward IV walling which surmounts the Roman Wall. For some reason, however, and to the bafflement of the Ministry of Works and the concern of the various parties involved, including Forty, the City Engineer, the Corporation refused to accept the LCC's amended conditions. Baillie Reynolds issued an internal memo of the 19th February 1960 saying that 'This section of London Wall – both the Roman and the medieval levels <u>must</u> be preserved intact and the planning of the area ought to be so designed as to leave it exposed to the public view and not built in as it is now, and as it seems proposed to be again' (MoW file Work 14:2041; emphasis original).

This planning application was subsequently dropped, but later that year, a new planning application was put forward by Bernard Sunley Investment Trust Ltd. Bernard Sunley and his architects, Seifert and Partners, were keen to retain the whole length and height of this section of City wall as a show piece and so Seifert conferred with Curnow at the Ministry of Works. It was hoped that the base of the Roman wall could also be exposed for public viewing, and that only one part of the wall would be over-scaled, where the upper storeys of the new building would be supported by columns in a paved area. Curnow pointed out that the scheduled area of the wall extended northwards and that this should not be disturbed. In a memo he said that 'from the A.M. [Ancient Monument] point of view, the new scheme should present a fine length of wall (comparable to our Guardianship length [the piece at Tower Hill]) to view from the West' (MoW file Work 14:2041). At the inquiry, various issues were raised. The Ministry of Works' report for the inquiry stressed that the proposed development 'affects some of the most important surviving stretches of the defences of Roman and Medieval London... its line still defines the City boundary in many places...'. The report from the inquiry of the 10th July 1960 notes that the Ministry of Works was very anxious that this section of London wall be properly and adequately 'emphasised and preserved'. Point 13 of the report noted that the two Authorities, the Ministry of Works and the applicants 'were most anxious to ensure any redevelopment of the site should provide for further excavation along the line of the wall – a considerable part of which is still below ground level – and for its permanent retention and display as a major feature of the design'. In order to achieve this, it was declared, in Point 14 that,

'it was necessary to provide within the site an open piazza of adequate size – together with the stilting over ground floor level of a 5 storey block and of a considerable portion of the main building, at its eastern end, with a resulting further loss of accommodation – to form a fit setting for the wall and one from which it could be viewed in its entirety. The piazza would be open to the public'.

The application was duly accepted (MoW file Work 14:2041). Furthermore, and to the evident surprise and relief of the Ministry of Works, the developers agreed to pay for the conservation works as part of their development. In relation to future maintenance they were non-committal, though they asked whether the Corporation might not adopt it, especially as it would be open and free to the public. For their part, the Ministry of Works, in recognition of the 'public-spirited action' of the company, secured special Treasury authority to waive all administration and professional overheads and to charge them only cost of labour and materials and to submit bills during work rather than expect payment in advance (MoW file Work 14:2041).

Unusually, some consideration was given to the display of the monument after preservation. Initially all parties concerned – the Corporation, LCC, the Ministry of Works and the applicants had stated in the process of the planning application that the presentation of the wall to the public was a factor to be considered. At a later meeting between the architects and the Ministry of Works the question of a commemorative plaque to explain the wall to the public was raised. In the report of the 6th April 1962 of that meeting sent to Seifert and Partners, the Ministry of Works expressed their willingness to collaborate in producing a suitable text for such a plaque and went on to say, 'There is no question but that something of outstanding archaeological quality is being preserved and incorporated in this new development and there would seem to be good cause for you to draw attention to it.' (MoW file Work 14:2041). A Ministry of Works memo, in response to a letter of the 9th May 1962 from Seifert and Partners requesting help with the wording and asking suggestions as to what material might be most suitable, noted that it should be of bronze and 'with the min. of wording'. At the beginning of 1963, the Ministry of Works wrote to Seifert and Partners suggesting that it would be better to consider the details of the plaque closer to the completion of the work on the wall, but explaining that they were having a survey done which the architects might consider displaying when the site was completed. The architects thought this an excellent idea (MoW file Work 14:2041).

In mid-1962 the Ministry of Works decided to generate some publicity for this section of the City wall, in which Bernard Sunley asked to be involved. This took the form of a press conference on the 13th June 1962 and resulted in articles the following day not just in national newspapers but also in regional newspapers, and all appeared complimentary. The then Minister of Works,

Lord John Hope was quoted in the *Daily Telegraph* as saying 'too often the surge of modern building threatens to obliterate historic remains', and in the *Scotsman* as saying 'Surely it is a good thing that this reminder of the insecurity of past ages should be preserved'. The *Financial Times* noted that,

> 'Interest in sections of the Roman wall of London is intensified when permanent provision is made for easy viewing. By incorporating a good section of this Second Century relic into a new building now being erected on Coopers Row... the Bernard Sunley Investment Trust is making a welcome present to Londoners and London visitors; not an object of beauty, but of great historical importance.'

The *London Illustrated News* of June 23rd had a photograph of the wall still covered in scaffolding with Richard Thompson, Parliamentary Secretary to the Ministry of Works; Lord John Hope, and Bernard Sunley, with a caption of 'Men who can determine the fate of this well-preserved section of London's Roman wall decide to restore it and leave it on show to the public'. The *Liverpool Post*, however, concluded its article with what perhaps contains a note of sarcasm, 'Other sections of the wall are being jealously preserved in the City where costly building sites are being kept clear after war-torn bombing so that they may be seen permanently to advantage among lawns and flower beds' (MoW file Work 14:2041).

This section at Coopers Row was in recent years redone and it has a temporary sign (which has been 'temporary' since 2002), and on a wall out on the street, it has been provided with an etched brass sign. The City wall forms an attractive backdrop to a courtyard that on one side has a café-bar, which used to advertise the presence of a '2000 year old Roman wall' at the street entrance, though this sign sadly, seems no longer to be used.

Temple of Mithras

The discovery of the Temple of Mithras (figure 18) at the Walbrook, and the subsequent furore concerning its preservation, has been well documented and discussed (Grimes 1968; Shepherd 1998; Lyon 2007). Whereas the City wall had been a known monument and had its conservation agreed on at an early stage, the Temple of Mithras was a chance discovery; the marble head of Mithras was only uncovered (rather typically) on the last day of the excavation, 18th September 1954 (Shepherd 1998, xvii). Unlike the occasional mention in the newspapers that archaeological discoveries normally get, this particular site erupted into a public and media storm which even reached the attention of the Prime Minister, Sir Winston Churchill. The blame for this public furore was laid on the way that the televised news of the discovery had fired public imagination in a way not experienced before (Eccles in letter to Nicholson 29/9/54). The reality of the situation was that the cost of conserving the remains of the temple *in situ* was estimated to be in the region of £500,000 (a not inconsiderable sum in the 1950s); they sat on soft ground in the middle of London's largest and most expensive development, Bucklersbury House, at the time. For all that, it was not considered to be the most important site discovered in London: both the Roman fort at Cripplegate and the archaeological remains discovered below St Bride's Church were considered to be of greater archaeological value (MoW file Work 14: 2592). A somewhat emotive letter from Nigel Nicholson (but most probably with some input from Grimes (G. Milne pers. comm.)), Member of the House of Commons and the only one to also be on the Ancient Monuments Board, to Eccles of the 26th September 1954 summed up the dilemma:

> 'If you decided not to make a grant towards the huge cost of preserving the Temple I would entirely support you. All my instincts lead me to plead with you to save it, but I feel it would be wrong to do so, for the preservation of the Temple, as distinct from its discovery, is really of little importance. Its archaeological value lies in its existence, its groundplan and the objects found in it. In itself it is not an object of beauty, and its dismembered stones would mean little to any but professional archaeologists. If it were preserved few people would visit it, and even those that did, would see it as part of a basement, surrounded perhaps by boilers and certainly cement walls, which would kill any atmosphere of Roman London. If there is to be any additional grant for archaeology, there are a dozen better ways of using it, for instance in the excavation of other blitzed sites in the City.' (MoW file Work 14: 2592).

The decision that £500,000 was simply too much to spend on one site, and the offering of the owner of the property involved, Leganland Property Company, to pay to have it dismantled and reconstructed elsewhere on the property sealed the temple's fate. When the time came, three years later in 1957, for the developer to complete the final phases of their development the City Planning Officer refused to give them planning permission because they had failed to provide for the sixteen car-parking spaces which, they claimed, were going to be taken up by the replaced Temple of Mithras. The City Planning Officer stressed, however, that the provision of these spaces was in no way to interfere with the agreement to re-construct the Temple of Mithras (MoW file Work 14: 2592). Leganland complained to the Ministry of Works, but a careful study of their plans revealed that the spaces were in fact being taken up by the proposed addition of a restaurant. The next problem was how the Temple of Mithras was going to be sited, but a rather abrupt internal memo from the CIAM, Baillie Reynolds, of the 6th June 1957 stated that 'Honestly I do not think it matters 1/2d where it is re-erected once it had been destroyed and moved from its original site. It could be in a museum or in a City backyard, but the public should be able to see it' (MoW file Work 14: 2592).

In effect the Ministry of Works wanted nothing more to do with the Temple of Mithras: a memo of the 18th December 1961 noted, that 'We are keeping away from the Mithras work as we have always felt the re-erection on the 'wrong site, at the wrong level and with the wrong orientation' to be something of a compromise' (MoW file Work 14:2592). They also declined to contract out specialist staff to Leganland to carry out the re-erection of the temple, though they did offer the advice of Ministry of Works architects, and provided a model and architectural drawings to Leganland. Although the huge public interest died off quite dramatically, and was not to prove as useful in generating more donations towards archaeological excavations in London as Grimes and others had hoped, interest in the Temple of Mithras did not die off completely. Right up until the temple remains were re-erected, the Ministry of Works continued to receive calls from the public about the site, though it had a policy of redirecting them to the developer and generally being non-committal about it. There was also a question asked of the Minister of Works in Parliament on the 16th May 1961 about when the re-erection of the temple was going to happen; he simply responded that the development had not proceeded to a point as yet to allow for the temple to be reconstructed. There seems to have been some regret in the Ministry of Works that they had not taken more interest – a memo of January 1962 suggests that perhaps they should not have taken Baillie Reynolds' suggestions so much to heart and been more involved with the reconstruction, but it was too late at that point (MoW file Work 14:2592).

The Temple of Mithras thus ended up a rather forlorn and badly restored monument in the open-air. In 2006, Legal and General, the current owners of Bucklersbury House, announced redevelopment plans for the entire site, and are taking no chances with the Temple of Mithras. There are definite plans for it; it is to be moved back to its 'original' location beside what was the Walbrook stream, and it will be located inside under Walbrook Square in a publicly accessible exhibition space (Legal and General 2006). These plans are expertly discussed by Lyon (2007).

Figure 18: Temple of Mithras

Ruined Churches

Within the City, three bombed churches, declared unfit for rebuilding, were acquired by the Corporation to turn into 'open spaces'. These were St Mary Aldermanbury, St Dunstan-in-the-East, and Greyfriars Christchurch. The preservation of churches was an important issue in the rebuilding of London (Forshaw and Abercrombie 1944, 140). In the City, one of the historic characteristics of the skyline was the number of church spires. In order to retain something of this, many of the towers were preserved while the destroyed churches to which they were attached were removed – for example St Alban's, Wood Street (figure 19), and both St Dunstan's-in-the-East and Greyfriars Christchurch had their towers rebuilt after World War II.

Figure 19: The surviving tower of St Alban's, Wood Street.

The idea of conserving ruined churches as war memorials was something suggested in a letter to *The Times* of 15th August 1944 signed by a number of notable people including T.S. Eliot, John Maynard Keynes and the Director of the National Gallery, Kenneth Clark. This suggestion was subsequently expanded into a small book, *Bombed Churches as War Memorials* (Casson *et al* 1945). This book and its ideas have been described as 'the last great fling of the British Picturesque' (Woodward 2001, 212). The idea of preserving church ruins to remind people of the violence of the Blitz while at the same time providing gardens for meditation and relaxation (Casson *et al* 1945, 4) seems extremely contradictory and perhaps was only possible in a country that did not feel responsible for the war and was confident of victory. In addition, while the shell of Coventry Cathedral is a rather stark reminder of the Blitz and a definite war memorial, and the remains of Holyrood Church, Southampton, are dedicated to seaman who died not just in World War II but also in the Falklands war, the ruined churches in the City of London are not formally identified as war memorials, and their wartime destruction is simply a fact of their history. Ultimately it may be suggested that the Corporation were simply interested in their provision of the all important open space, and if people wanted to regard them as war memorials, so be it. This is clear from some of the minutes of the meetings of the Corporation's Improvements and Town Planning Committee. In 1951 the London Diocesan Reorganisation Committee listed St Mary Aldermanbury, amongst others, to be rebuilt as a Guild church (IR 37:148). By 1959 the Church Commissioners had amended their proposals and agreed to allow St Mary Aldermanbury to be demolished, and the site to be sold, let or exchanged. It was, however, stipulated that the east wall be preserved either *in situ* or taken down and erected elsewhere to the satisfaction of the Diocesan Board, and that it be maintained after that by whoever acquired the site (CoL 1959, 525). The Improvements and Town Planning Committee minutes go on to say that it was the intention to acquire the site of the church so that it could be laid out as an open space, but they had objections to preserving the east wall, as it would require supporting, which would be unsatisfactory aesthetically and would take up space in the open space (CoL 1959, 525). In the end the site was conserved as a small garden (figure 20), and the remains of the church, with the exception of the lower courses of the exterior walls and internal pillars that remain *in situ*, were shipped off to Fulton, Missouri, to be rebuilt as a memorial to Winston Churchill (where he made his famous 'Iron Curtain' speech; the site also now includes a section of the Berlin Wall). There seems to have been no apparent consideration given to the site as either the remains of an historic building, or to its potential as a war memorial.

Figure 20: St Mary Aldermanbury

Today St Mary Aldermanbury, St Dunstan-in-the-East and Greyfriars Christchurch provide garden space with benches and have signs that give details of, for example, the church's construction history, people involved with the churches and of when the Corporation acquired them. St Dunstan's (figure 21) has fig trees and ivy growing up and near the walls, and a small water feature sits in what was the main aisle of the church – the space being very much reminiscent of a garden folly of the English Picturesque aesthetic traditions. Greyfriars Christchurch (figure 22) is something similar though more ordered – for example rose bushes marking out the position of the inner columns of the aisle – and the garden more formal; no vegetation growing over the walls and no grass – but the idea is the same, with benches and an invitation to sit for awhile (the busy traffic passing the site, however, makes this space considerably less inviting that St Dunstan's). Their treatment is considerably different to that given to sites considered to be of archaeological interest, as will be demonstrated by the site of St Alphage's.

Figure 21: St Dunstan-in-the-East

St Alphage's Tower

The Tower of St Alphage's Church (figures 3 and 23) is synonymous with the term survival (Sandes 2008). It survived the Reformation, the Great Fire of 1666, the demolition of the rest of the church in the 1920s, bombing during World War II and, lastly, the best efforts of the Corporation and their developers to have it demolished in the post-war period. Its post-war treatment was diametrically opposite to that of the stretch of City wall of St Alphage's Churchyard, which is only metres away, across the small street of St Alphage's Garden.

Figure 22: Greyfriars Christchurch

The site of this second parish church of St Alphage, replacing the first church of St Alphage located against the City wall, was the site of the hospital and priory founded in 1329 by Sir William Elsing. The lowest two stages of the surviving tower date from this fourteenth century period. When the first Church of St Alphage fell into disrepair, the parishioners were allowed to take over the tower and chancel of the St Mary Elsing priory church for their new parish church, when it became St Alphage's (Milne 2002, 104). The church was rebuilt in 1777 incorporating the remaining medieval stonework. In 1913 a neo-Gothic façade was added to the front, but in 1923 the parish was amalgamated with that of St Mary Aldermanbury (Milne 2002, 104). Although at this point the nave of St Alphage's was demolished and the land around it used for commercial properties, the ancient tower and vestibule were retained, probably because St Alphage's had some income by way of a tithe, until they were abolished in 1948, that St Mary Aldermanbury's did not, and it was believed that this, along with the rents from the warehousing on the property, gave the rector about £1200 a year (Henry n.d. in IR file IR 37:148). The tower and vestibule did, however, continue in use as a place of prayer (Henry n.d. in IR file IR 37:148).

St Alphage's was gutted by fire from the bombing of 1940, and although an initial decision by the Church authorities that it was beyond repair was withdrawn, by July 1951 it was once again, along with nearby St Alban's on Wood Street, considered not worth restoring (IR file IR 37:148). The remains of St Alphage and of St Alban were sitting on property needed for redevelopment for the Barbican and for Route 11 and so were included in the City of London (Area 4): Compulsory Purchase Order (CPO) of 1954 put forward by the Corporation (MoW file Work 14:2588). The proposed CPO required that an inspection be made by the Ministry of Works of St Alphage's, which was completed in September 1954 by A.H. Brookholding-Jones. His report concluded that the structure was stable and that 'For £500 the remains could be cleaned down and consolidated and the second memorial repaired' (MoW file Work 14:2588).

According to a letter from the Comptroller and City Solicitor at the Corporation of the 7th October 1954 to the Ministry of Works, the Corporation was intending to preserve the tower of St Alban's, and to incorporate the remains of St Alphage's tower in a redevelopment scheme. The then CIAM, O'Neil, responded to the latter idea by suggesting that 'The method of preservation of this medieval masonry... [is that the two chambers] should have their walling and monuments cleaned and repaired, that they should have a ceiling put across them just above the top of the masonry ... They should be incorporated within a modern building, just as they were in 1939 not left standing as a ruin'. He goes on to suggest that the space could be used as a museum 'especially as one of the last surviving parts of the [City] wall is almost opposite and is intimately connected with St Alphage' (MoW file Work 14:2588; emphasis original). The City Planning Officer's response was to hone in on the words 'incorporated within a modern building' and to agree to consider the other ideas should the CPO go through (MoW file Work 14:2588).

Although the towers of both St Alban's and St Alphage's were noted as ancient monuments in the CPO, it would seem that the tower of St Alphage's was only scheduled as a protected monument sometime in 1956: there is a reference to the Ministry of Works being in discussion with the Church authorities about preserving and scheduling St Alphage's in a letter of the 23rd April 1956 to London County Council (MoW file Work 14:2588). The Church, however, having agreed with the Ministry of Works to allow for the scheduling and preservation of the tower and remains, were then informed by the Corporation that the site was worth some £5000 less because of the presence of the monument. The Church was unimpressed by this and wrote to the Ministry of Works threatening demolition and asking for compensation, but the Ministry of Works informed them that they, the Church, would have to take the matter up with the Corporation as it did not involve the Ministry of Works (MoW file Work 14:2588).

On the 13th March 1958, the City Planning Officer wrote to the Ministry of Works asking for a meeting as he was now examining how the tower was to be treated with the proposed redevelopment. This is followed by a report by Brookholding-Jones to the CIAM, Baillie Reynolds, of the 18th April 1958 regarding St Alphage's, in which he suggested that,

> 'the remains could have been enclosed (as they partly were before) in a new commercial building built over and around them provided always that what is now visible remained so [but] the City Architect would like to know to what height we would insist the ruins be retained as there is to be built a 'pedestrian level' at 18ft above the road ...If we allow the walls to be demolished below 18ft the remains will be engulfed and disappear

beneath a roof, never to see the sun again. If not, then holes will have to be left in a concrete platform so that parts of [the tower] may penetrate it, stretching up multi-stone fingers from the ... petrol-laden depths' (MoW file Work 14:2588).

At an official level, there was no question about the tower of St Alphage's not being retained. On the 29th July, the Ministry of Housing and Local Government wrote to the Ministry of Works stating that the planning requirements set out in the Report to the Common Council is for 'the developer to make provisions in the first instance for the inclusion of part of St Alphage Church tower within the curtilage of his building, the tower being given a suitable setting within the walkway, and restricted access from the lower level must be provided' (MoW file Work 14:2588). The Corporation, however, wanted to have at least some of the ruin removed, and even within the Ministry of Works, it would seem that not everyone was of the opinion that the remains of St Alphage were worth conserving. There is a note in the file from Baillie Reynolds of the 30th June 1958 that states that he was 'strongly of the opinion that those slight remains of the medieval church of St Alphage are not worth preserving, but should be properly recorded, and allowed to go.' Brookholding-Jones was clearly unimpressed by this, replying curtly 'CIAM you kid, I think. I have not acknowledged' (MoW file Work 14:2588).

It would seem that there was a move by the Corporation to get unofficial permission from the Ministry of Works to have the remains demolished; a report to Baillie Reynolds of the 6th August 1958 noted that when the City Corporation had wanted to demolish St Alban's tower on Wood Street, the Ministry of Works had refused to allow them, not because the Ministry of Works felt strongly about St Alban's but because 'the City had ducked possible objections to their acquisition of the land by giving us this undertaking to preserve and that a subsequent withdrawal would have looked like bad faith – to which we would have been party.' The report goes on to say that presumably the same applies to St Alphage's. Baillie Reynolds responded, however, on the 11th August 1958 that,

> 'The two cases of St Alban's and St Alphage's are very different. Mr O' Neil was anxious to preserve St Alphage's for purely archaeological reasons. A small fragment of the medieval church (14th cent.) survived before it was incorporated in the church of the 18th and 20th centuries (Medieval churches which survived the fire of 1666 were few). It was not a thing which could stand by itself, nor is it of any particular architectural distinction. ... Most of the 18th cent. church was destroyed by bombing, really only the 14th cent. fragment and the 20th cent. porch now survive. They are not an entity in themselves, and if preserved by themselves, not incorporated into some other building, they would be an architectural oddity. The City have not consulted us to my knowledge about the proposed treatment, and their plan shows Route 11 impinging upon the site. St Alban's Tower on the contrary is an architectural entity even if divorced from its church, and is an example of work not in his [Wren's] usual style of a very famous architect. It is also (or was until modern buildings overtopped it) part of the skyline of the City of London, lifting its Gothic head among Renaissance spires to give a spire of rarity...'.

It seems that Baillie Reynolds was initially unaware of the undertaking given by the Corporation to protect both St Alban's and St Alphage's. He was duly informed of the response given by the Ministry of Works to a request by the City Planning Officer, two years earlier in 1956, to redevelop the site of St Alban's: the Ministry of Works had stated in a letter of 25th January 1956 that 'The undertaking to the Minister of Works to preserve the tower of the Church of St Alban's, Wood Street, was given by the Corporation in accordance with the terms of paragraph 12, part III, of the first Schedule to the Acquisition of Land (Authorisation Procedure Act 1946). It was accepted by the Ministry of Works as being sufficient to enable a certificate to be issued to the Corporation that the ancient monuments on the sites to be acquired were being satisfactorily provided for' (MoW file Work 14:2588).

Despite this, however, the general attitude seems to have been to sit back and wait to see what would happen; there did not seem to be any concrete proposals from the Corporation in relation to how they might be planning to redevelop the area. Baillie Reynolds, in a memo of the 25th August 1958, noted that,

> 'If the remains [of St Alphage] could have been incorporated into a modern building, as I find Mr O'Neil did suggest, then they would have been worth keeping. But we know from experience that modern architects can not or will not do anything other than remove everything on a site before they erect (Mithras Temple, St Swithin's London Stone - or even the Whitehall wine cellar!), and the v. small-scale plan sent with the letter of 10th July 58 just shows the remains standing there (but shorn of one corner of the medieval structure) which is no way to preserve them. I think we should ask the City what they really have in mind for the site a) preserving the remains, b) demolish then' (MoW file Work 14:2588).

This led to a certain amount of going round in circles as the Corporation would not give any indication of its plans for the site until the Ministry of Works had stipulated what had to be preserved, but the Ministry of Works would not do this until it knew what the Corporation was planning. In due course a line was chalked around the ruins at the height of the proposed walkway to indicate what would be removed, but it was put at such a low level on the tower that it cut through some of the arches. The City Planning Officer then suggested, in a letter to the Ministry of Works of the 28th November 1958, two proposals: the first was to remove the whole building down to the white line, but this was unacceptable to the Ministry of Works, particularly in regard to the south portion. The second proposal was to remove the three walls of the northern section, including the large traceried window (considered as an example of 'good modern Gothic architecture' (IR file: IR37:148), down to the level of the white line, so as to allow pedestrian circulation on the upper level. If this was not acceptable the next option was to remove the east and west walls of the northern portion but leaving the northern wall with its window *in situ* supported from the southern part with flying arches (MoW file Work 14: 2588). The Ministry of Works considered both of these last two options suitable, though it was suggested in an internal memo that 'the front wall with window would be a bit odd on its own'. The response, therefore, from the Ministry of Works to the City Planning Officer on the 3rd February 1959 was that 'It is agreed that in our view the southern portion of the building should not be removed down to the level of the white line … With regard to the northern portion, either of the proposals outlined in your letter would be satisfactory … although we think that the first proposal, to remove the three walls down to the white line, is preferable to leaving the south wall standing on its own without the East and West walls to give it meaning' (MoW file Work 14: 2588).

It was to be almost a year later before there were any further discussions between the Corporation and the Ministry of Works about St Alphage's. The Ministry of Works was shown plans by the developer's architect, Sanders, that showed the church breaking into the central façade of a new building on Route 11, which would extend above it in height; access to the church was to be from the northern entrance in the new building. It seems that Sanders was not allowed to develop this idea further, and the question of the stability of the ruins, especially when the later brickwork was removed, arose. A meeting was held on the 31st May 1960 between Ministry of Works representatives and the developers' architects and a provisional decision was made to retain all four sides of the tower for aesthetic reasons, while the blocking of the top of the walls would be deferred until later, as would be the treatment of the medieval work. This was officially confirmed to the City Planning Officer Department on the 15th June 1960 (MoW file Work 14: 2588).

What followed was to be two years of almost farcical delay, presumably because the developers hoped St Alphage's would collapse of its own accord: in the process of removing the later brickwork, the contractors had caused the tower to become unstable and a Dangerous Structure Notice had to be placed on it at the beginning of July 1960. The Ministry of Works, however, was not going to release the Corporation from its undertaking to preserve the site. By April of the following year, despite communication between all parties concerned, nothing had been done even to make the tower safe. At last, to the evident relief of the Ministry of Works, a letter from the City Engineer, Mr Forty, arrived on the 27th April 1961 explaining that recently St Alphage's had come within his remit, mentioning that the developers' consultants were of the opinion that the only option was to demolish the remains, but that he, Forty, was aware of the undertaking given to the Ministry of Works, and that the site was to be preserved to their satisfaction. By the end of June, still nothing had happened, and it took a legal reminder from Forty via the Comptroller and the City Solicitor to the developers to cause any action. This instantly resulted in a letter from the developer's architect, Sanders, to the Ministry of Works, explaining that they had been instructed by their clients to arrange the reinstatement of St Alphage's, and asking the Ministry of Works if would recommend a suitable consultant (MoW file Work 14: 2588).

There were, however, several more delays involved, much to the evident exasperation of the Ministry of Works, including, suddenly, permission needed from the GPO as St Alphage's sat on the fringe of GPO demised land, followed by a rather impertinent complaint to the Corporation from the developers' architect about the lack of co-operation from the Ministry of Works.

At long last, some eight years after the CPO and two and a half years from the point when the tower was served with a Dangerous Structure notice, there is a memo of the 8th November 1962 in the Ministry of Works files advising that the restoration job had been completed. The work was carried out by the developers, MacAlpine, and the area between the remains and Route 11 was to be laid out as a garden by the Corporation, but there was some consternation on the part of the Ministry of Works about the finishing of the wall endings facing Route 11 (figure 23). Not surprisingly, it was decided to let the matter rest, and the job was considered completed and the file closed on the 4th March 1963 (MoW file Work 14: 2588).

There is a letter in the City Engineer's file on St Alphage's, London Wall, dated to November 1964 from a member of the public, who writes to commend the idea of keeping such pieces of the past alive in such a way but complaining that there was no information about the site. The writer continues his letter by suggesting that a sketch of the completed church might be shown together with the relevant information such as the name, age, builder, the extent of the parish and some associated names, and ends by asking that don't they think that this would make the site much more interesting (CoL 1964).

Today, the tower of St Alphage's is 'the most neglected and least known medieval monument in the City' (Milne 2002, 113). It has had at least one metal girder inserted, which is now expanding with corrosion and causing problems to the monument, has been unsympathetically repointed and has weeds growing from the top; the air pollution has also caused considerable blackening and flaking of the stonework (figure 3). It is fenced off at ground level, and as Brookholding-Jones predicted (MoW file Work 14:2588), it does protrude up out of a hole in the insensitively placed concrete walkway. There is a single antiquated sign not at the level of the walkway or by the pavement along Route 11, but in the place where it is least likely to be found – at the end of the cul-de-sac of St Alphage's Garden where people park their cars.

Figure 23: St Alphage's Tower

V. DISCUSSION

London suffered considerable physical damage from the Blitz and parts of the City were still in ruins in the 1950s, but the main fact about London at the end of World War II was that it was the capital city of a victorious, united and comparatively guilt-free country. The main aim was now to rebuild a modern city free of the problems, such as slums, traffic and uncontrolled growth, that had plagued it before the war. The modernist ways of solving these problems, as expressed in the 1933 Athens Charter and expounded by the likes of Le Corbusier, were seen as the way forward particularly for London outside the City. In the City, however, these ideals were moderated somewhat by a desire to respect the historic street layout and many of the City's historic buildings, particularly St Paul's Cathedral. The exception was the ultra-modernist Barbican Estate development.

Urban archaeology in a living city was a comparatively under-developed discipline in 1945, so Grimes and the RMLEC led the way in this respect. Grimes' strict application of archaeological methods and his inclusion of post-Roman layers set a certain standard for other urban excavations (Gerrard 2003, 96). There was, however, no overall plan, and sites were dealt with on a site-by-site basis; the main difference between pre- and post-war urban archaeology was that, as with urban planning, there was suddenly a much greater opportunity. Because, however, of the bias towards rural prehistoric and Roman archaeology, the interest seems to have been muted, and as with the inter-war years, it was a case of a small number of interested, able and independently-minded individuals taking the initiative, backed up by their respective organisations. The sites that were excavated tended to be because archaeologists could access them or, on occasion, because Grimes did not want to lose his small team while waiting for another site to become accessible. It was, then, quite an ad hoc selection, except in the Cripplegate area where the wall sites were visible, and where there were specific research questions about the city defences.

A considerable portion of conserved archaeological sites in the City of London date, in fact, to the period between 1945 and the late 1960s, but this is somewhat misleading. Despite the insertion, at the last minute, of a listing requirement for buildings worthy of preservation into the 1947 *Town and Country Planning Act*, there was no immediate fundamental or widespread change in attitude or thought towards conservation. In reality, wide scale removal of old or redundant buildings and building anew continued to be considered the best policy throughout the 1950s and into the 1960s. This was encouraged by the prevailing modernist beliefs and arguably supported by the public (Hall 2002, 245). By the 1960s, however, there seems to have been a dramatic change in attitude, exemplified later in the conservation crisis of Covent Garden, mentioned previously. That is not to say that destruction of the built heritage stopped at this point, Euston Arch was demolished in 1961 and it took a three week public inquiry in 1964 to save the listed National Provincial Bank, Bishopsgate, built in 1865 by John Gibson, from demolition (Earl 1996, 72). In fact throughout the 1970s, the destruction both of historic buildings and of archaeological sites within cities became worse.

In relation to the archaeological sites that were conserved, it was on a site-by-site basis, and the influence of interested individuals was significant in their conservation. O'Neil, as CIAM during the war years and up to c.1955, appears to have been instrumental in encouraging Forty's appreciation of the City wall and in getting the Corporation's support to conserve sections of it. O'Neil's interest in preserving St Alphage's tower, followed by that of Brookholding-Jones, did at least ensure that this site was not demolished in the first instance. Ultimately, though, it would seem that it was the willingness of the Ministry of Works, specifically the Board of Ancient Monuments, to take their responsibilities towards these archaeological sites seriously that ensured the conservation of many of them – their refusal to let the Corporation out of their undertaking to preserve the remains of St Alphage's being a prime example.

One site where the Ministry of Works did not follow through was the Temple of Mithras but they did not consider this site as worthy of preservation as, for example the West Gate of the Roman fort. An interesting aspect of this seems to have been the lack of appreciation of public interest. Although the importance of keeping sites open to the public is expressed both by the Ministry of Works and the Corporation, there is a sense that public interest was assumed but considered as secondary or not especially relevant. The fact that a site was listed and protected as an ancient monument was the main concern. The values that the Ministry of Works considered of foremost importance were archaeological and historic, in other words academic. It is suggested that they considered urban archaeological sites the same way that they considered rural sites and so conserved them for 'ancient monument' values. The aim was to ensure preservation; there appears to have been little overall thought given to context and presentation.

The Corporation, however, appears to have had a different set of values. The city wall sites were conserved with, for the most part, the co-operation of the Corporation. Furthermore, they financed the conservation of the Cripplegate sites, though in the case of the West Gate, not without some persuasion. There is little in the Ministry of Works files currently available to the public about the section at Tower Hill Underground station, and since it is in the guardianship of English Heritage (the eventual successor of the Ancient Monuments Board), it is possible that the Corporation did not finance the conservation of this section. They were also unhelpful and clearly uninterested in the section on Coopers Row. The conclusions that may be tentatively drawn from this and the Corporation's blatant disinterest in other monuments, such as St Alphage's and St Alban's, perhaps suggests that their interest in the City wall may have been a product of Forty's enthusiasm rather than from any inherent regard for the built heritage. For this reason it is worth examining the Corporation's apparent interest in the Cripplegate sites.

Several different reasons seem to apply as to why the Cripplegate City wall sites were conserved. From the very beginning there was a general interest in these sites: Cripplegate was one of the worst bombed areas in the City and this in itself was a tourist attraction. Some of the tallest surviving buildings were, in fact, the remains of the Roman-medieval City wall and its associated bastions. There was also, as noted, a professional or archaeological/historical interest in these sites and their conservation. The reasons why the Corporation was especially interested in them seems to have been entirely for socio-political reasons. These City wall pieces conveniently appeared on the edge of where the Corporation planned their new huge and ultra-modern Barbican Estate. The redevelopment of the Cripplegate area essentially involved the developing of a new local community, which required, amongst other things, a sense of the past (Eade 2000, 119). As Eade explains, the Corporation understood that a thriving, multi-cultural London was likely to be more attractive to global businesses than old memories of World War II and the British Empire; 'The transnational aesthetics of the City's new buildings and the modernist formality of the Barbican estate established a local/global identity to which the few remnants of the past, especially St Paul's Cathedral and the other Anglican places of worship, provided a gloss of authenticity' (Eade 2000, 118). So, the presence of the City wall in convenient and attractive sections at the edge of this development must have suited the Corporation perfectly. It is evident from the documentation that nothing was actually done to conserve these sites until the Barbican complex had been worked out, and it is quite clear from the presence of, for example, unsympathetic walkways and the relationship between the City wall sites, St Giles Without and the Barbican buildings that the built heritage was very much expected to fit in with the new development.

The Corporation's interest in social and aesthetic values over historic and archaeological values is further emphasised by the conservation of the ruined churches of St Mary Aldermanbury, St Dunstan-in-the-East and Greyfriars Christchurch. The Ministry of Works appears to have had less to do with these. They were acquired from the Church authorities principally, it would seem, to create open spaces, and they are considered as informal war memorials. The maintenance and display of these ruins by the Corporation is entirely different to that of the archaeological sites, even though they are historic monuments. Their primary value is not so much as monuments but as gardens. The Corporation's neglect of St Alphage's is in contrast to the treatment of both the Cripplegate and other ruined churches. The most obvious reason for this was, and still is, is that St Alphage's Tower did not fit into the urban landscape design.

CHAPTER FOUR

BERLIN SINCE WORLD WAR II

I. INTRODUCTION

Berlin, along with many other cities in Germany, suffered extensive damage during World War II: some 40% of the city was destroyed and it lost half of its four million population (Taylor 1997, 287). In the immediate aftermath of World War II, Germany and Berlin were divided between the four Allied powers, Great Britain, France, the USA and the USSR. This division was assumed to be temporary but as the political gulf between the Western Allies and the USSR increased, Germany and Berlin became increasingly divided in two rather than four. The city over the following forty-five years, developed into two very separate cities, not least because East and West Berlin were used by the Soviet Union and the Western Allies respectively to demonstrate their power and the 'success' of their respective political systems. Berlin has two post-World War II redevelopment phases. The first is between 1945 and 1989. The second is the post-Cold War phase starting in 1989 when the Berlin Wall came down.

Figure 24: The Reichstag after the allied bombing of Berlin, 3 June 1945

Much war damage was sustained by Berlin's historical buildings. The Reichstag, built *c.*1890 to house the new parliament of the unified Germany, was badly damaged by bombing and completely gutted by fire (figure 24). The Stadtschloss, the Berliner Dom (cathedral) and, in the western part of the city, the Charlottenburg Palace also suffered. While appreciation and conservation of historical monuments has a long history in Germany (Jokilehto 1999; Koshar 2000), as in Britain, the damage to the built heritage was not confined to the duration of the war. In the competitive and politically motivated rebuilding of East and West Berlin, there was further destruction of the historical fabric (Taylor 1997, 298). The development of urban conservation and medieval archaeology, as in the UK, were due to the damage caused in urban areas and the necessary rescue excavations (Wolfram 2000, 185).

This chapter will concentrate on the historic centre of Berlin (see figure 36 for map). The city began as a medieval foundation based on what was originally two towns – Berlin itself and Cölln across the Spree river on the west bank. When they came into existence is unclear but they were granted civic status in the 1230s, flourished as trading centres and were formally amalgamated in 1432 (Taylor 1997, 11-13). This historic centre, the Mitte, came to be within the Soviet sector and subsequently the centre of East Berlin. A new city centre had to be created for West Berlin which came to be around the Kurfürstendammn – Kaiser-Wilhelm Gedächtniskirche area, just to the south-west of the Tiergarten. The sections of this chapter, the urban context and conservation and archaeology sections will be subdivided into three – East and West Berlin and post-1989 Berlin. The section on the sites is, however, divided by site type.

II: THE URBAN CONTEXT

The Urban Context 1945 to 1989

Berlin, like London and other urban centres in Europe, grew dramatically in the nineteenth and early twentieth centuries due to industrialisation and rural to urban migration. Many people had to live in the slums of the overcrowded 'Mietskasernen' – 'rental barracks' as they derisively came to be called – apartment houses that were built between 1860 and 1914 (Ladd 1998, 100). At the time of German unification in 1871, Berlin had a population of 827,000 but by 1933 it was four million, making it the third largest urban community after London and New York (Reader 2004, 147, 284).

The war-time destruction of Berlin was such that by the end of the war there was an estimated 55,000,000 cubic metres of rubble throughout the city – by far the largest amount in any of Germany's cities (Diefendorf 1993, 15). Since two-thirds of the surviving two million population were female, much of the clearance was done by hand by the 'rubble women' (Taylor 1997, 287). Initially, reconstruction plans for Berlin were for the city as a whole. The first plan, the 'Kollectivplan' was by architect Hans Scharoun, an ex-Bauhaus member who had remained in Germany throughout the war. It was unveiled to the public in an exhibition at the Stadtschloss (Royal Palace) in August 1946. In keeping with modernist ideals, it aimed at physically separating functions such as housing, industry and government. The plan also proposed a ribbon development along the Spree river, which ignored the city's historic concentric development, and a high-capacity motorway grid. Although Scharoun was in favour of maintaining the major governmental and cultural buildings in the centre, he wanted to disperse the population to outlying neighbourhoods and to relocate industry to the Havel district west of the city (Diefendorf 1993, 192). Scharoun's plan was condemned because it would require clearing away vast parts of the city, not all of which was in ruin, and replacing all the underground services and supply lines, 90% of which were believed to be still intact (Ladd 1998, 178). Financially it was not feasible and, furthermore, it was rejected as too radical by the Allies and by the public (Diefendorf 1993, 192; Gutierrez 1999; Schildt 2002, 145).

In May 1949 the Federal Republic of Germany (FRG) was established, created from the British, American and French zones. In October of the same year, the Soviet Union followed suit by creating the German Democratic Republic (GDR) from its zone. Berlin, situated within the GDR, was likewise divided into West and East Berlin respectively, and proceeded to become a focal-point of the highly strung political and military tensions of the Cold War (Clay Large 2002, 438; 456). In practice the redevelopment plans for Berlin as a single city were no longer feasible, and the rebuilding of East and West Berlin became highly politically competitive.

This competition between East and West was not, however, the only socio-political factor influencing Berlin's post-war redevelopment. A sense of guilt about World War II and all that Hitler and the Third Reich had meant pervaded Germany but especially Berlin. This guilt was effectively hidden under a process of forgetting that characterised the post-war period. West Germany preferred to see itself as a victim of Hitler's dictatorship, while East Germany felt exonerated by becoming a socialist republic. In 1989 Germany became one country again and in 1995, this united Germany felt confident to celebrate the fiftieth anniversary of Hitler's surrender as a day of liberation (East Germany had always celebrated it as such). Habermas (1998, 164) argues, however, that it was not 1989 but 1945 that was the real turning point in German history; that the events of 1989 and the country that it has become today cannot be understood without acknowledging this history. He suggests that Germany has had to learn to 'publicly confront' a traumatic past (Habermas 1998, 164). The forgetting and the confronting has been very much reflected in the treatment of the built heritage in both East and West Berlin, and in the subsequently unified city.

East Berlin

In 1949, despite the GDR not having official international recognition, and in direct contravention of the Potsdam Agreement, East Berlin was established as its capital. The Soviet Union felt it was important to have a strong visible influence and presence in East Berlin and so they built a large new embassy on the Unter den Linden in 1953, in which Stalin took a personal interest (Balfour 1990, 160). It was also seen as of fundamental importance that their portion of the city compare favourably with West Berlin. Consequently the rebuilding of East Berlin was designed to be a socialist showcase and there was considerable Soviet influence on its redevelopment. Planners and architects, of whom Hermann Henselmann emerged as Chief Architect, were organised into collectives, and a delegation was sent to Moscow in early 1950. The theories applied to the post-war replanning of East Berlin were based on an adoption of a post-Lenin Soviet, or Stalinist, artistic theory, which was effectively neo-classicism, or rather 'ornate monumentality' (Balfour 1990, 162; Ladd 1998, 182). The instructions, that the architects and planners came back with from Moscow were for a centralised, monumental East Berlin (Ladd 1998, 182). Walter Ulbricht, the First Secretary of the SED (Socialist Unity Party) and leader of the GDR, had considerable interest in urban planning and architecture, and while there appears to have been no clear idea of what socialist urban planning really was, there was political interest in developing some form of German architectural identity. Consequently, East German urban planning and redevelopment was dominated by an adherence to a national architectural tradition combined with the social realism advocated by the Soviet Union (Schildt 2002, 150).

On the 27th July, 1950, the GDR government issued 'General Rules for Urban Development', often referred to as the Sixteen Principles. The aim of the Sixteen Principles was 'the harmonious satisfaction of the human right to work, housing, culture and recreation'; the city was to 'become the image of socialist society and its public life'; and the centres were to be the centres of all political, cultural and other such activities, and the location for the most important buildings (Paul 1990, 174; 175). Rather than following the idea prominent amongst socialist thinkers since the nineteenth century that a prerequisite for a socialist society was the dissolution of large cities, the Principles promoted the idea that further urbanisation was essential if socialism was to foster scientific and technical progress (Paul 1990, 174). They were also promoted both as doing justice to the 'national consciousness of the people', and as a counter-model to the 1933 modernist Athens Charter (Schildt 2002, 150). Modernism had been scorned as a result of 'bourgeois intellectualism' but in many aspects the Sixteen Principles reflected some of the fundamental elements of this Charter, particularly in relation to the functional structuring of the city (Paul 1990, 174; Schildt 2002, 150). This is unsurprising as some of East Germany's more influential architects including Hermann Henselmann, had been staunch modernists and dedicated to the Bauhaus tradition before the war. They had spent the war in the Soviet Union and/or now considered it prudent to at least formally renounce modernism (von Beyme 1990, 190). Consequently, some of the Sixteen Principles would have been acceptable to Western modernists: Principle 4, for example, stressed the need for the limitation of growth of towns; Principle 6 emphasised the importance of the monumental city centre, and Principle 13 promoted the construction of high-rise buildings (von Beyme 1990, 193, 194).

In practice a prototype originally developed for Moscow was used to redevelop many of East Germany's cities, including East Berlin. This prototype had little time or space for the existing urban fabric, requiring the construction of a vast square necessary for political parades, a correspondingly wide Magistrale, or main avenue, and a tower (Paul 1990, 176). In central East Berlin, in order to make way for such a vast square, the Marx-Engels Platz, Ulbricht ordered the demolition in 1950 of the historic Stadtschloss, which although war-damaged was not beyond repair. In 1951 construction work began on a vast avenue, the Stalinallee (renamed Karl-Marx Allee in 1961), of tall, neo-classical buildings decorated with various worker motifs and statues. This 'boulevard of epic character' is probably the best-known and most discussed of all the planning projects of the GDR and was considered to be of the highest priority; it was provided with considerable resources, to the detriment of redevelopment projects not just in East Berlin but also in other East German urban centres (Balfour 1990, 166; Schildt 2002, 150).

Stalin died in 1953, and with his death came not only a denouncement of Stalinist architecture by Khrushchev, but a realisation that such architecture was too expensive, as the Stalinallee was proving. By the end of the 1950s the 'international style' of modernist architecture was in favour in East Berlin, and blocks of plain concrete and steel became the norm (Ladd 1998, 186, 187). In 1958 there was a series of architectural and planning competitions for central East Berlin. One of the more controversial designs was by Hermann Henselmann who proposed the dominant structure should be not a large government building on the site of the Stadtschloss but a television tower. This was initially rejected but ten years later it seems that technological modernity rather than German socialist characteristics was in vogue and a tower based on Henselmann's designs was built on the western side of Alexanderplatz (Ladd 1998, 190) (figure 25). The project was planned by a collective under the architect Peter Schweitzer, and was further revised after the Berlin Wall went up in 1961 (Balfour 1990, 179, 180). The construction of the Stalinallee and then the television tower moved the centre of the city to the east of the Marx-Engels Platz, away from the more traditional centre that was now close to the border. Priority was to still given, however, to the rebuilding of the Unter den Linden that led down to the Brandenburg Gate because of its visibility from West Berlin, at least until the Wall was built (Balfour 1990, 180).

There was yet another change in direction in the 1970s and 1980s, instigated, as would be expected, by political change. In 1971, Erich Honecker succeeded Ulbricht as party leader. Unlike the latter, he had no interest in planning and his priority was housing. As a result numerous mid- and high-rise apartment buildings of prefabricated concrete panels were built creating satellite cities all over East Germany, including three on the outskirts of Berlin (Ladd 1998, 191). In the 1970s, he also oversaw the building of the Palast der Republik (Palace of the Republic) on the west side of the Marx-Engels Platz on part of the site of the demolished Stadtschloss. The Palast was the official seat of the Socialist government and it was built in the style of 'high-gloss international modernism' (figure 25) (Ladd 1998, 59).

Figure: 25: The Palast der Republik with the Fernsehturm (Television Tower) behind

Figure 26: Reconstructed Nikolai Quarter, and the Nikolaikirche

It was also during this period that the historic Nikolai Quarter, including the medieval Nikolaikirche, was rebuilt (figure 26). Very little had survived that was original to the area and there were excavations in the 1950s. By the 1970s it was still mostly empty land or ruins. In 1979, a plan to recreate the area by architect

Günter Stahn was authorised. The vast majority of the buildings constructed in this quarter were examples of seventeenth and eighteenth century merchants' houses (Ladd 1998, 46). Due to a lack of financial resources for authentic materials, they were reconstructed in prefabricated concrete, which will no doubt make them interesting pieces of built heritage in their own right in the years to come.

Other than to encourage tourism, one of the main reasons for this 'reconstruction' of the Nikolai quarter was the 750th anniversary of the founding of Berlin to be celebrated in 1987 – an anniversary first celebrated by the National Socialists in 1937, but a new practice on the part of the GDR. It had been proposed that East and West Berlin should celebrate this anniversary jointly, but the East Germans refused, rendering it yet another point of competition between the two Berlins (Clay Large 2002, 480). The other reason was that throughout the 1980s there had been something of a change of attitude towards the past in the GDR as the state attempted to place itself historically on a line of progressive development that led naturally to the socialist state (Ladd 1998, 46). This renewed interest in the past, if for different reasons, was also seen in West Berlin during this period.

West Berlin

After the division of Berlin in 1949, there was concern by both the western Allies and Berliners that West Berlin, having lost its capital city status, should at least remain as a *Weltstadt* (world city). The guiding principles for the rebuilding of West Berlin were to be modernism and democracy (Strom 2001, 138; von Beyme 1991, 138). Modernist planners such as Hans Scharoun saw the destruction of Berlin as an opportunity to build anew. Berlin's architectural past was considered by many, perhaps somewhat harshly, as 'aesthetically unpleasant', or as an 'incoherent clutter', and worse, there was now the taint of Nazism (Clay Large 2002, 418; Strom 2001, 138). Since Scharoun's plans were considered too radical and too expensive, he was replaced by Karl Bonatz as the head of the planning department.

As Berlin's historical centre was now within East Berlin, Bonatz decided to concentrate on planning just parts of West Berlin, such as the areas of Bahnhof Zoo and the Kurfürstendamm around the Kaiser-Wilhelm Gedächtniskirche in 1948. This area to the south-west of the Tiergarten had been a popular and fashionable centre before the war. His modernist-style plans to develop it, although based on the pre-existing radial patterns of the city, caused much debate in the newspapers because of the predominance of radical traffic considerations and whether or not he was aiming to make this area West Berlin's city centre. Bonatz originally denied the latter but in fact this is what happened after the plans were approved in 1954 (Diefendorf 1993, 194). The area became a 'genuine capitalist showcase' with expensive shops, cafes, cinemas, tourists and, at night, nightclubs and prostitutes; there were few old buildings and no apparent governmental presence (Ladd 1998, 181). New buildings included the Europa Center and a church with free-standing campanile, designed by Egon Eiermann, on either side of the bomb-damaged spire of the Kaiser-Wilhelm Gedächtniskirche that had come to be popularly considered as a symbolic war memorial (figure 27). In true Berliner fashion, this ensemble was soon irreverently known as the broken tooth flanked by a lipstick tube (Clay Large 2002, 471).

Figure 27: Kaiser-Wilhelm Gedächtniskirche with Eiermann's church (behind) and campanile.

Despite the planning of Berlin as a whole being a practical impossibility, in 1955 the Federal Republic government and the Berlin Senate announced an international competition, 'Capital Berlin' for the rebuilding of Berlin's war-damaged central part (which suggests that much of it, whether in East or West, was still in ruins), comprising an area between the Tiergarten in the west and Jannowitzbrücke in the east, centred on the north-south Friedrichstrasse, meaning that half the area was in fact in East Berlin. The 'spiritual task' was to 'fashion the centre in such a way that it will become a visible expression of Germany's capital and that of a modern metropolis' (quoted in Rürup 2003, 204). The plan included a street network dominated by roads but with fixed points that included a number of buildings to be conserved 'because of their artistic or historical significance' or 'because their preservation seemed desirable for financial or other reasons' (quoted in Rürup

2003, 205). These buildings were highly selective and did not include, for example, the Martin-Gropius-Bau, the Museum of Ethnology or the Anhalter Bahnhof (Rürup 2003, 205). Not only was historic building conservation of minor importance, but it is evident that tackling the major problems inherent to a divided city occupied by foreign powers was not a feature either. Not surprisingly the competition was treated as little more than a theoretical exercise by the international architects and planners who entered it (Johnson-Marshall 1966, 116).

Figure 28: Kulturforum: Hans Sharoun's Philharmonic (Reichstag visible in left of centre background; Sony Center (Potsdamer Platz) to right)

In 1953, a competition had also been announced for the redesign and rebuilding of Hansaviertel, a residential area built during the nineteenth century just to the northwest of the Tiergarten but badly bombed during the war. The aim was to 'demonstrate what [West Germans] consider modern city planning and proper housing, in contrast to the false ostentation of Stalinallee' (quoted in Ladd 2005, 125). All the renowned modernist planners of the day were invited to submit designs, including Le Corbusier, Walter Gropius, Alvar Aalto, Oscar Niemeyer and Hans Sharoun. The result was a collection of comparatively modest modernist buildings of both high-rise towers and low-rise slabs that were built not along a street but dispersed in a park-like setting (the exception was Le Corbusier's design which was too large for the area and had to be built elsewhere). This apparent showcase of international modernism was the centre of the 1957 International Building Exhibition *(Internationale Bauausstellung*, or Interbau), and was extensively praised by Western politicians and architects as 'the embodiment of Western liberal principles of freedom, individuality, and the nonauthoritarian order of democracy and the marketplace' (Ladd 1998, 188). Others, however, considered the whole enterprise simply an uninspired collection of glass and concrete boxes (Clay Large 2002, 424). This rebuilding had also resulted in the demolition of a large number of nineteenth century buildings, not all of which were in ruins. As with East Berlin's Stalinallee it soon became relegated to a one-off. In the case of the Hansaviertel, the low residential densities of the area made it too expensive to copy because land prices began rising (Clay Large 2002, 424). Furthermore, in order for this project to be carried out, private property was expropriated and not only property lines but also street layouts had been extensively changed – practices that were simply not repeatable elsewhere in West Berlin (Ladd 2005, 126). West Berlin's love affair with modernism continued, however, into the 1960s and 1970s. This 'second wave' of modernism unfortunately lacked the flair and innovation seen in the modernist architecture of 1920s Berlin. Consequently the result was endless impersonal steel and glass boxes and 'a deluge of unspeakably bad architecture' (quoted in Strom 2001, 138), while older buildings continued to decay.

In 1961 the East German authorities constructed the Berlin Wall, rendering the city physically divided for an unforeseeable forty years and reducing the areas through which it passed, including the Potsdamer Platz, to no-man's land. Before the Berlin Wall was built, the high political tensions ensured that West Berlin remained at the centre of political activity. With the building of the Wall, the increased physical isolation and the lessening off of tensions between West and East over Berlin, West Berlin threatened to slide into some sort of backwater. So, while the East Berlin planning authorities turned their attention away from the border, with the exception of Unter den Linden, the West Berlin authorities decided in the early 1960s on the construction of the Kulturforum just west of the Potsdamer Platz and the Berlin Wall. This area was completely redeveloped with buildings designed by leading modernist architects; they included the Berlin Philharmonic Hall with its golden walls (figure 28) and the State Library both by Scharoun, and the National Gallery by Mies van der Rohe (a building purportedly originally designed for the Bacardi Rum company in Cuba but not required once Fidel Castro took over). The Kulturforum was in fact a result of the massive subsidies paid into West Berlin to counteract the loss of political significance; the aim was to make West Berlin a cultural centre. West Berlin also, however, became the centre for the 'alternative scene', mainly centred in the district of Kreuzberg, a forgotten and undeveloped district south of the old centre and very close to the Wall. In Eastern Kreuzberg many buildings from the 1860s and 1870s survived, and these provided cheap accommodation not only for the many Turkish immigrants invited to West Germany to solve labour shortages, but also to an often violent collection of illegal squatters, draft dodgers (unlike West Germany, there was no military draft in West Berlin), students, artists, anarchists, and punks. Needless to say, by the 1980s, and the change in attitude towards the past and historic architecture that affected both East and West Berlin, these solid and adaptable old houses became much sought-after properties. In 1979 a new, multi-year International Building Exhibition (*Internationale Bauaustellung*, IBA) was opened which continued until 1987. This recognised the value of older buildings, including the Mietskasernen, and the aims were now not demolition but the transformation of historic areas by a combination of renovation and small-scale new construction that complemented the historic environment (Strom 2001, 139). From the outset the IBA was important and the ideas developed during this period continued to be very influential in the redevelopment of Berlin after unification.

The Urban Context since 1989

Dramatic and historic changes occurred in November 1989, signalled, on the 9th of that month, by the opening of the Berlin Wall. Although these were for the most part, unforeseen both nationally and internationally (O'Dochartaigh 2004, 178), a number of events, such as the peaceful protest in Leipzig in October of that year, and various political developments, not least Gorbachev's new policies of *glasnost* and *perestroika* in the Soviet Union, and East Germany's dramatically worsening financial situation at that time all lent themselves to the process.

Berlin, a city so radically divided for forty years suddenly found itself undivided. Germany was formally 'reunited' on the 3rd October 1990. In reality, however, it was not so much a re-unification as an annexation of the GDR by the FRG. Along with this came the general attitude that the GDR should be forgotten as quickly as possible. Needless to say, after a time many former East Germans resented this as exemplified in protests to save buildings and monuments suddenly now considered politically tainted, such as the Palast and various statues, for example the huge one of Ernst Thälmann, in Berlin. The general attitude of 'superiority' on the part of the West Germans caused, not surprisingly, a considerable amount of antagonism and resentment amongst East Germans.

The decision to move the capital of Germany back to Berlin was not automatic. The Federal government had been established by Chancellor Konrad Adenauer in Bonn – a convenient business-like city with no inconvenient associations with Prussian militarism or the National Socialists. It should be remembered that right up to 1989 and the subsequent unification, Germany was still overseen by the respective World War II Allies and neither Britain or France had been keen to see a re-united Germany; only the USA was supportive. As a consequence, moving the capital back to Berlin was accompanied by a number of political and historical issues that made many people somewhat uncomfortable. This had been the capital of the country that had caused two world wars, not to mention being capital of the socialist GDR, and even many West Germans disliked the capital of Prussia on principle. There were also a number of practical issues, not least the cost, so that although it had been agreed in 1991 to move the government back to Berlin, it was not until 1994 that it was formally announced: the relocation would be carried out by 2000 at a maximum cost of DM 20 billion ($10 billion) (Strom 2001, 163).

As Strom (2001, 153) points out in her book, *Building the new Berlin*, the job of building a new government and business centre into a living city is almost unprecedented. Architecture has long played an important role in political symbolism in Germany. With the IBA of the 1980s, there had been a change in West German architectural and planning thought towards an appreciation of the historic environment, and this was to continue into the official redevelopment plans for post-Cold War Berlin. In 1991 Hans Stimmann, a top-level Social Democratic Party (SPD) planning official, came to Berlin to take up his appointment as Building Director of the Department of Construction. Under his guidance, the Planwerk Innenstadt was produced – a controversial and ambitions master plan for the whole of Berlin. Stimmann and his supporters were very keen to return to the Berlin of around the 1900s and out of this was born the notion of 'critical reconstruction', which was aimed at returning the city to its prewar density and variety (the slums of the Mietskasernen having been conveniently forgotten). Two of the main principals of critical reconstruction were retention or restoration of the historic street network and associated frontage lines of streets and squares with new buildings conforming to nineteenth century block sizes, and a height restriction of a maximum of 30m (Stimmann 1995, 13). Those streets that were considered to be excessively wide, such as the Leipziger Strasse, Glinkastrasse and Friedrichstrasse, would be narrowed with the implication of favouring public transport as opposed to private cars (Stimmann 1995, 13). The modernist ideas of separation of functions and the car-friendly city were replaced with a somewhat nebulous idea of the 'European city'. The notion of the European city ran alongside the concept of critical reconstruction. The principal requirement was the strict division between public space – streets, squares and parks – and private space (Stimmann 1995, 17). This was to be applied mostly to those areas that had lost most of their buildings – for example the Alexanderplatz, the Potsdamer Platz and the area of the Palast. As a result its greatest effect would be in the former East Berlin.

The Planwerk Innenstadt caused immediate controversy when it was unveiled in 1996. Though it was praised for dealing with the city as a whole and for promoting what is now called sustainable development, it ignored some of the principles of German planning law, including the right to appeal decisions, and it left no room for the input from either local governments or local inhabitants. Furthermore, as it was concerned mostly with what had been East Berlin, it was seen by many as simply another way of obliterating the physical evidence of the GDR; critics noted that 'critical reconstruction' aimed at conserving the historic environment would provide little more than a pastiche of the idealised nineteenth century dreamt up by Stimmann and his supporters (Strom 2001, 111). There seems to be an overall attachment to the Berlin of the turn of the century and a rejection of anything 'too' modern, which perhaps reaches its peak in the plan to have the Stadtschloss rebuilt as a cultural centre, the Humboldt Forum (Senate Dept of Urban Development website 2006). The main contradictions to the idea of critical reconstruction have been new Federal government buildings which are modern and light in appearance to ensure no comparisons with the architecture of Third Reich government buildings (Strom 2001, 145), and the redevelopment of the Potsdamer Platz.

Figure 29: Potsdamer Platz (with traffic light tower left centreground))

Figure 30: Looking towards Potsdamer Platz from the Kulturforum (Sony Center on left)

The Potsdamer Platz was the commercial and entertainment hub of 1920s Berlin and was reputably Europe's busiest square (figure 29). The bombing of World War II and the division of Berlin turned it into an empty wasteland; the Berlin Wall ran right across it. In the months following the coming down of the Wall, large plots of land were sold off at prices greatly below their value to a number of multi-national corporations, the principal two being Daimler-Benz and, later, Sony. In a rather post-modernist superficial fashion the redevelopment of the Potsdamer Platz has been feted as 'unique' in Europe: 'In the very heart of a European capital, on historic ground, a completely new section of the inner city is being created for 20,000 workers, many more visitors, customers and business partners. ...it knits the city together into one functional and spatial unit' (Burg 1995, 173) (figure 30). What is noticeable about Potsdamer Platz is the successful eradication of this 'historic ground'. So, while a replica of what was apparently Europe's first ever traffic light, which was erected on the Potsdamer Platz in 1924, has been put up in the same spot (Schulte-Peevers 2004, 110), the only surviving historic building, the Grand Hotel Esplanade, which Sony was instructed to conserve within their complex was 'conserved' in such a way that it has merited inclusion here as a fragmentary site. Furthermore, all remnants of the Berlin Wall have been removed, with two token pieces replaced at either side of Leipziger Platz, and the line of the Wall is symbolically but discreetly marked out by a narrow row of rectangular bronze cobble-like insets across the square.

III: CONSERVATION AND ARCHAEOLOGY

Conservation and archaeology prior to World War II

The appreciation of historic monuments, and the practices of conservation and archaeology in Germany has a long history. In the late eighteenth – early nineteenth century, German Romanticism encouraged a rediscovery of medieval and Gothic architecture, which was seen as the national, German architecture (Jokilehto 1999, 112). The architect, planner and painter Karl Friedrich Schinkel (1781-1841), Berlin's most renowned architect and responsible for, amongst others, the Altes Museum building, was sent to report on the state of the public buildings of the Rhineland, an area handed over to Prussia at the Conference of Vienna in 1815. The report resulted in a document which was to become fundamental for the conservation of cultural heritage in Prussia, containing as it did basic principles for the conservation of ancient monuments and antiquities (Jokilehto 1999, 113). These included proposals for establishing a special state organisation for the listing and conservation of valuable historic monuments, and for preserving these monuments 'in order to have the people respond to a national education and interest in their country's earlier destinies' (quoted in Jokilehto 1999, 115). From 1815 onwards there were legal changes in the way old buildings and monuments were treated, including starting state care for the conservation of historic buildings in Prussia. Various circulars released in 1819, 1823, 1824 and 1830 provided for the protection of abandoned castles and convents, for the care and protection of historic monuments against change that may result in loss of character, and in 1830 there was also a cabinet order on the preservation of city defences (Jokilehto 1999, 115). The concept of a monument, as defined in a circular issued in 1844, was very broad and included any construction provided it had 'some artistic or monumental significance', though private property was not included. By the 1890s, Germany's state laws and regional organisations for monument protection were such as to be at the forefront of monument conservation in Europe (Koshar 2000, 52).

From 1903 however, local associations, *Heimatschutz*, that supported the 'restoration' of towns and buildings were set up. This usually meant altering buildings to match some idealised notion of what they should or would have looked like in a specific period – for example Baroque houses would be given 'medieval' facades, or old buildings would be demolished to be replaced by new buildings in a traditional style. The Nazi party also supported this traditionalism (Diefendorf 1993, 68, 73). Conservation of historic buildings, however, became somewhat tainted by National Socialist promotion. The Nazis were quick to assimilate monuments and historical places into 'the goals of racial hygiene' (Koshar 2000, 116). Even in the destruction of Jewish monuments, the Nazis had ideas to establish a museum for what they planned would be an extinct race (Koshar 2000, 126). The urban policies for historic towns during the Nazi period aimed to 'thin out' historic cores and modernise them; in Cologne, urban renewal saw buildings torn down only to be reconstructed elsewhere to create 'historical' districts (Koshar 2000, 133). In terms of architecture, Hitler and others favoured 'historical' styles, and neo-classicism was the main style of Albert Speer's plans for redesigning central Berlin. Speer also developed a 'theory of ruin value', which acknowledged the eventual decay of buildings and led Speer to promote the idea of constructing buildings that would look imposing even in a state of ruin, an idea that impressed Hitler and is reflected in the plans that Speer subsequently drew up (Koshar 2000, 130).

Archaeology, as with monument conservation, was also a political tool under Hitler; as has been commented, 'there can hardly be a better case study of the interrelation of archaeology and politics than Germany' (Härke 2002, 12). In the mid-nineteenth century the concept of archaeological culture being equivalent to ethnicity emerged, not only in Germany but elsewhere such as in Russia (Dolukhanov 1996, 202). As with much of Europe, in Germany, after unification in the 1870s, there was the development of the notion of the 'national' monument (Koshar 2000, 53). Archaeological discussion towards the end of the nineteenth century tended to be dominated by an assumption of a constant 'west-east slope'; in other words Germanic finds were considered superior and progressive when compared to Slavic finds (Wiwjorra 1996, 175). After the First World War there was a prejudicing of Slavic culture and the use of archaeological and historical material to justify German borders with Poland (Wiwjorra 1996, 175). The largest single influence on the linking of ethnicity and archaeology in Germany was the work of Gustaf Kossinna. In 1920 he published a book, *Die Herkunft der Germanen*, in which he attempted to show how a Nordic, Aryan, German race had descended from Indo-Germans and from this 'superior' core, all cultural development stemmed (Hodder 1991, 1). The Third Reich, after Kossinna's death, used his ideas and methods to help develop their 'master race' ideology (Hodder 1991, 1).

In 1935, Himmler founded the *Deutsches Ahnenerbe* (German Forefathers' Heritage), which then, from 1938, began conducting excavations partly carried out by the *Schutzstaffel* (SS). Every SS unit in Germany was supposed to have a 'Germanic' excavation in order to have a cultural focus for 'German greatness' and to provide evidence to support aspects of Nationalist Socialist ideology. Some of these excavations were directed by scholars and carried out to a high standard but this use of archaeology was to have serious repercussions for German archaeology, leading to a general shunning of archaeological theory (sometimes referred to as the 'Kossinna Syndrome'), for many decades after World War II (Hodder 1991, 2; Härke 1991, 204).

Urban and medieval archaeology were, however, in their infancies prior to World War II: indeed urban archaeology in Germany prior to 1945 was a barely recognised practice, and it only developed as a response to the destruction of the war (Fehring 1991, 9).

Conservation and archaeology after World War II

The politicisation of the built heritage is nothing unusual but it is a primary issue with Germany's built heritage, particularly in Berlin, since 1945. In his books on Germany's architectural monuments and cultural history, *Germany's Transient Pasts* (1998) and *From Monuments to Traces* (2000) Koshar explores this in great detail. In both East and West Germany there was a desire to get away from the immediate past of Hitler's Third Reich; to forget all those horrors and to generally portray Germans as victims of that dictatorship. There was no desire to face up or confront this period of Germany's past, nor to acknowledge any form of complicity with it. Many buildings and remains of buildings associated with this period were quickly demolished or changed beyond recognition in the post-war period in both parts of Berlin. Despite this desire to break with the past there was still a simultaneous need for a level of historical orientation – a need to know where one was both in time and place. This led to complications when deciding what to remove and what to rebuild, and what form the rebuilding should take. Koshar (2000, 154) writes about an 'allergy to ruins', and that this collective allergy was not so much a result of the desire to forget the war but more an attempt to resurrect a particular version of history, something that appears to have continued at some levels into post-Cold War Berlin. Consequently different buildings and the arguments relating to their reconstruction or removal became permeated with the respective political beliefs, aims and, indeed, contradictions active during this period.

East Berlin

The establishment of the GDR in 1949 provided a political framework in which to start large-scale rebuilding. East German cities had suffered extensively during the war but this destruction continued in the process of rebuilding. There was a requirement to show that the development of East Germany into a socialist state was a natural historical development for the country (Koshar 1998, 250). There was no clear idea, however, of what was wanted in terms of socialist planning, and confusion over what to conserve. The unofficial cut-off point for monuments in both East and West Germany was 1830. This, combined with a general desire for a break with the past meant there was little protection for later buildings.

East Germany's Sixteen Principles for urban redevelopment do not appear to have concerned themselves with the built heritage. The required break with the immediate past saw the demolition and alteration of what were considered politically significant areas, for example the centre of Leipzig and the remains of Dresden's centre (Jokilehto 1999, 256; Paul 1990, 178-180). This desire for a break with the past also resulted in the demolition of a number of notable buildings, particularly the historic Stadtschloss, in East Berlin. The Stadtschloss was originally a fort built in the sixteenth century. It was greatly expanded and elaborated by the architect Andreas Schlüter starting in 1698 for Elector Friedrich III (figure 31). It was situated at the east end of the Unter den Linden and was the major focal point of central Berlin. During the war it was badly damaged but not entirely beyond repair. Several exhibitions, including one concerned with the rebuilding of Berlin, were held in it in the first few years after the war. There were various arguments put forward as to whether it could be restored or not but in the end Ulbricht ordered its demolition in 1949 in order to free Berlin from its 'dishonourable' past with total disregard for any protest, which came from not only West Germans but also East Germans, including some of his own advisors (Koshar 2000, 159; Stangl 2006, 354). It had been agreed that some pieces should be preserved but all that has survived is Portal IV from the Lustgarten façade, where the revolutionary Liebknecht had proclaimed a socialist republic in 1918, some other sculptures and statues that have ended up in various museums, and a couple of capitals that sit in the grass beside the ruins of the Klosterkirche (figure 32) (Ladd 2004, 73). The doorway was finally inserted into a government building on the Marx-Engels Platz in 1963. On the site of the Stadtschloss itself, nothing was built despite various grand schemes until the 1970s when the comparatively smaller Palast was constructed.

It seems that considerably more of central Berlin's historic architecture would have been demolished but for the fact that progress tended to be slow; for example the ruin of Schinkel's huge Berliner Dom was to be demolished in the early 1950s but the job was never started, leaving the shell to be carefully restored in the 1970s (Clay Large 2002, 500). The medieval Marienkirche, on Marx-Engels Platz, now somewhat overshadowed by Henselmann's television tower amongst other buildings (figure 33), was also threatened with demolition but international pressure was enough to save it (Clay Large 2002, 460).

One of the areas of East Berlin that did have extensive restoration work carried out was the Unter den Linden – the historic avenue that leads from the Brandenburg Gate to the site of the Stadtschloss and the Lustgarten at its eastern end. There were many historic buildings lining the Unter den Linden route and of course it was clearly visible from West Berlin until the Berlin Wall was built. One of the factors that appears to have saved some

Figure 31: The Stadtschloss, c.1900

Figure 32: Surviving Royal Palace capitals

Figure 33: Marienkirche and the Television Tower

of these buildings from being demolished and replaced with modern buildings was the adoption of the Leninist-Marxist ideology of socialist realism (Stangl, 2006, 354). This concerned the relations between art, architecture, urban design and society, and considered architecture to be both functional and artistic (Stangl 2006, 354). Essentially, Prussian architecture, although sponsored by the monarchy, had been designed and built by German architects and labourers, therefore making it national cultural heritage. Historic buildings could be preserved as 'living witnesses to these traditions from which everyone learns' (quoted in Stangl 2006, 355). In the 1950s there was the beginning of a change of attitude away from getting rid of politically-tainted buildings to conserving a broader and more traditional range such as churches, castles, city halls, and *Bürger* residences (Koshar 1998, 254). In 1954 a new law for the protection and conservation of monuments came into effect. The legal framework for this had been drawn up by W. Unverzagt – considered the organisational and intellectual figurehead of East German archaeology. He had always firmly believed in keeping archaeology free from ideology and had managed to maintain this stance both during the Nazi period and after World War II (Coblenz 2002, 312). As a result, the new law was comparatively free of any ideological basis (Coblenz 2002, 327). It was very specific about protecting monuments and defined all portable antiquities and sites of cultural monuments as objects in need of protection, which could be extended to include a site's surroundings if proposed alterations would impair the impression of the monument (Coblenz 2002, 327).

In 1953 the governmental *Institut für Denkmalpflege* (Institute for Monument Preservation) had been re-organised, and sites and monuments of German history as a whole were distinguished from those which could be integrated into 'progressive traditions'; the Brandenburg Gate in the late 1950s, for example, was stripped of its Prussian symbolism and, despite previously featuring heavily as a backdrop to Hitler's military parades, became a 'monument of peace' (Koshar 1998, 254). In fact, the restoration of the Brandenburg Gate in the 1950s was an extremely rare joint project between East and West Berlin. The East Germans restored the gate itself and the West Germans, who had the casts of the quadriga that had surmounted it, recast the quadriga to place back on top of the gate. The West Germans left this on the border in 1958, but the East Germans did not place it on the Brandenburg Gate until they had removed two controversial symbols of German militarism – the Prussian eagle and the Iron Cross (Koshar 2000, 163).

The principle of conservation of cultural heritage in East Germany was reaffirmed in Article 18 of the Constitution of April 1968, and the concept of the built heritage as a 'witness' to history continued to be a primary value, as seen in a new preservation law that came into effect in June 1975. It recognised that because monuments are 'witnesses of political, cultural, economic, and historical development [and] because of their historic, scientific, and artistic value, their preservation is of great interest for the socialist society' (Deiters 1979, 142, 147). This 1975 law included a number of other important concepts that reflected socialist thinking at that time. There was an acknowledgement that people came across sites and monuments in their daily lives in urban areas; that these monuments were documents that helped people to understand the past and also that the 'chain of achievement' that they were evidence of both taught people about historical development and helped 'to achieve [socialist] political goals'. Added to this, it was stressed that 'more and more the value of old cores of settlements is recognised for the knowledge of history that they give and for their artistic conception' (Deiters 1979, 145). It is evident that the law had a wide definition of the term 'monument', including those of cultural history as well as monuments of art; the latter was particularly wide in its scope and included architecture, garden cultivation and landscaping, and the fine arts (Deiters 1979, 145).

Dieters (1979, 145), General Conservator of the *Institut für Denkmalpflege* in East Berlin, identified four main tasks the Institute faced in 1975. These were to rebuild monuments destroyed in the war; to restore and equip them in such a way that 'people can experience their historical and artistic impression; that means to open the valuable monument to the general public'; the third was the proper use of space in a monument 'according to the present requirements of society'; and the fourth task was to deal with the efforts 'to increase the effectiveness of the monuments in developing urban areas and cities.' The paper also mentions that 'in the process of reconstruction it is important to continue all humanistic traditions, to safeguard all historic architectural values, in order to preserve the characteristic appearance of the town' (Dieters 1979, 146). It is worth noting the comments of two respondents, both from American universities, to Dieters when he presented a paper on the 1975 law to a seminar on architecture and historic preservation in Central and Eastern Europe in New York in that same year. One was complimentary of the work done on, for example restoring Schinkel's Altes Museum in East Berlin that had been badly damaged (H.G Pundt in Dieter 1979, 147). The second noted that preservation in East Germany appeared to be a combination of 'excellence and frustration'; the latter caused by the vast amount of destruction from the war and also to a long period of indifference towards the historic environment by the government (C. F. Otto in Dieter 1979, 147).

Amongst this 'excellence and frustration', and not an inconsiderable amount of destruction, there were also confusions and contradictions that emerged in relation to the built heritage in East Berlin. This is exemplified in the case of the large equestrian statue of Frederick the Great. This statue had dominated the east end of the Unter den Linden since 1851 but in 1950, the statue was removed because Fredrick the Great was now no longer considered a military hero but a militarist aggressor. In 1980, however, he was rehabilitated as an advocator of the enlightenment, and his statue was restored to its original position (Ladd 1998, 46).

The comparatively slow pace of redevelopment in East Germany, and a therefore necessarily greater acceptance of 'ruins' compared to West Germany (Koshar 1998, 225), possibly aided urban archaeological research. As mentioned previously, urban archaeology was in its infancy in the immediate post-war period and medieval archaeology only really became a focus of interest with the post-war development of urban archaeology in the 1950s (Coblenz 2002, 328). By 1975, Joachim Herrmann of the *Zentralinstitut für alte Geschichte und Archäologie, Akademie der Wissenschaften der DDR* (ZIAGA) in East Berlin was able to announce at a conference in Oxford that 'The period of major archaeological studies of the origins of large modern towns [in the GDR] is now for the most part over' (Herrmann 1977, 244). The paper goes on to say how over fifty towns and cities, including Berlin, Dresden and Leipzig, had been investigated during the post-war period between 1948 and 1974. These intensive and 'more or less' systematic investigations of the larger urban centres had taken the form of large-scale excavations, careful observations and some small-scale excavations during redevelopment. A comprehensive archaeological base had been established from which the origins of towns in the high Middle Ages could be studied, along with the history of their settlement and their social and economic significance (Herrmann 1977, 244). In the introduction to the proceedings of the Oxford conference, it was noted that,

> 'the surveys of some countries of Eastern Europe may appear to western readers to have a self-satisfied flavour, both in terms of the amount of work done since 1945 and in the ability to interpret the results. There are clearly grounds for self-satisfaction: the opportunities for archaeological research on historic town centres presented by war-time destruction were taken with such energy that the results may now be presented in tabular form (Herrmann, fig 2). Whether all that might be done has in fact been done, the papers themselves do not allow a western reader to tell' (Barley 1977, ix).

The political exploitation of archaeology and the dominance of a particular line of thinking did not, however, stop with the demise of the Third Reich; in East Germany it was merely swapped for another, that of Marxist archaeology. There were some positive sides to this, for example the racist theories were gone, as noted by Barley (1977, ix), because as a general rule Marxist ideology included the rejection of cultural-ethnic models (Dolukhanov 1996, 204). The role of ideology in the post-war period appears, however, to have been considerably less influential than it had been under the Nazis. In the immediate post-war period, those few archaeologists that had survived the war had been trained before the war or were trained after the war by people not yet trained in Marxist ideology. For the greater part archaeology in East Germany was, it seems, able to stay clear of most of the ideological demands placed on it by the regime; in fact, the ratio of Marxists to non-Marxists was a persistent source of annoyance to the SED right up to 1990 (Coblenz 2002, 311). Certainly archaeology did not suffer the same level of interference that modern history did, and towing the Party line of historical materialism was often only to be found in the forewords of books or pandered to in special publications (Coblenz 2002, 333). Having said that, however, all archaeologists of the post-war generation were educated in Marxist Leninist ideology and, as the older generation retired (or defected), the ideology and the political control did increase (Starling 1985, 229). The building of the Berlin Wall in 1961 and the problems of such things as foreign currency shortages and travel restrictions did result in the isolation of East German archaeologists. The theoretical debates that occurred in archaeology in Britain and the USA beginning in the 1960s could not occur in East Germany (Härke 1991, 188), though it should be noted that such theoretical issues were not extensively debated in most other continental European countries either or, indeed, in the course of rescue archaeology in Britain at that time.

West Berlin

Once the FRG was established in 1949 the political and legal framework for planning and rebuilding could be developed. Unlike the GDR, however, there was no law specifically dealing with the protection of the built heritage. Individual states were left to decide on their own practices, which led to great disparity in how conservation was approached. In some cities, such as Münster, Freiburg, and Nuremberg, serious attempts were made to preserve the historic character of the inner city. In other cities, such as Lübeck, Cologne and Munich, there was a combination of modernisation and attempts to conserve historic architecture. In many cities, however, it was modernisation that was the driving force, resulting in the conservation of only isolated monuments or 'archipelagoes' of built heritage (Koshar 1998, 210). These cities included Frankfurt, Hannover, Stuttgart, and West Berlin (Diefendorf 1993, 74-75). The constitution of West Berlin, along with states such as Lower Saxony, had no mention at all of the importance of protecting monuments (Koshar 1998, 216). The lack of protection of the historic urban landscape was further compounded by having no consistent theoretical basis, or even a list of fundamental priorities (Diefendorf 1993, 73), added to which was the desire to be rid of Nazi-tainted architecture. The result was very mixed approaches to conservation, and ensured as many losses, if not more, as in East Germany. Bavaria for example, a state that had always been at the forefront of monument preservation, took an active role in restoring historic architecture, spending more than 30 million DM in Munich alone between 1945 and 1950 (Koshar 1998, 216). Yet, those of Munich's historic buildings that had been appropriated by the Nazis, such as the famous Wittelsbacher palace built *c.*1845 for Ludwig I but later occupied by the Gestapo, were demolished regardless of their state of repair or architectural significance (Koshar 2000, 171). Other aspects added to the assault on the historic architecture: whereas in East Germany rebuilding progress was slow due to a lack of resources, in West Germany the Marshall Plan and a keen commitment to modernism and the capitalist market meant that redevelopment happened at a faster pace, and any loss of architectural heritage was easily written off (Koshar 1998, 202-3). Unlike in East Germany where directives about replanning and rebuilding came from the government in East Berlin, city authorities in the FRG were left to their own devices. The destruction of West Berlin's built heritage in the post-war period has been described as 'cultural barbarism with a vengeance', as buildings and ruins, including many of the Wilhelmine period and most of what remained of the famous Anhalter Bahnhof (train station), disappeared into a huge, 120 metre mound, Teufelsberg (Devil's Mountain) (Clay Large 2002, 423). This was in the grounds of a former Wehrmacht school in the Grunewald and was high enough for the Americans to put a radar station on the summit. There is no doubt that the remains of the Kaiser-Wilhelm Gedächtniskirche would have ended up there as well were it not for public resistance.

The burnt-out Reichstag was also left to moulder on the basis that there was no money for its restoration; the only work carried out on it was when its decaying dome was demolished in the 1950s. Part of the problem was what it had represented – a discredited monarchy and Germany's imperial past; not something that seemed appropriate for the FRG government in Bonn to be associated with (Ladd 1998, 90). It was not until 1961, when the Berlin Wall was built passing just behind it, did anybody begin to show any interest in restoring the building and this was because it suddenly took on the mantle of being a symbol for the future re-unification of Germany (Clay Large 2002, 423). Even this 'restoration', however, saw much of the façade's architectural ornament removed and inside it was given modern offices and meeting rooms. The Soviet Union objected to any political use of the building, so from 1971 it was used for an exhibition on German history (Ladd 1998, 90-91).

This general desire to move on was counteracted somewhat by simultaneous interest in the past and, as with East Germany, some need of historical orientation, expressed in popular celebrations of anniversaries such as the 700th of the laying of the foundation stone of Cologne Cathedral in 1948 (Koshar 1998, 206). The 'democratisation of architecture' was also reflected in what came to be restored, despite occasional reservations by conservationists, because local citizens' groups demanded it (von Beyme 1991, 142). There was, for example, a long-running and heated debate about whether to restore Goethe's house in Frankfurt am Main; in the end the public won and the house was completely rebuilt. The influence of politics did sometimes have a positive effect. The decision to restore the badly bombed eighteenth-century Charlottenburg palace in West Berlin was mostly a political reaction to the political decision to demolish the Stadtschloss in East Berlin in 1950, and because the latter caused such public outcry (Koshar 1998, 210). A long and careful conservation programme starting in 1951 was carried out and resulted in what has been described as one of Germany's pre-eminent historical showpieces (Clay Large 2002, 422). The other building carefully restored was the Schloss Bellevue on the edge of the Tiergarten. This palace was built in the 1780s for Fredrick the Great's brother, Prince August Ferdinand. The majority of historic buildings was not so fortunate and, despite the reasons of denazification, there are still questions over why so much was destroyed (Diefendorf 1993, 106). As in East Germany, there was, however, a slow change of attitude so that by the 1960s and 1970s, critics were arguing that the policy of modernisation without a proper commitment to the conservation of the built heritage had been a mistake because city dwellers no longer felt 'rooted' in their cities (Diefendorf 1993, 107). As a consequence, a little more care of what survived began to be taken, and by the 1980s when the IBA was launched, there was an active interest in incorporating what was left of the historic environment and its conservation into redevelopment (Strom 2001, 139).

West German conservation practices were not the only ones that lacked any comprehensive theoretical basis, West German archaeology had a similar problem. After the ideological horrors inflicted on it by the Third Reich, there was a general distrust of theory. As a consequence, there was almost no theoretical discussion after 1945, a situation that actually worsened in the 1970s and 1980s. The new theories, such as New Archaeology, coming from the USA and Britain in the 1960s were ignored (Härke 1991, 187, 191-2). So, while German archaeology maintained its reputation for careful excavations, studies of artefacts and extensive publication of its findings, Härke noted in the late 1980s that both Roman and medieval archaeology had developed no theory or methodology to handle the combination of different types of evidence, and that medieval archaeology was still 'somewhat uncertain' about its aims, methods and even its definition as it was still seen to a greater or lesser extent as part of, yet inferior to, medieval history (Härke 1991, 197-8). Urban archaeology suffered from much the same problems. In 1982, a conference had been held in Münster on the situation of urban archaeology in Germany in comparison with the rest of Europe. It was acknowledged that in neighbouring countries urban research had long been part of urban renewal and large building schemes, but this was not the case in West Germany (Fehring 1991, 193). It was admitted in 1988 that 'unlike in neighbouring countries, there is no generally agreed aims for or concept of urban archaeology in the German Federal Republic' (Fehring 1991, 10).

That is not to say no work was done but it would seem that there was little provision made for archaeological excavation in the post-war period and that this continued to be the case (Lobbedey 1977, 128, 129). Uwe Lobbedey, the state conservator for Westfalen-Lippe in Münster, presented a very pessimistic future for urban archaeology in 1975. In the introduction to a paper he presented to the Oxford conference for the European Architectural Heritage Year (Barley 1977), he outlined the state of play for urban archaeology for north-west Germany. As with the protection of monuments, archaeology was the responsibility of the *Länder* (individual federal states), so there was a variety of legal and organisational approaches. Each state employed its own state archaeologist who, with their staff and sometimes outside help, was responsible for archaeological monuments. There were also a number of full- and/or part-time officers, often based with museums and supported by local authorities or societies, who would carry out local archaeological surveillance; in 'some special cases', archaeological research institutions, museums or university departments would carry out urban excavations (Lobbedey 1977, 129). Lobbedey (1977, 129) stressed how there were rarely the resources for even qualified observers to observe demolition work, let alone carry out extensive rescue excavations, and that this situation was unlikely to change. There were systematic post-war excavations, despite difficulties of conditions, in Hamburg and Emden, and work had also been done in such cities as Lübeck, Münster and Hannover, but despite ongoing or planned restoration work in many urban centres, Lobbedey (1977, 127) said in his introduction that 'the prospects for further archaeological activity is viewed with scepticism'.

Conservation and archaeology since 1989

Since the unification of Germany in 1990 was, in effect, a take-over of the GDR by the FRG, the GDR and all its national laws and practices disappeared. This meant that conservation and archaeology of the former GDR lost their central organisations, for example the Central Institute for Monument Conservation of the GDR was dissolved, and became the responsibilities of the respective states, as had been the tradition in the past and is still the practice in the FRG. In each state, conservation was thus handled by the ministry for either arts and culture or for building and town planning. As might perhaps be expected, in Berlin protection of the historic environment then came under the remit of the Senate Department of Urban Development, even though it was criticised for failing to prevent the demolition of many prewar buildings. In December 1992, the federal government, then still resident in Bonn, announced that all Third Reich and GDR government buildings would be demolished, and new buildings would be built to house the new government ministries; Chancellor Kohl referred to this decision as 'the extinguishing of the unloved witnesses of history' (quoted in Neill 2004, 47). This decision resulted, not surprisingly, in loud protests on the basis that this was not the way to come to terms with Berlin's or Germany's past. The issue was not resolved until 1994 when the Federal Finance Minister announced that for financial reasons existing buildings in Berlin would be used to accommodate over 80% of the estimated ministerial office requirements (Neill 2004, 47).

A report on the legislation and practice of urban conservation in the FRG, which includes comparisons with the British system, was published in 1996 (Akers 1996). As mentioned above, because there is no central authority to oversee conservation and archaeology, there are considerable disparities between states. While sites are listed for protection, there are no separate categories for archaeological sites and no grading of listed buildings – all come under one list (Akers 1996, 58). Public finance is available for conservation at state and, in cases of 'cultural goods of national value', at federal level (Akers 1996, 55; ICOMOS website 2001). Despite state and federal legal protection for all aspects of the built heritage, Germany found itself the subject of an ICOMOS Heritage at Risk report of 2001-2002. It commented specifically on the threat to urban heritage due to large development companies (ICOMOS website 2001). It also commented on the considerable number of buildings in Berlin, particularly governmental buildings from the GDR that had by that stage been out of use for up to ten years and were in need of maintenance. Even though Berlin is a city with one of the smallest number of listed monuments, and receives substantial subsidies granted by the Federal Ministry of Buildings for urban conservation particularly in the former East German states including East Berlin (ICOMOS website 2001), lack of funds is a problem. There are, for example, insufficient financial resources to complete conservation works started on buildings, such as the baroque Parochialkirche, built in 1700, and Schinkel's St. Elizabeth Church, built c.1830. The subsidies for urban conservation were part of an urban renewal and conservation programme for the five eastern states as it was quickly recognised in 1989-90 that due to East Germany's less aggressive development programmes, there was much urban fabric worthy of conservation still surviving. This was in contrast to the destruction of built heritage in the 1960s and 1970s in West Germany, mistakes that should not be repeated in the urge to redevelop the former GDR too quickly (Akers 1996, 56). In 1992, a Federal competition was announced, 'Conservation of the historic urban environment in the new Länder [states] of the FRG'. Its main objective was to allow eastern municipalities to demonstrate what they were doing with their funds; most schemes were commended (Akers 1996, 56).

In terms of archaeology, the end of the GDR had a serious impact on archaeological research. While, for the most part, the quality of work carried out during the period of the GDR is not in question, there had been efforts made by scholars from the ZIAGA and other institutions to prove the existence of principles from prehistoric times on that led to communism, and there was also the problem that criticising a Marxist-Leninist approach was seen as criticism of the communist political system, and so there had been little critical theoretical discussion; this issue was, however, quickly recognised after 1989 (Gringmuth-Dallmer 1993, 135, 136, 137). Since most of the leading positions in research, teaching, museums and archaeological heritage management were held by SED members, once the FRG took over, all of these people were replaced by people from West Germany (Gringmuth-Dallmer 1993, 137). In addition some positions were abolished and some organisations, such as the ZIAGA, were dissolved, with leading figures forced to resign. It was difficult for some professionals to come to terms with the transition and the problems of being politically marked. Joachim Herrmann, for example, was forced to resign in 1990.

In Berlin the *Denkmalpflege* (protection of monuments) offices were amalgamated into an archaeological regional government office with its main seat at the Charlottenburg Palace, and a branch office in central Berlin. This Office for the Archeological Monument Preservation comes under the Senate Department of Urban Development. On their website they detail a number of archaeological sites, along with various historic buildings (Senate Dept of Urban Development website 2006). Berlin now contains two World Heritage Sites – the first listed in 1990 are the castles and gardens of Potsdam and Berlin, the second is the Museuminsel of central Berlin, listed in 1999.

Berlin still has to contend with controversy when it comes to the built environment. Three sites show clearly the different socio-political ideas and arguments that wash back and forth in the city. The first is the Palast (figure 25) (see also Sandes forthcoming). This was built as the seat of the government of the GDR on part of the site of the Stadtschloss. It was, however, very much a palace of the people as it also contained a theatre, bowling alley, restaurants and was a major place of entertainment for East Berliners. After reunification there were moves to have the building demolished, on the superficial basis that it had asbestos problems. There was huge outcry from ex-East Berliners, many of whom had fond memories of the building. An impasse resulted and the building stood mostly empty, internally stripped to remove the asbestos, except for hosting a number of exhibitions (including one of the Emperors of China). Only in 2006 was a decision finally made to demolish the aging and decaying building. The socio-political sensitivities surrounding the building were such, however, that the Senate Department of Urban Development's website went to great lengths to demonstrate that this was a 'democratic decision', and officially the building was not demolished but 'dismantled' (figures 34-35); and could be viewed via a webcam on the internet (Senate Dept of Urban Development website 2006). In its place will be built a cultural centre, the Humboldt Forum, that will have a façade that replicates the Stadtschloss (Senate Dept of Urban Development website 2006).

Figure 34: Dismantling the GDR's Palace of the Republic, 2007

Figure 35 : Dismantling of the Palace of the Republic, 2007. The banner reads 'A Project of Prestige – East Germany Asserts its Legitimacy'.

The Olympic Stadium, built by the Nazis for the 1936 Olympics, is a building that has been completely rehabilitated and carefully restored (to host the 2006 football World Cup), including the Nazi sculptures that decorate some parts of it. The willingness to restore this stadium, one of the iconic sites of the Third Reich, is perhaps due to certain aspects of its history – Jessie Owen's spectacular performance that won him a gold medal during the 1936 Olympics and the fact that the British occupying forces used it as their headquarters in the aftermath of World War II helping to balance some of the associated Nazi past – but also perhaps due to Germany's slow coming to terms with its past. It was also pointed out on a BBC Radio 4 programme on the stadium and its restoration 'that you can't blame it all on the building' (BBC Radio 4 2006). An obvious statement perhaps, but it does highlight how symbolic architecture and monuments become and how they are seen as a legitimate target to vent emotions on.

The third site that continues to cause much controversy is Hitler's Bunker. The site has been known about from immediately after the war; it had many visitors including Winston Churchill. In 1948, however, the Soviets closed the bunkers and levelled the ruins of Hitler's chancellery. After 1961, the Berlin Wall covered much of the former chancellery grounds, with the rest remaining vacant until the late 1980s when it was decided to build apartment blocks on the site; part of the bunker was destroyed in the process. After the fall of the Wall, one of the strongest advocates of preserving remains of the Nazi past, including what remained of Hitler's bunker, was the then head of the municipal archaeology office, Alfred Kernd'l. His basis for doing this rested on the belief that the continuing destruction of the Nazi past was a reflection of many Germans' failure to confront their own past. This continuing destruction also meant that many of the remains of sites now only survive underground, and his office had jurisdiction over all below ground sites. Hitler's bunker along with others had been rediscovered in the process of checking what appeared to be empty land before the staging of a Pink Floyd rock concert in summer of 1990. It caused great embarrassment as the site had been chosen because it was thought to have been

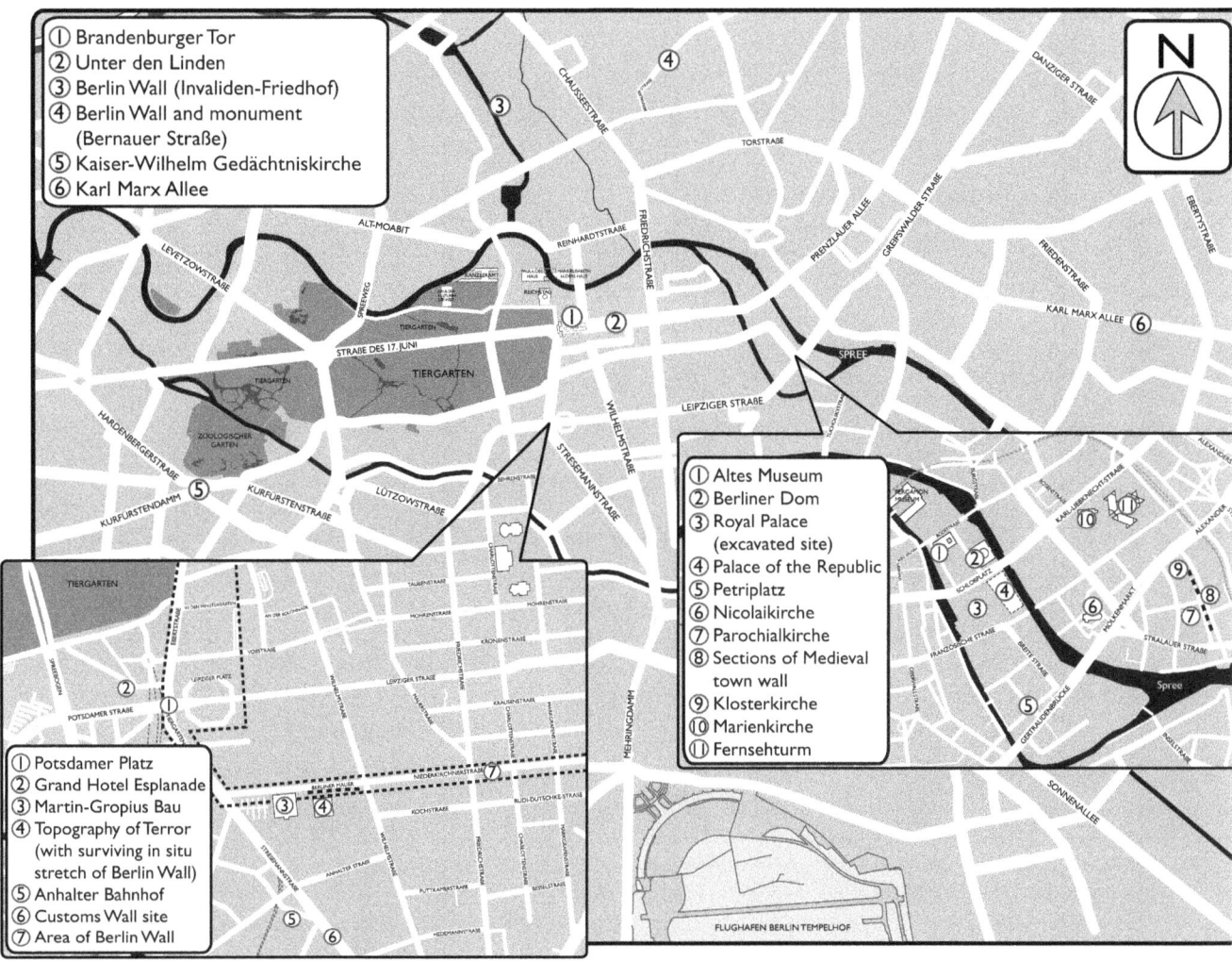

Figure 36: Central Berlin: sites mentioned in the text

free of such Nazi evidence. Kernd'l was able to open the bunker two years later and make an inventory. In fact little remains of Hitler's bunker, though there were some intact SS bunkers also found (Ladd 1998, 130-134). The site was subsequently buried under a park and unmarked for fear of encouraging neo-Nazis. In June 2006, however, it was decided to mark the site with a sign (BBC News Online website 2006).

IV: THE SITES

There are comparatively few fragmentary sites conserved for display in central Berlin. Apart from the fact that Berlin unlike, for example, Cologne, was not a major medieval centre, conservation of sites in both East and West Berlin appears to have been a comparatively random process based mostly on political considerations. In total, nine sites are detailed below: the medieval and customs wall sites, two ruined churches; the Anhalter Bahnhof façade; the Topography of Terror; the Berlin Wall remains; foundations of the Stadtschloss, and the Esplanade Hotel (figure 36). In East Berlin, the sites conserved for display between 1945 and 1989 comprise only the medieval town wall fragments and, nearby, the ruins of the Klosterkirche. There were widespread excavations of some 70 acres of the medieval core of central East Berlin (Taylor 1997, 6). These included excavations around the medieval town wall in the area of the Nikolaikirche – the heart of the old medieval dairy market – and in the area of the fish market centred on the Petrikirche across the Spree in Cölln. These two areas provided evidence of some of Berlin's earliest settlement dating to sometime in the late twelfth century (Herrmann 1977, 253). Between 1956 and 1958, the Nikolaikirche had been excavated and the remains of a Romanesque basilica dating to about 1220 had been discovered built over an earlier Christian cemetery (Taylor 1997, 5). Starting in the late 1970s, the Nikolaikirche was restored and the area around it reconstructed (figure 26). The Nikolaikirche is now a museum devoted to the area, and includes a small exhibition on the excavations and the finds. Unlike the Nikolaikirche and quarter, however, all that survives of medieval Cölln are the names of Petriplatz and Fischerinsel. The Petrikirche, originally a medieval church but replaced by a nineteenth century neo-Gothic church, was badly damaged in street fighting in 1945 and was demolished in the 1960s (Taylor 1997, 12).

There are slightly more sites conserved in what was West Berlin, mainly by default rather than because they were specifically marked for protection. These are the bomb damaged spire of the Kaiser-Wilhelm Gedächtniskirche, a small section of the eighteenth century customs wall on the Stresemannstrasse, the façade of the Anhalter Bahnhof and the excavated remains of the Gestapo Headquarters of the Topography of Terror site.

Since 1989, while there have been sites conserved outside of Berlin's centre (Senate Dept of Urban Development 2006), there have been very few conserved within the centre. There are some medieval foundations of the Heiliggeist-Hospital on Spandauer Strasse and the eighteenth-century foundation remains of the Stadtschloss. Added to these are a number of surviving sections of the Berlin Wall, and in the Sony Center, Potsdamer Platz, there are the remains of the Breakfast Room of the Esplanade Hotel.

Town Wall Sites

The Medieval town wall

There are several surviving portions of the Berlin's medieval town wall or *Stadtmauer* (figure 37). They are all located on the eastern edge of the Berlin Mitte, just south of the Klosterkirche ruins, in what is now a quiet park setting. The town wall was built of brick with the lower courses being of boulders and dates to the fourteenth century (Ladd 2004, 72). The oldest map showing the town wall is dated to 1652 (Senate Dept of Urban Development 2006). These sections survived because they became incorporated into the houses built along Waisenstrasse when the wall was replaced by new fortifications in the eighteenth century (Ladd 2004, 72). In the process of building these new fortifications, the medieval double ditch was backfilled, and between the old wall and the new wall, the Littenstrasse was developed. This street is still intact, and between it and the surviving wall fragments is a small grassed area. Parts of the medieval wall were excavated in 1961, when Berlin's oldest pub, Zur letzten Instanz, was being rebuilt, and in 1965 near the Klosterkirche (Senate Dept of Urban Development 2006). The conservation of about 120 metres of the wall was completed in 1984, though some more remains of it were discovered in 1996 when some buildings on Littenstrasse were demolished (Senate Dept of Urban Development 2006).

There is a stone plaque attached to one section from 1963 (figure 37) which gives brief details of the site's history including the work carried out on it in the early 1960s. To date there has been no apparent attempt to update this signage nor to give the visitor some idea of the larger monument that the town wall would have originally consisted of.

Figure 37: Berlin medieval town wall and its 1963 plaque

Eighteenth-century Customs Wall

Figure 38: Remains of the 18th century Customs Wall, Berlin; ivy-clad reconstruction in background

Figure 39: Sign for Customs Wall

In the middle of the Stresemannstrasse is a small fragment of the eighteenth century customs wall (figure 38). This was built by Fredrick William I in the 1730s to prevent the importing of undeclared supplies and also to prevent soldiers from deserting. The original Brandenburg Gate was part of the same complex, though the present gate was built in the 1790s to replace the less grand original (Ladd 2004, 48). The wall itself was redundant by 1867-68. The Berlin Wall later followed some of the course of this wall. The piece on the Stresemannstrasse was discovered and a section rebuilt in 1987, the year of the 750th anniversary celebrations of Berlin's founding. The site is right in the middle of a busy road, on a central traffic island. It does have a sign giving details of what the wall was part of, along with a map, and mentions its excavation and conservation in the 1980s (figure 39). The site is just within what would have been West Berlin.

Ruined Church sites

As in Britain after World War II, a considerable number of Germany's churches lay in ruins. In East Germany, church ruins were often not removed for no other reason than there was no money either to remove the ruins or to restore them. The ruins of the famous Baroque Frauenkirche in Dresden were purposely left as a reminder of 'capitalist warmongering' and had a sign that exhorted people to 'join the struggle against imperialist barbarism, [and] for peace and happiness of mankind' (Koshar 1998, 256). The keeping of the ruins of this particular church backfired as, from 1982, it became a site for protests against the GDR (Woodward 2001, 210). Prior to the Berlin Wall coming down, there had been plans to rebuild this church, partly it would seem, as a tourist attraction (Diefendorf 1990, 11). Since the demise of the GDR, it has been completely and painstakingly rebuilt as it was prior to World War II (Frauenkirche Dresden website 2006).

There was some commitment by planners and architects in West Germany to rebuild historic buildings but as they usually only considered the most 'imageable' landmarks, they were often churches (Koshar 1998, 204). In Cologne, for example, where extensive damage had been done to many churches, including to a number of important Romanesque ones, a series of lectures on their restoration was held in 1946-47. These included a debate on whether any should be left as ruins or rebuilt exactly as before. Adenauer (then Mayor of Cologne), supported by many conservationists, wanted complete restoration on the basis that ruins were 'out of place', and that 'the churches are places of peace and reconciliation. Everything reminiscent of war and hate should be kept away from them and their surroundings' (quoted in Koshar 1998, 220). This argument is reminiscent of that of Riegl's relating to the keeping of ruined churches (Riegl [1903] 1996, 79). It was further argued that those who wanted to keep such evidence of the destruction of the war and of Nazism wanted to continue with such war and hate, added to which was the argument that conserving monuments when people were still homeless was an unacceptable luxury (Koshar 1998, 222, 225). In Cologne, it was decided not to conserve any of the ruins of the city's famous Romanesque churches as a war memorial but instead those of the seventeenth-century St Alban's Church. These 'cultivated ruins' were a set piece within an ensemble that included the reconstructed Gürzenich assembly hall complex. To add to its role as war memorial, St Alban's was also given in 1955 a copy of Käthe Kollwitz's 'Mourning Parents'[5] (Koshar 1998, 221).

There are examples of conserved war-damaged churches in both East and West Berlin, both kept as war memorials.

Klosterkirche

Figure 40: Entrance to Klosterkirche, 2007

---

[5] The original 'Mourning Parents' comprises two separate statues, a mother and a father, that Kollwitz created for a memorial to her own son, killed in World War I, in 1931 that are at the Roggevelde German war cemetery near Vladslo, Belgium (Koshar 2000, 96).

The Klosterkirche was the church of the former Franciscan monastery that was founded in the mid thirteenth century. It was built just inside the town wall enclosing the eastern part of the medieval town. It was closed after the Reformation and the buildings converted into a grammar school, which it remained as until its destruction during World War II. The church itself was Berlin's oldest brick church and the first church to be completely vaulted (Senate Dept of Urban Development website 2006). It seems that the monastery buildings and church were badly damaged as late as April 1945, and the remains were cleaned up and stabilised in the 1950s (Ladd 2004, 72; Der Förderverein Klosterruine e. V. website 2007). Sometime between the 1960s and 1983, the ruins of the monastery buildings were removed due to road construction, and a small park between the surviving ruins of the Klosterkirche and the widened Grunerstrasse to the east was established (Ladd 2004, 73; Der Förderverein Klosterruine e. V. website 2007). This small park has been described by Ladd as a 'small oasis', and contains, incidentally, the two carved stone capitals that came from the destroyed Stadtschloss (figure 32) (Ladd 2004, 73).

Today the ruins of the Klosterkirche survive to roof height in some places, and the west arch and some window tracery also remain *in situ* (figure 40). Since 1982, the church ruins were used for theatre performances, and for exhibitions between 1987 and 1990. In 1992 an organisation that concerns itself specifically with the Klosterkirche ruins, *Der Förderverein Klosterruine e. V.*, was established and since then they have held annual cultural projects at the site. The site was undergoing conservation works in 2005 but these have now been completed and the site given a plaque explaining its bombing in 1945.

The Kaiser-Wilhelm Gedächtniskirche

This church was built to commemorate Kaiser Wilhelm and completed in 1895. It was designed by the architect Franz Schwechten as an historicist monument and built at the intersection of four major streets in what later became the centre of West Berlin. Unfortunately, historicism went out of fashion just after its completion and the church was generally ridiculed as a memorial to imperial pomposity (Ladd 2004, 277). In the process of post-war clearance and reconstruction in the late 1950s, the remains of the Gedächtniskirche were going to be cleared along with everything else. The surviving ruined tower with its jagged roofline where the spire had been destroyed had, however, quickly become a popular monument and there was public pressure to keep it (Diefendorf 1993, 75). Consequently, it was conserved as a war memorial – to remind occupiers as well as Germans of the destruction Germany had caused. Many Germans, though, tended to see it as a reminder of their suffering rather than as a symbol of their guilt (Ladd 2004, 277-278). The ruined church tower became a focal point and a symbol of West Berlin, somewhat overshadowing Eiermann's modern church and campanile that sit either side of the tower (figure 28). This rather strange ensemble sits on what is effectively a traffic island. Inside the ruined tower, on the ground floor, there is a small exhibition of the church's wartime history which includes, incidentally, a small Cross of Nails donated by Coventry Cathedral.

Anhalter Bahnhof

The original Anhalter Bahnhof was built *c.*1840, but it was redesigned and rebuilt on a colossal scale, opening to the public again in 1880 (figure 41). It was, at that time, one of the largest terminal railway stations in the world, being 170 metres long by 60 metres wide and almost 35 metres high at its apex, and cost more than fourteen million marks (Presner 2001, 418). When the station first opened in 1840, it was as the terminal for Germany's longest stretch of railway, connecting Prussia and Anhalt. It was one of Berlin's busiest stations and one of the most important railway stations in Europe, being the departure point for Prague and Vienna amongst others. An important later feature of the Anhalter Bahnhof was the eighty-metre underground tunnel with its shops built in 1928 connecting it to Berlin's largest luxury hotel, the Excelsior (Ladd 2004, 129; Presner 2001, 418). This passage has been considered as analogous to the Parisian arcades of the nineteenth century, and the whole complex 'a dream place of modernity' (Presner 2001, 418).

Figure 41: Front of the Anhalter Bahnhof, c.1910

In the 1930s, however, it was from this railway station that some 3000 Jewish children were sent south out of Germany by their parents and later it became, along with the notorious Grunewald Bahnhof, a departure point for the concentration camps. It was bombed during World War II but continued to function on a much reduced scale until it was closed in May 1952. In 1959, after much debate and despite plans to convert it into a new transport museum, it was demolished, leaving only the ruined north portal. In 1983, a museum for Transport and Technology was opened in one of the surviving brick buildings of the station; this museum was subsequently extended and exhibition buildings were opened in 1985, 1987 and 1988 (Gottwaldt 1994, 210). In 1987, the site was also used extensively as part of West Berlin's celebrations of the 750th anniversary of Berlin's foundation, including an exhibition called 'Mythos Berlin' that was held here (Presner 2001, 427).

The surviving central section of the north façade has, Ladd (2004, 129) suggests, become a symbol of postwar Berlin's 'broken connection to its past' (figures 42). It represents a number of contradictory aspects of Berlin's history – Prussian expansionism, the hopes of a unified Germany, the possibilities of being connected to the world at large but at the same time the destructive capacities of all these things, and what now remains has also been considered as representing both the dream and the nightmare of modernity (Presner 2001, 418).

Figure 42: Surviving portion of the Anhalter Bahnhof façade

The area behind the façade, which would have originally been covered by the main station platforms, is now a sports ground dedicated to a world-record holding Jewish sportswoman, Lilli Henoch, who was murdered in 1942. In 2004 the site underwent conservation works. While the sports ground has a sign explaining its dedication, the façade itself remains without any signage at all.

Topography of Terror

The Topography of Terror is a very specific monument comprising the remains of the building that housed the Gestapo Headquarters located on what is now Niederkirchnerstrasse. Prior to East Berlin's municipal administration's renaming of streets in May 1951, it was Prinz-Albrecht-Strasse (Rürup 2003, 200) and ran along the edge of the Wilhelm Strasse quarter – the location of government offices from the 1930s. This street had a number of historic buildings which were appropriated for Nazi offices. The Prinz-Albrecht-Palais – an eighteenth-century palace renovated by Schinkel in c.1830 for a Hohenzollern prince, the brother of Friedrich Wilhelm IV (Ladd 2004, 126) – became in 1933 the headquarters of the SS's Security Service (SD; *Sicherheitsdienst*,), under the directorship of Reinhard Heydrich, Himmler's closest aide. Next door to the Prinz-Albrecht-Palais was the Museum of Applied Art that was designed by Martin Gropius and Heino Schmieden in c.1880, and also on the same street and built about the same time were the Ethnology Museum, the Hotel Prinz Albrecht and the State School of Applied Art (Ladd 1998, 155). In 1933, Prinz-Albrecht-Strasse 8 became the headquarters for the new *Geheime Staatspolizei* (Gestapo). In 1934, when Heinrich Himmler was appointed head of the Gestapo, he moved the SS headquarters from Munich to the Hotel Prinz Albrecht, next door to the new Gestapo Headquarters. In 1939, the Gestapo, the criminal police and the SD were amalgamated in the *Reichssicherheitshauptamt* (Reich Main Security Office) under the directorship of Heydrich with their official headquarters at Prinz-Albrecht-Strasse 8 (Ladd 1998, 156). The Prinz-Albrecht-Strasse quickly became one of the most feared addresses in Europe. It is here that Himmler and Heydrich made plans for the terror and mass murder associated with the Nazis. Furthermore, it was here that arrested people were held for what was called 'intensified interrogation', i.e. interrogation using torture. People were not generally held here for very long, some were released but most were sent on to concentration camps. Some, however, died in custody or, during the war, were executed here; the full story of the horrors that emanated from these buildings are detailed in the exhibition catalogue for the site (Rürup 2003).

Figure 43: Former Gestapo Headquarters, 1949

In the period immediately after the war it was just one area of many of ruins (figure 43). The border, and later the Wall, between East and West Berlin ran down Prinz-Albrecht-Strasse. This put the area into West Berlin, and in 1949, the West Berlin authorities had the palace and the other buildings, with the exception of the former Museum of Applied Art, levelled. This caused some outcry amongst architectural historians as the palace was one of the few of Schinkel's buildings in West Berlin, though the outcry was muted compared to that at the destruction of the Stadtschloss by the East German authorities in the 1950s. After the Berlin Wall was built, the area quickly became one of those forgotten places; part of the land was leased to a dealer in construction debris, the mounds of which are still on the site, and part to an 'Autodrome' (unlicensed car driving) business (Ladd 2004, 127).

It was not until the late 1970s-early 1980s that any interest was taken in this part of West Berlin. Since 1957 there had been a plan to put in an integrated network of Autobahnen and expressways that would have involved widening and extending Kochstrasse across the area of the former Prinz-Albrecht-Palais. This plan remained in place, though unrealised, until the 1980s when attention was drawn to the history of the area by local architectural historian, Dieter Hoffmann-Axthelm (later involved with post-Cold War redevelopment and the idea of 'critical reconstruction'). When the organisers of the IBA learnt of this historic significance they successfully campaigned to have the plans for Kochstrasse dropped (Rürup 2003, 205, 208). The former Museum of Applied Art, which had survived almost accidentally, was restored, renamed as Martin-Gropius-Bau and opened in 1981 with an exhibition entitled 'Prussia – an attempt to take stock' (Rürup 2003, 198, 208). At that point a temporary sign was erected giving some information about the site: 'You are standing on the grounds of the former torture chambers of the Gestapo' (quoted in Ladd 1998, 159). There was at this time a new and growing interest in the past, especially that of the Nazi era, particularly amongst the younger generations, and this combined with an acknowledgement that something had to be done about the commemoration of this particular site and its grim history (Rürup 2003, 208).

A motion was passed in Berlin's parliament that a memorial be erected. A competition to design such a memorial was announced in 1983, but its task was contradictory, as contestants were expected to come up with a plan that 'would reconcile the historic depth of a location with practical applications such as the establishment of parks, playgrounds, space for exercise etc.' (Rürup 2003, 208). It was, however, decided not to proceed with the winning entry as the Senator for Cultural Affairs took over responsibility for the area in order that at least some provisional arrangement be reached in time for the 750th anniversary of Berlin's founding to be celebrated in 1987.

Various other uses were put forward for the area – a favourite project of Chancellor Kohl's was a German Historical Museum. This was opposed by others who felt he was trying to bury the history of the site under something that would generate national pride; a proposal to rebuild part of the palace as a Jewish museum met with similar opposition (Ladd 1998, 159; 160). A grass-roots organisation, the Active Museum of Fascism and Resistance in Berlin, set up to protect the site, decided on another course of action, when on May 5th 1985, Helmut Kohl and Ronald Reagan made a controversial visit to a cemetery in Bitburg, where Waffen-SS soldiers were buried, the Active Museum held a symbolic dig on the site. This and the unexpected discovery of surviving remains of the buildings, generated further public interest and a significant though not uncontroversial desire to have the site commemorated appropriately. Such an example was an organisation called 'Citizens Concerned with the History and Future of the Gestapo Terrain' who wrote an open letter to the then Lord Mayor of Berlin, Eberhard Diepgen, in December 1985 expressing their concern that the public had not been informed as to what was going to happen to the site, stressing the international importance of the site and putting forward that what was required on the Prinz-Albrecht-Palais site was, 'an international site of contemplation (*Denkstätte*) on an European scale, including a centre with documents and exhibits (an Active Museum)' (Rürup 2003, 216). The letter went on to stress the need for wide-reaching discussion on the site, to include Berliners and people from outside the city who had both the relevant expertise and a genuine personal concern in order to determine the terrain's future appearance and to safeguard the physical remains.

The various calls for the site's conservation, including requests by the West Berlin's municipal archaeologist, Alfred Kernd'l, following the Active Museum's symbolic excavation, resulted in a reluctantly government-sponsored archaeological excavation of the site between July and September 1986. Not only were the foundations of the old buildings along both Niederkirchnerstrasse and Wilhelmstrasse uncovered, but also the layout of several of the cells of the prison the Gestapo had set up in 1933 (Ladd 1998, 160; Rürup 2003, 217). The impression is that the West Berlin city government was loath to do anything formal with the site. Not only did they shelve the design for the site that had won the competition that they themselves had organised but would only agree to a temporary exhibition and this was only because it could hardly be ignored when the main historical exhibition to mark Berlin's 750th anniversary was to be held next door in Martin-Gropius-Bau (Rürup 2003, 216).

In July 1987 the 'Topography of Terror' exhibition was opened. The entire site covers some 62,000 square metres and the site has been cleared and restored in such a way as to emphasise its historic significance without eliminating the site's post-war history and attempts to 'render invisible and to repress' (Rürup 2003, 218). Initially, temporary structures were put up over the excavated remains and the site was given signage to indicate what had gone on at various places and to encourage visitors to explore the rest of the overgrown site. In the small exhibition building was a documented explanation of the Gestapo's activities and of the ordeals of prisoners held here, many with their personal details and sufferings individually documented. It also attempted to put the SS and the Gestapo into the wider context of both Berlin and Europe by documenting their general activities such as espionage and the organising of their reign of terror, including the transportation of people from all over Europe to Auschwitz (Ladd 1998, 161).

Up until 1989, this area of West Berlin was marginal land – it lay right next to the Berlin Wall and was far from the centre of things. With the coming down of the Wall and the unification of Berlin it suddenly came to be in the centre of things. The former Prussian House of Deputies – the building facing Gropius-Bau – became the new home of Berlin's municipal parliament and so, at the very least, the Topography of Terror was found to be taking up valuable real estate (Ladd 1998, 164). Fortunately the overwhelming consensus to conserve the site had come prior to the Wall coming down and so removing the exhibition was not an option. In 1997 it was decided to replace the 'temporary' exhibition with a more permanent one but the costs of constructing the new building, designed by Swiss architect Peter Zumthor, became prohibitive. Consequently a new temporary exhibition was put in place. A re-designed permanent documentation centre is now scheduled to open in May 2010. The initial exhibition buildings were removed and replaced by an unobtrusive, flat-roofed building that houses the documentation centre. The excavated foundations below Niederkirchnerstrasse are in the open air but sheltered under a simple roof, and are lined by a collection of signs using details from original documents and photographs on the activities of the Gestapo, the SS, and their prisoners (figures 44-45). The rest of the site remains in a state of 'paradoxically preserved neglect', which ensures that the post-war decades of attempted forgetting is also demonstrated (Ladd 2004, 127). The lack of a permanent exhibition has been seen as an attribute; as Ladd (2004, 127) points out, a more permanent exhibition would probably lend the site a sense of formality of a more traditional museum which would detract from it remaining a deliberate 'open wound'. This is a point worth noting – there is little of the sanitisation or detachment that more formal monuments or objects in glass cases tend to allow the visitor, nor is the site 'faceless' or dehumanised; the identification, photographs and details of individuals of both Gestapo and prisoners ensure this. A confrontation with some of the realities and horrors of history is what indeed the visitor has to contend with, and to this end, the use of the physical remains of the buildings are well-utilised and presented.

The exhibition was critically acclaimed when it first opened and very popular; within the first year the exhibition had over 300,000 visitors, including foreigners and it continued to have some 3,000 visitors a week after that, resulting in the exhibition being continued indefinitely (Ladd 1998, 162; Ladd 2004, 127). One of the notable points was the concentration on documentation and an avoidance of interpretation or judgement; it was also recognised as a place different to other Third Reich sites in that it was a place of perpetrators more than victims (Ladd 1998, 162). The site as a record of the perpetrators of violence in the Third Reich is important to note – Germany for the previous forty years had studiously worked to forget the horrors of the Third Reich and even when there was movement to commemorate it, it was, and still is, largely about honouring and remembering the victims. This is not, however, the same as accepting responsibility and the Topography of Terror is perhaps one of the few sites that puts the perpetrators up for examination in an accessible and public way, and provides for a degree of confrontation with that history.

Figure 44: Basements, Topography of Terror (Berlin Wall above)

Figure 45: Topography of Terror (Berlin Wall above)

The Berlin Wall

By the late 1950s the 'brain drain' from East Germany to West via West Berlin was considered a major problem by the Soviet and East German authorities as causing a significant loss to the economy of the GDR. Consequently, with no other option to stop this – the USA under President Kennedy had implied that they would rather go to war than hand over West Berlin – Ulbricht in June 1961 suggested building a barrier, which was approved by Moscow in August 1961

(O'Dochartaigh 2004, 67). Construction of the first 'anti-fascist rampart' began on 13th August of that year. This was replaced and elaborated three times; the final, fourth generation, 'Wall' was built in the 1970s (Klausmeier and Schmidt 2004, 16). The Wall as is generally known was this fourth generation 3.6m high West-Berlin facing border wall of pre-cast steel-reinforced high density concrete (Baker 1993, 716). It was this face with its rounded top that provided the perfect surface for the graffiti that, at least in the West, became so associated with it. This border wall was only part of the defences which comprised a double wall – the border wall (*Wand*) that faced West Berlin and a hinterland wall (*Mauer*) that faced East Berlin. Between these two walls was the 'death strip' that comprised a variety of features such as a patrol road and watch towers for the border guards, guard dog runs, trip-wires, spikes to impale any wall-jumpers, and, of course, extensive lighting. The extent and nature of this defence system varied from place to place and often pre-existing features were incorporated – for example the railway walls originally built in 1900 at the Norweger and Behmstrasse in the Pankow district, or the Spree river itself at the site that is now the East Side Gallery in the Kreuzberg-Friedrichshain district.

The Berlin Wall may have put an end to the emigration and some of the international political tensions over the city, but it divided Berlin physically in two, cutting friends and families off from each other, with no opportunity to see each other for years. According to Ladd (1998, 30), it also inadvertently served a number of psychological functions such as stimulating discussion about German identity and allowing West Berliners in particular to be considered victims, implying a certain amount of redemption from the horrors of World War II. The sudden collapse of the GDR in November 1989 and the famous breaching of the Wall resulted in the rapid transformation of the Berlin Wall, almost overnight, from a death-threatening border to a historic monument and ruin. 'The Wall must go!' was the initial public response, and in fact most of it was hastily and happily destroyed by the public both in celebration of the end of the regime that had built it and as means of forgetting yet another problematical chapter in Germany's history (Baker 1990, 167). The Active Museum of Berlin, responsible for drawing attention to the Gestapo headquarters were one of the few organisations that began very quickly to campaign to conserve what was left of the Wall (Baker 1990, 167).

One of the more unusual aspects of the Berlin Wall's sudden demise was the consumption or commodification of it. This is examined by Frederick Baker in his paper, 'The Berlin Wall: production, preservation and consumption of a 20th-Century Monument' (Baker 1993, 719ff). Although the East German authorities, before the East German state disappeared, tried to protect it and issued a preservation order for the piece along the Niederkirchnerstrasse (they even put up signs to this effect but they were stolen within a day), they were also quick to auction off some of the more colourful sections of the border wall to art galleries in order to make some much needed money (Baker 1990, 167). At the opposite end of the scale were the 'wall-peckers' who were initially souvenir hunters but were soon joined by those who realised they could make some money by chipping off pieces to sell or to make into products such as key rings. This led to dubious practices such as the spraying of unmarked pieces of the wall, including surviving *Mauer* sections, converting the 'originally grey pieces of a *Mauer* in which 189 people died trying to cross…into the harmless *Wand*, West Berlin's colourful scribble pad' (Baker 1993, 720), in order to sell the pieces to tourists. Sections of the Berlin Wall were also presented as a kind of trophy to, for example, US president Ronald Reagan, and there is a slab sitting, rather forlornly, in an overgrown public garden within the EU quarter in Brussels. There is also a piece now positioned next to the reconstructed St Mary Aldermanbury Church in Fulton, Missouri, where Winston Churchill made his famous 'Iron Curtain' speech (see London Chapter).

Figure 46: Berlin Wall along Niederkirchnerstrasse (bordering the Topography of Terror site)

From 1990 and the demise of the East German regime, the Wall became the responsibility of the *Landesdenkmalamt* (Berlin Monument Authority) within the Senate Department of Urban Development of Berlin. The *c.*200 metre stretch of border wall along the Niederkirchnerstrasse was badly damaged by wall-peckers, the concrete chipped away down to its steel frame in a number of places, which is how it remains today (figure 46). It runs along the road bordering the Topography of Terror exhibition. Whereas the Topography of Terror site comprises the remains of the Gestapo Headquarters and thus of the Nazi era, the Wall is from the post-war period and the two thus represent two separate phases in history. It has been argued, however, that it is appropriate to have a section of the Berlin Wall as part of this exhibition because ultimately it is a consequence of Nazi crimes and the historical relationship should be remembered (Baker 1990, 167). The Wall and the Topography of Terror are in fact displayed as two separate sites. There is a sign on the street explaining this section of the Berlin Wall, which is protected behind fencing from the street side. The Wall is inaccessible, though clearly visible from the Topography of Terror side, but the remains of the Gestapo headquarters are below street level, sheltered under a roof structure that visually splits the two sites up. Its position next to the Topography of Terror site is, however, appropriate: up to 189 people were killed during confrontations at the Wall, including a number of border guards shot by their own colleagues for attempting to escape to the West (Baker 1993, 716, 718; Ladd 1998, 24, 25).

In 1995, Dr Volker Hassemer, the senator responsible for both urban development and for historic conservation argued for the retention of sections of the Berlin Wall:

> 'It is our duty to retain proof of this madness to guard against any possibility of its return. We should take the 'incredibility of the Wall' seriously. Quite soon nobody will believe that such a thing was put into the middle of a metropolis. Therefore we need the remnants of this horrible edifice as enduring witness. ... These are depressing locations in our city. Therefore one must also have sympathy for those who ask – now that we have been freed of this pressure – why they should have to bear these depressing aspects in our city in the future...' (quoted in Klausmeier and Schmidt 2004, 8).

Hassemer's words highlight the difficulty of trying to protect a socio-politically tainted monument in the early years following the event/period that the monument was a part of. It was not until 2001 that there was a Senate initiative to protect the Berlin Wall more thoroughly, and sites were still being listed in 2005. A survey has since been conducted of all the remaining evidence of the Wall and is published as a comprehensive guidebook, *Wall Remnants – Wall Traces* (Klausmeier and Schmidt 2004). Remains of the Berlin Wall have been divided between listed 'monuments' and 'traces'. Traces of the Wall include street lamps, scars where it was attached to existing buildings and surviving barriers. It is accepted that many of these will gradually disappear but they are at least recorded. There are twenty-five listed and thus protected Berlin Wall monuments, which comprise several hundred metres in total of wall and three watch towers. They are located in four districts of Berlin: Pankow, Mitte, Kreuzeberg-Friedrichshain and Treptow-Köpenick and, in most cases, comprise several structures.

A Wall monument in Mitte is at Bernauer Strasse. This is the infamous street where people jumped from upper floor windows of a building right on the border to escape from East to West in the early days of the Wall. The occupants of these border buildings were later evicted and the houses demolished in 1965. It is also the street where a church, the neo-Gothic Church of the Reconciliation, that ended up in no-man's land with the building of the Wall, was blown up by the GDR authorities in 1985. Although it was the former pastor of this church who first campaigned to have a Wall monument here (Baker 1990, 727), there were strong protests about keeping this particular stretch of the fortification from the pastor of another church, the Sophienkirche. The Wall crossed its cemetery and the pastor declared that a monument to the Wall here would represent a second desecration of the cemetery (Ladd 1998, 34). Furthermore, the Lazarus home for the chronically ill stands on the opposite side of the street and there was considerable concern that for the patients to have to look out over a Berlin Wall monument would be a cause of unnecessary depression (Baker 1993, 728; Ladd 1998, 34). Nevertheless the monument was approved, though due to property claims, financing problems and design indecisions, nothing was done with it for a number of years (Ladd 1998, 34). As it is now, it appears to straddle a line between an archaeological monument and an art installation (figure 47). The Deutsche Historische Museum (Museum for German History) wanted this to be a 'didactic installation for history'. This is the only section where both *Wand* and *Mauer* have been conserved along with the other features of the defence system such as the patrol strip and lighting. The display was designed by Stuttgart architects Kohlhoff and Kohlhoff. This section of the Wall had been badly damaged by wall-peckers, so it was completely restored. The architects then cut through the listed Wall with two six metre high steel walls that sandwich a 64-metre stretch of the Wall between them. The outer side of the steel walls are corroded to provide an association with the 'Iron Curtain' of the Cold War; the inner ones are polished to reflect the Wall into infinity as a way of representing its much greater original extent (Sentate Dept of Urban Development website 2006).

Figure 47: Bernauer Strasse Wall monument

The Wall has also been conserved, though only in comparatively relocated small sections, at the Leipziger Platz (Klausmeier and Schmidt 2004, 153). There was a larger section of *Mauer*, listed since 2001, just off the to the south of the Platz on the corner of Stresemannstrasse/Erna-Berger-Strasse (figure 5). The corresponding *Wand*, none of which survive, crossed the Potsdamer Platz to the west. The *Mauer* in this part of Berlin was constructed to resemble the *Wand*, apparently to make the Wall look better – the Potsdamer Platz being one of the areas where Western tourists came to view the Wall during the Cold War (Sentate Dept of Urban Development website 2006). The piece on the Stresemannstrasse/Erna-Berger-Strasse corner also retained the original knee-high red and white barrier. The Wall itself linked up with a former fire protection wall of a neo-classicist extension added to what had been the Prussian Ministry of Agriculture between 1913 and 1919. There had been plans to incorporate this piece of the Wall into the entrance area of the Berlin seat of the Federal Ministry for Environmental Affairs (Sentate Dept of Urban Development website 2006), but by 2007 this piece of wall had been removed and the property was being redeveloped. Not far away, on the Erna-Berger-Strasse, is a surviving watch-tower. This was listed in 2001 but has been moved about eight metres to the east as it was obstructing a development (Sentate Dept of Urban Development website 2006).

These surviving pieces of *Mauer* on the Leipziger Platz have graffiti on them. The Stresemannstrasse/ Erna-Berger-Strasse piece exhorted the viewer in English 'Don't destroy history' (figure 5). There is a very strong link between graffiti and the Berlin Wall. Some of it was of artistic merit – for instance that done near Checkpoint Charlie by American artist Keith Haring, who died in 1990. Being at such a 'popular' part of the Wall, this section was destroyed very quickly by the wall-peckers (Ladd 1998, 10). Graffiti was part of the *Wand* and therefore of the Western perception of the Berlin Wall and this is what has persevered in the present day presentation of it. The *Mauer* was painted white with grey framing; East Berlin residents were not allowed anywhere near it, let alone deface it with graffiti. Although some of the Wall monuments are now maintained with this colour scheme, for example the piece of *Mauer* in the Invaliden-Cemetery (figure 48), the majority of the Wall monuments, even though most are in fact *Mauer*, are maintained in such a way as to allow, even to actively encourage, graffiti – for example the piece in the Wall Park at Prenzlauer Berg in the Pankow district, and the East Side Gallery in the Kreuzeberg-Friedrichshain district. The latter site is the longest surviving stretch of Wall at 1.3km. It was listed in 1991 and artists were invited to illustrate it. The aim had been to then send the panels on an international exhibition before auctioning them off; this did not materialise. Its various art works have since become quite faded and themselves require conservation and cleaning up from later graffiti (Sentate Dept of Urban Development website 2006). In terms of the Wall's graffiti, it is extremely rare for a historic monument to have something of what it means to some people demonstrated in such a graphic manner, and also for this ongoing expression to be a part of the monument. The perceived connection between the Berlin Wall and artistic expression is, however, very much a Western perspective, and while it is arguably more practical to allow an unprotected piece of wall to become a graffiti canvas, the dominance of this perspective may perhaps be seen as another demonstration of the dominance of West German memory over East German memory.

Figure 48: *Mauer* (east-facing Wall) in the Invaliden-Cemetery, painted in the original grey colour scheme

The website of the Senate Department of Urban Development in Berlin, which carries information on the archaeological sites of the city, goes into great detail on the surviving pieces of the Berlin Wall. It has even developed a special city walk that takes in various sites (Sentate Dept of Urban Development website 2006).

The Stadtschloss

The gigantic Stadtschloss was the focal point of Berlin, until its demolition almost entirely for political reasons in the early 1950s (figure 31). The site, the large Marx-Engels Platz, then provided the requisite large public rallying space and later, in the 1970s, the Palast, the seat of the GDR and also an entertainment centre for East Berliners, was built on part of the site. After the fall of the Wall, there was growing interest in removing the Palast and rebuilding the Stadtschloss. This movement was led by a Hamburg businessman Wilhelm von Boddien, and in 1993 and 1994, a huge mock-up of the palace using scaffolding and painted canvases was exhibited on the site. This proved hugely successful, even converting some who were initially against the rebuilding proposal (Ladd 1998, 60). The restoration proponents did not, however, realise that they had to contend with East Berliners' desire to keep their Palast. As a consequence the whole site became mired in the confusion of conflicting histories and identities until very recently, when the decision was finally made to demolish the latter to rebuild something resembling the old Stadtschloss. In the 1990s excavations were carried out in the square to the immediate west of the Palast to discover if anything of the Stadtschloss foundations survived. Evidence of the aborted eighteenth century Coin Tower and, further to the west towards the Lustgarten, of settlement dating to the twelfth to fourteenth centuries – the oldest settlement evidence to date on Cölln – was uncovered. The site is to be integrated into the new building and displayed (Senate Dept of Urban Development website 2006). At present, however, it has been left exposed and growing weeds (figure 49), though it does have signage explaining the site.

Figure 49: Excavated foundations of the Stadtschloss

The Grand Hotel Esplanade

The Grand Hotel Esplanade, Bellevuestrasse, opened in 1911, was one of Berlin's grandest hotels and was even frequented by the Kaiser, so it included an elaborate Kaisersaal (Imperial Room). The Hotel Esplanade was badly damaged during the second world war, but it was the only extant building on this part of the Potsdamer Platz, and part of the large plot subsequently bought by Sony after the Wall came down. The surviving portion, which included the historic façade, the neo-Baroque Kaisersaal and a neo-Rococco Breakfast Room, were listed for preservation. The architect of the Sony Center, Helmut Jahn, was forced to go to great lengths to incorporate the Esplanade within the Center. Sony did, however, have an ulterior motive to conserve the Esplanade: Sony had paid a suspiciously low price for the plot on Potsdamer Platz and this was duly investigated by an EU commission. In the end, the EU approved this low price because Sony promised to conserve the listed Esplanade, and to provide low rent premises for a film museum (Strom 2001, 191). Incidentally, the Grand Hotel Esplanade was in fact used in the famous, award-winning film 'Wings of Desire' set in West Berlin and directed by Wim Wenders in the 1980s.

Jahn's Sony Center gives the impression of being a single glass and steel structure, but it is in fact a complex of seven different buildings (figure 30). His attitude towards the Hotel Esplanade was, as Ladd (2004, 141) puts it mildly, one of disdain. The façade on Bellevuestrasse remains, but it is 'sheathed in glass and virtually crushed' by the apartment block, the 'Esplanade Residence', that has been suspended over it on a steel bridge (Ladd 2004, 141). As, according to the official Berlin website (Berlin.de 2006), it was apparently not possible to integrate the interior of the Esplanade within the new development, two historic rooms – the Kaisersaal and half of the Breakfast Room were 'translocated'. This involved lifting and moving the 13,000 tonne Kaisersaal some 75 metres away and dismantling half of the Breakfast Room. The ceiling, the floor and two walls of the latter were dismantled and then reassembled as part of the interior of the new Café Josty (a reference to a famous café of 1920s Potsdamer Platz) within the complex, leaving just two walls *in situ* (figure 50). These two walls, at right angles to each other, are now behind glass and face outwards onto an open paved space that is part of the huge central, publicly-accessible area of the Sony Center. It has to be asked whether this is really 'conservation' of a listed building – to divide it up and move the portions around as if it were a collection of artefacts rather than a single piece of built heritage?

Figure 50: Half of the Esplanade's Breakfast Room behind glass in the Sony Centre

The signage, however, demonstrates an ability for euphemism that the corporate world has honed to perfection. It has an extensive sign in both German and English that begins with identifying the Esplanade Residence and the former Grand Hotel Esplanade as 'a historical landmark for the future'. It goes on to explain how due to zoning plans and the subsequent widening of the Potsdamer Strasse, the Breakfast Room and the Kaisersaal had to be moved, and that the building of the Esplanade Residence apartments over the former hotel 'represent a "bridge" to the modern and rejuvenated spirit of Berlin today'. It then explains how the surviving two walls of the Breakfast Room 'is a significant exhibition commemorating the old Esplanade'.

The interesting point of the so-called conservation of the Grand Hotel Esplanade is that, as architects and developers have discovered, it possible to destroy, or at least to neutralise, while simultaneously appearing to conserve, the original significance of a site. Furthermore the reconstituting but destroying of the site as a cultural and historical symbol and the plundering and ridiculing of the past that seem to be an integral part of postmodernism (Clarke 2003, 38; Jencks 1992, 23) could not be more clearly demonstrated.

V: DISCUSSION

The dominating fact of Berlin was that between 1949 and 1989, the city was a major front of the Cold War: East and West Berlin represented two opposing political systems, communism and democracy. The other dominating aspect was the need to forget or disassociate from the horrors of the Third Reich and, to a lesser extent, the stigma of Prussian militarism. East and West Berlin appear to have reacted differently to these problems and in the process the treatment of the built heritage was affected. In East Berlin, the attitude to the immediate past was due mostly to the fact that as a socialist regime, East Germany felt automatically exonerated of any responsibility for the Nazis. With the exception of the demolition of Hitler's chancellery, many Third Reich government buildings were simply stripped of National Socialist paraphernalia and re-used. Lack of finances due to reparations to the USSR and no aid from the Marshall Plan meant that rebuilding was at a much slower rate than in the FRG. The huge redevelopment of Stalinallee also took finances away from rebuilding elsewhere not only in East Berlin but throughout the GDR. As a consequence of this, more urban heritage survived in East Germany, as was appreciated after 1989, and it may also have allowed greater time for urban archaeological work. Nonetheless, the East German government did not care specifically for the built heritage, and where it was expedient to remove it, they did, particularly if it got in the way of development, as seen in the destruction of the remains of the monastery that the Klosterkirche was part of, or if it could be used to send a political message to the West, as seen with the demolition of the Stadtschloss.

West Berlin aimed to forget the immediate past, and utilised modernism in its rebuilding. This part of the city lost a considerable amount of its built heritage in the immediate post-war period due mostly to deliberate demolition, and what survived was either through chance, public demand or as a reaction to what was happening in East Berlin. This desire to break with the past was very much supported by modernism, and may also explain the mixed reactions to urban archaeology.

Urban archaeology, as in Britain, only developed in Germany in the aftermath of World War II. While there appears to have been extensive archaeological work carried out in East German cities, including in East Berlin (Herrmann 1977, 244; Taylor 1997, 6), in West Germany it was much less regulated. As late as 1988 there was concern that urban archaeology in West Germany was not up to the standard of other European countries (Fehring 1991, 10).

The international broad-based socio-cultural change that began in the late 1960s-70s and the change of attitude towards the built heritage, exemplified by, for instance, the 1975 Year of European Architectural Heritage and twelve years later in the 1987 Washington Charter, as discussed in Chapter 2, may have gradually been felt in Germany. By the 1980s in both East and West Berlin there had been a change of heart towards the past. In East Berlin, the desire to establish some sort of historical base or precedent for the socialist GDR saw a growing interest in the built heritage, for example the reconstruction of the Nikolai Quarter that began in 1979. In West Berlin, planning ideas began to take on board the historic environment, partly due to pressure from local citizens' groups and other interested parties, as seen in the IBA of the 1980s. Both East and West decided to celebrate the 750th anniversary of Berlin's foundation in 1987, and a variety of work was carried out on the built heritage for this reason. The other aspect behind this growing appreciation of the past was an increasing desire, and indeed financial need, to encourage tourists to both East and West Berlin.

From 1989, there is a different attitude towards different components of the built heritage, depending on what it represented. This is reflected in the desire to return to an imagined late nineteenth-century Berlin in the redesign of the centre of the city, compared to the desire to demolish buildings associated with the Third Reich or the GDR. The desire to forget and move on is still strong, though this time it is former West Germany's desire to forget about former East Germany. This is not a sentiment appreciated by many former East Germans, as battles over whether to save or demolish the Palast demonstrated. Consequently, the politicisation of the built heritage is as strong now as ever.

The Senate Department for Urban Development is responsible for Berlin's sites and monuments (something that may give rise to conflicts of interest). They detail many of them on their website, and provide examples of walking tours for visiting some of the sites (Senate Dept of Urban Development website 2006). As noted, there are in fact very few fragmentary archaeological remains conserved for display in central Berlin, and only a small number of these are 'traditional' sites – i.e. fragments of medieval town wall, or foundations of historic buildings, such as those of the Stadtschloss, kept principally, though not exclusively, for their historic value. The medieval wall fragments and other medieval remains conserved about the wider city since 1989 (Senate Dept of Urban Development website 2006) may reflect a suggested tendency to look back to the medieval city of the early German Empire for inspiration as a period prior to Prussian militarism, the Nazis and division (Hain 2001, 70).

The majority, it would seem, have been conserved for very specific socio-political values. Both the Klosterkirche and Kaiser-Wilhelm Gedächtniskirche ruins in East and West Berlin respectively were kept as war memorials. The Klosterkirche is one of Berlin's oldest medieval churches and has great academic and historic value for this reason. The Gedächtniskirche, on the other hand, has arguably relatively little inherent architectural or historic value except as a war memorial and as a, if not the, symbolic site of West Berlin; a role it continues to play today. Something to note about both sites is that the Klosterkirche ruins are used for exhibitions and various cultural events, and the ground floor of the Gedächtniskirche was restored and is used for an exhibition on the war. This use of archaeological sites and ruins is important and will be returned to in the Discussion chapter.

The keeping of the remains of the Anhalter Bahnhof just inside what was West Berlin may represent several things. It was, during the late nineteenth century, one of the largest railway terminus buildings in the world but by the late 1930s it was being used, as were most German railway stations, to transport people to concentration camps. It thus represents one of the best followed by the worst period of German history. Its demolition illustrates West Berlin's tendency to demolish in order to forget. The subsequent conservation of part of its façade perhaps illustrates a belated attempt to save something, and perhaps as a reaction to the fact that West Berlin did not have the historic roots that East Berlin could claim by having the traditional, historic centre of Berlin. The same may be said for the conservation of the small piece of eighteenth-century customs wall on the Stresemannstrasse. Conserving this site in 1987 may have made a certain amount of sense when West Berlin was competing with East Berlin over the celebrations of Berlin's 750th anniversary, but in reality it is a rather uninteresting site stuck in the middle of a very busy road. The Senate Department of Urban Planning website does not mention either site in its monument section.

The most clearly political sites are, however, the Topography of Terror and the remains of the Berlin Wall. They highlight three important aspects of post-war conservation, which will be more fully examined in the Discussion Chapter. Briefly, however, these are first, the issue of built heritage being considered politically tainted. Many historic buildings were demolished in the post-war period because they had been associated with the Nazis. This causes two problems: the first is the loss of important historic architecture due to only one period of their usually multi-period existence; the second is the loss of physical evidence of this negative but none-the-less historic phase which thus, arguably, makes it more difficult for people to come to terms with it, to commemorate it and, particularly in the case of following generations, to remember the actuality of war-time events and atrocities. The Topography of Terror is a rare attempt to right this typical imbalance. Second, as demonstrated by the presentation of some of the remains of the Berlin Wall, the 'winner' is often reflected in what is conserved or not, or how it is conserved in the post-war period. It is the graffiti covered *Wand* sections of Berlin Wall that are considered to be most representative of it and are consequently to be found all over the world, from Seoul in South Korea to Reagan's Library in Washington, and it is this aspect that is highlighted in the conservation of pieces in Berlin itself, not the ominous white and grey *Mauer* and all its lethal trappings that East Berliners had to live with. The third issue is that of time. It was some thirty-five or forty years before it was felt that the history of the Third Reich could be dealt with, as exemplified by the interest in the Gestapo Headquarter remains. Although there were attempts to save the Berlin Wall as an historical monument from an early stage, it was 2001 before their was any official attempt to survey and protect thoroughly what was left, though pieces of it are still being destroyed, judging by the removal of the piece near Potsdamer Platz, illustrated in figure 5.

CHAPTER FIVE

BEIRUT AFTER THE 1975-1990 WAR

I. INTRODUCTION

Beirut has a long, distinguished but battle-scarred history. By 1990 it had seen fifteen years of yet another war, generally referred to as the Civil War but in fact consisting of several conflicts and involving foreign groups and armies as well as the many Lebanese militias that generally represented individual religious sects. Since the establishment of Lebanon's First Republic in 1943, there had been numerous occasions of unrest, and civil war had broken out previously in 1958 (Hourani 1991, 430; Diab 1999, 34). Diab (1999) puts forward the argument that the huge social inequalities and complexities, the 'development without growth', and the imbalances between Beirut and the rest of Lebanon are some of the principle causes of the war that broke out in 1975. Another cause put forward is the lack of an universally accepted national history, as Kamal Salibi (1988) argues in his aptly titled *A House of Many Mansions*. The complexities of that civil war, the involvement and interferences from outside powers with other agendas and the horrific brutalities that occurred in that tragic fifteen years are detailed by Robert Fisk (2001) in his book, *Pity the Nation: Lebanon at War*. Central Beirut became a shelled-out and abandoned no-man's land divided between Christian East Beirut and Muslim West Beirut by the Green Line that ran straight through Martyrs Square and on down the Damascus Road. One of the main, and most notorious, crossing points was the *Mathaf*, right outside the National Museum. By the time the Ta'if Accord was signed in 1989 to stop the fighting, between 150,000 and 170,000 people had been killed, *c.*300,000 injured, scores missing, many people were displaced, and estimates of the cost of the economic damage range from US$25-40 billion throughout Lebanon (Hamdan 1994; Stewart 1996, 494; UN 1993).

The damage done to central Beirut was extensive – due not only to direct war damage such as shelling and small-arms fire (leaving many buildings looking as if a giant rat had gnawed at them) but also to fifteen years of neglect. Such historic buildings as the twelfth century Al-Omari Mosque (originally the Crusader Cathedral of St John), and many of the later French Mandate buildings were in bad states of repair or reduced to bullet-ridden shells, and the areas of the souks had suffered extensive damage (see figure 57 for map). Much of the type of damage inflicted is still visible in buildings or shells of buildings around the Beirut Central District (BCD) (figure 51).

At the time of my first visit to Beirut, in April 2005, it was only fifteen years since the cessation of hostilities. Furthermore, the various recent events, namely Rafiq Hariri's assassination in February 2005, the Israeli bombing of the summer of 2006 (the July War) and subsequent social and political unrest means a perpetually changing socio-political climate that has taken its toll on the redevelopment and conservation works in the BCD. Added to which there is still considerable sensitivity surrounding the archaeological work of the BCD, and it may be many years before the dust has settled enough to be able to ascertain a clear, less subjective, and overall picture of the post-war redevelopment, including the archaeological work, under Solidere's (Société Libanaise pour le Développement et la Reconstruction du Centre-Ville de Beyrouth) direction.

Figure: 51: War damaged building south of the BCD, in 2005

II: THE URBAN CONTEXT

As mentioned previously, Beirut, or at least the area that became Beirut, has a long settlement history stretching back to the Palaeolithic. Beirut was at its height during the Roman period when it was famous for its Law School, set up in the second century AD. An earthquake in 551 destroyed much of Roman *Berytus*, and the city became something of a backwater. Beirut appears to have been a walled city by the time the Crusaders arrived in 1110, and by 1130 it was a wealthy city with a fortified harbour (Jidejian 1997, 171). Once the period of Crusader control ended in 1291, Syria, including what is now Lebanon, remained within various Islamic empires ruled by caliphs or by sultans. The last of these was the Ottoman sultanate that existed from 1379 until 1918 when it lost its Arab territories to the Allies (Salibi 1988, 5-6).

Beirut in the nineteenth and early twentieth centuries saw a level of growth similar to that experienced by cities in Europe at that time. The Ottomans in the nineteenth century made dramatic changes to the city, particularly after they agreed to pleas made by Beiruti notables to make it a provincial capital (Hanssen 1998, 47). Up until about 1800, Beirut had a population of about *c.*6,500 and was of minor importance. It served as an administrative centre for the area, the main industry of which was silk, which was mostly traded eastwards (Diab 1999, 12). Change came in 1827 when the French were forced to withdraw from Tripoli and so moved their trading houses to Beirut. In the 1830s, Beirut's port was also made an official quarantine station, which meant all passing ships had to dock there (Jidejian 1997, 214). Growing colonial interest in the Orient by the main European powers, the Industrial Revolution and other such factors saw a quick development of foreign commercial interests in Beirut as it was recognised as an ideal point of entry to the east in terms of trade and markets, preferably for new European goods. In the 1840s, the town was still walled and its image was one of mosques, castles and fortification towers but shelling by the British in 1840 destroyed the medieval castle and many other buildings (Jidejian 1997, 202). Throughout the second half of the nineteenth century, the Ottoman administration made efforts to reorganise central Beirut. By 1875, Beirut's population had grown to 80,000 (Diab 1999, 13), and most of the medieval gates were gone, the fortified harbour had been replaced by long jetties and quays, and church and school towers had joined the minarets of the skyline (Hanssen 1998, 49). In the 1850s the Ottomans built the Grand Serail on a ridge overlooking the city, and in the 1860s added the smaller Military Hospital. The Petit Serail for local administration was built in c.1883. In the 1890s, it was decided to put in a road connecting the port to the souks and the town centre – an idea that was to appear in virtually all later plans for Beirut – and consequently a number of houses and buildings were demolished, causing much protest (Hanssen 1998, 52). In 1898, the Clock Tower, a specifically Ottoman symbol that, rather than being of local origin, came from Istanbul, was built in front of the Grand Serail, and was the tallest building in Beirut at that time.

French and British interest in the region, especially in Beirut, had been growing throughout the nineteenth century, and the silk industry continued to create wealth particularly for the merchants. Regional roads and railways were built and telecommunication systems set up. The complicated social relations that developed during this time, the problems of unemployment caused by the later collapse of the silk industry and the great disparities in wealth are detailed by Hassan Diab in his book *Beirut: Reviving Lebanon's Past* (1999). Beirut continued to grow, as did west European power in the region, particularly after World War I and the defeat of the Ottoman Empire. As a consequence of the controversial 1916 Sykes-Picot Treaty, France was given the mandate from the League of Nations for Lebanon and Syria in 1920. At this point, Lebanon became the State of Greater Lebanon, and then in 1926 the country was given a constitution, essentially a version of the French constitution, with Beirut officially the capital. The French, during the period of their mandate, wanted to make their own mark on the city, which consequently led to more demolition of central Beirut, though also to some excavation (see below). They are responsible for the Place de l'Etoile with its radiating roads, based on the Place de l'Etoile in Paris, and the Foch and Allenby roads that run straight from the centre towards the sea, and now form the centrepiece of the Conservation Area. The star design was not completed on the east side as to fully implement it would have involved demolishing a number of historic religious buildings. By 1938 Beirut's population had reached 180,000 (Diab 1999, 13), requiring further urban changes. One of the more influential early master plans was the first Ecochard Plan of 1942. This was a very comprehensive plan and included zoning for industry and housing; detailed transport links and roads; a study of open and green spaces; and marked out where the airport should go (Ghorayeb 1998). This plan, as was the fate of many of Beirut's urban plans, was never approved but many of its aspects could be found in later designs (Salam 1998, 125).

In 1943 Lebanon was made an independent state to be ruled under an unwritten National Pact which attempted to balance the concerns of the Christian communities with those of the Muslim communities. It was at this time that the top positions in the government were assigned by religion: the President was to be Maronite Christian, the Prime Minister Sunni and the Speaker of the House, Shi'a. Other ministries were likewise allocated, for example the Director General of Antiquities must be a Maronite Christian, while the allocation of seats in parliament was maintained at a ratio of six Christian-held seats to five Muslim-held seats. By 1975, however, it was estimated that, due to increasing emigration amongst the Maronite community, increasing birth rates among the Muslim communities, and an influx of Palestinian refugees, Shi'as were in the majority, followed by Sunnis, with the Maronites being only the third largest community (Stewart 1996, 491).

After independence in 1948, Beirut continued to grow rapidly without much control or planning. The private and commercial sectors were very strong and development was guided by no more than a building code. Furthermore traffic congestion intensified and commercial activities invaded residential areas (Salam 1998, 126). Even though the French had introduced a law of antiquities in 1933, there was no practical protection at all for the urban fabric, for natural sites or for historic buildings and any archaeological features that surfaced; the destruction of the built heritage at this time has been described as 'barbaric' (Salam 1998, 125; 126). From 1958, governmental reforms were attempted and various new institutions, such as the Council for Public Administration, were established. The first legislation for urban planning was also introduced and with it the Higher Council of Planning and the General Directorate for Town Planning. In terms of urban planning and architecture, the influences of the 1933 CIAM Charter of Athens and modernism were evident in some of the architecture built in Beirut at that time (Verdeil 2005; Trad 2005). They were also evident in plans designed for Beirut, both its centre and the suburbs, such as those by Egli of 1954 and Ecochard in 1963 (Ghorayeb 1998, 113).

By 1975 Lebanon's population was about three million, 40% or 1.2 million of whom lived in Beirut (Diab 1999, 70). Beirut was considered the 'Paris of the Mediterranean', with its wealth and comparatively liberal business practices and lifestyle. The city had flourished as a gateway between the Middle East and Europe. Many businesses and banks had headquarters there and after the formation of Israel in 1948, oil-rich Middle Eastern countries such as Saudi Arabia began transporting oil out via Beirut rather than Haifa. Although traditionally considered, in terms of Islam, as being Sunni, Beirut's image, prior to 1975,was of being a multi-confessional and, indeed, multi-ethnic city, particularly in the centre (Nagel 2002, 719). Martyrs Square with its cinemas, cafes and transport hub was considered the epitome of this apparently harmonious mixing of people. One of the over-riding characteristics of Lebanon is, however, religion. There are seventeen different religious groups of which the main ones are Sunni and Shi'a Muslims, Maronite Christians, Greek Orthodox and Greek Catholics, but also include Druze, Armenian and Jewish. As with, for example, Northern Ireland, these religious groups are not just a matter of different places of worship but represent seventeen different cultural traditions with their corresponding histories, as discussed by Salibi (1988). Indeed the lack of a single accepted national history is one of Lebanon's problems (Salibi 1988), and these issues are reflected in attitudes to the built heritage including archaeology. The mixing pot that was Beirut prior to 1975 provided a superficial cover to the underlying tensions that stemmed not just from religion but also from issues such as Arab nationalism, for example Maronite Christians tended to look west to Europe while some Muslim Arabs saw themselves as part of the larger Arab world; added to which there were deep economic disparities (Nagel 2002, 720; Diab 1999), for example the Shi'as of southern Lebanon have always been, generally, less well-off than their Sunni compatriots – an issue that has lent itself to the rise of Hezbollah. These divisions had been played upon by European powers in the nineteenth and early twentieth centuries, particularly demonstrated by the French favouring the Maronite Christian community in terms of business, consequently making the latter more wealthy (Nagel 2002, 719). Acknowledgement of these divisions is perhaps best exemplified by the National Pact of 1943. As noted previously parliamentary power was distributed confessionally, but there were two other terms worth noting here, one included ensuring an independent, sovereign and natural Lebanon in which Muslims renounced any idea of union with Syria or any other Arab state, in return for which Christians would renounce separatism and their special ties with France or any other foreign power. The second term was that Muslims accept Lebanon's 'Christian character' in return for Christian acceptance of Lebanon's 'Arab face' (Diab 1999, 33). War, however, broke out in 1975 and shattered any notion of inter-confessional unity. Between 1975 and 1976 considerable damage was inflicted on central Beirut, and the city became divided between predominantly Muslim West Beirut and predominantly Christian East Beirut along the infamous Green Line. The Ta'if Accord of 1989 maintained the allocation of the top parliamentary positions, except for an important shift in power where the Sunni Prime Minister, a position later held by Rafiq Hariri, was given far greater power than the Maronite president. It has been suggested that this reduction in Maronite Christian political influence allowed for an important shift in Lebanon's identity – that being Lebanese could now mean also being Arab (Klaushofer 2007, 23).

A feature of the war that lasted from 1975 to 1990 was that it subsumed several conflicts and that there were periodic lulls in this fighting. Lulls that were long enough to give people the impression that the fighting had stopped for good. The first such lull came in 1977, and a master plan to repair the damage done to central Beirut was commissioned by the newly formed government body, the Council for Development and Reconstruction (CDR). It aimed to restore Beirut's centre as a meeting place for all communities while improving the infrastructure, but it also aimed to preserve Beirut's historic Mediterranean and Eastern character. Unfortunately war broke out again at the end of 1977 and was further intensified by foreign invasions but there was another lull in 1982, after UN peacekeepers arrived. In 1983, OGER Liban, an engineering company owned by Lebanese-born but Saudi-based billionaire Rafiq Hariri commissioned another master plan for the redevelopment of central Beirut from the international consultancy, Dar al-Handasah. This was the first of a number of plans from this consultancy and they ultimately produced the master plan that Solidere have based the redevelopment of the BCD on. It also marks the official beginnings of Rafiq Hariri's involvement in the reconstruction of central Beirut. From the late 1970s, when he had returned to visit the city, he was interested in rebuilding it and had begun almost straightaway making such plans (Becherer 2005, 6). Towards the end of 1983, 'cleaning up' started in central Beirut involving the demolition, without any apparent government authority or constraint, of a number of important buildings and the Souks Al-Nouriyeh and Sursuq, along with a large part of Saifi (a residential area to the east of Martyrs Square), and blatantly ignoring the recommendations of the 1977 plan (Makdisi 1997, 667). Fighting resumed again until 1986, when more demolitions were carried out to a plan that recommended some 80% of central Beirut be cleared (Makdisi 1997, 668).

The fighting was finally brought to an end by the Ta'if Accord. Despite the countrywide destruction, including much of the infrastructure – schools, hospitals, housing, roads and bridges – and the displacement of large sections of the populations, the government decided that a priority was to rebuild central Beirut. Beirut had been the financial and commercial centre of the country prior to the war so great significance was attached to its rehabilitation (Schmid 2006, 366). The overall aim was to put Lebanon back on the international economic map in a way that reflected its historical role as a centre for trade, skills and financial services (*Al-Hayat* 19/05/93 in Diab 1999, 1), for which the redevelopment of central Beirut was to be the flagship. The CDR designed a redevelopment plan for Lebanon, Horizon 2000, which aimed to restore Lebanon by the year 2000 but was soon put back to 2007 (Stewart 1996, 494). The 1996 and 2006 Israeli invasions and their bombing of Lebanon's infrastructure, particularly in 2006, have, however, long since rendered these deadlines obsolete.

After the end of the war in 1990, the head of Hariri's OGER Liban company was appointed head of the CDR. This appointment meant that the head of one of the largest private companies involved in Lebanon's construction industry became head of the government's council that oversaw redevelopment and planning, effectively allowing OGER Liban to legitimise its own plans (Sarkis 1993, 114; Khalaf 2006; 129). Unlike previous master plans for Beirut, plans after the war were developed for specific areas of Beirut rather than the whole city, so the southern suburbs and the coast to the north, along which there had been considerable unregulated building during the war, were allocated to the consultancies of Elisar under government jurisdiction and Linord as a joint venture respectively (Rowe and Sarkis 1998, 16). In 1991, a new master plan for central Beirut commissioned by the CDR and designed by Henri Eddé for Dar al-Handasah was unveiled. With shades of Le Corbusier's 1920s plans for central Paris and indeed Scharoun's initial plans for central Berlin, Eddé produced a dramatic modernist-type plan that seemed to virtually wipe out all of central Beirut. In its place would be a city centre with a 'majestic Champs-Elyseés-type' layout and a 'mini-Manhattan' island, cut off from the rest of the city as an 'island of modernity' (Tabet 1993, 95). This 1991 plan was severely criticised both by those who owned or had rights to property in central Beirut and by specialists such as the Urban Research Institute and the Engineers Union (Beyhum 1992). There were serious concerns over the traffic flow and control, over the huge 'fortresses of glass and iron' that were planned, and the massive and no doubt hugely profitable development on the island of accumulated war-time debris that had formed just off the coast (Beyhum 1992). It was argued that this plan would lead to a wealthy central Beirut isolated from the rest of the city (Beyhum 1992). Ultimately, the plan, as also happened to Sharoun's Berlin plan, was condemned by the general public as too radical and had to be scrapped (Makdisi 1997, 670). Its scrapping was aided by a surge of negative feeling towards the plan when a large number of historic buildings, condemned as unsafe, were hurriedly demolished in such a way as to damage nearby buildings, thus requiring them to be demolished also (Beyhum 1992; Fisk 2001, 665). It seems a rare surviving piece of the medieval town wall was also demolished at this time (Fisk 2001, 665)

Solidere is the private real estate company established to oversee the redevelopment of the BCD. In December 1991, the government had passed Law 117 that would allow for the establishment of such a company. This company would be exempt from tax for ten years but would have to undertake to finance the complete reconstruction, including the infrastructure, of the BCD. The State would refund it by allowing development rights on reclaimed land (principally that created by the waste dumped into the sea just north of the BCD during the war) (Gavin and Maluf 1996, 16). The debate over this potential real estate company and its powers was somewhat overshadowed by the elections held in 1992, in which Rafiq Hariri was elected prime minister. One of the last things the out-going government did was to pass a law allowing for the setting up of Solidere and to ratify the latest Dar al-Handasah plans (Makdisi 1997, 674).

There were several factors that made the idea of a public-private partnership to redevelop the BCD attractive. Firstly, the city centre had been severely damaged; most of the buildings had been deserted by their owners or tenants, only to be reoccupied towards the end of the war by refugees and squatters. The government was in a weak state and certainly had little funds available for such a massive redevelopment project. Hariri had vast experience in urban development from working in Saudi Arabia, as did his OGER Liban company and Dar al-Handasah, and it does not appear to have been difficult for him to persuade the Lebanese government of the benefits of this course of action (Schmid 2006, 366). There was also the major complicating factor of property rights. While property owners and their descendents have rights, of course, to their own property, so do, under Lebanese law, leaseholders, tenants and their descendents; consequently there was something in the region of 250,000 individual claims to property within the BCD alone, along with some 15,000 squatters (Makdisi 1997, 671; Stewart 1996, 500). This had potentially serious consequences for any attempts at comprehensive rebuilding, and so it was suggested that a single real estate company be set up to expropriate the property and oversee the redevelopment of central Beirut. Those with bona fide claims to such property would not be paid for their property but would be given controlling shares in this real estate company.

Solidere was formally established as a joint stock company with a majority shareholding of pre-existing land and property owners and other rights holders in the city centre, and with cash assets of $650 million (Gavin and Maluf 1996, 14). Those existing property owners and other rights holders gave up their property in return for controlling shares in Solidere, and Solidere was granted title over all land and retained buildings, with the exception of twenty-six retained public and religious buildings (Gavin and Maluf 1996, 17). Effectively, the centre of Beirut for all intents and purposes had become privatised. Schmid (2006) describes the success of Solidere's expropriation of central Beirut as a clear example of the re-orientation that has taken place in urban politics in recent decades, and which is termed 'new urban governance'. The most obvious expression of this new urban governance is the development of the public- private partnership, where, since the 1980s, there has been a gradual adoption by the private sector of tasks and functions normally carried out by the public sector. It is been particularly evident in the area of urban redevelopment as seen, for example, in the USA in Baltimore and Boston and then in London in the London Docklands Development Corporation. The consequential transfer of power and threatened undermining of state authorities is very controversial. A further issue is the primary orientation towards profit, a lack of transparency, and the exclusion or integration of particular protagonists and interests, leading to accusations and problems of playgrounds for the elite, and conflict with those excluded from the process (Schmid 2006, 366ff). In the case of Beirut, the state monopoly of planning was partly transferred to Solidere headed by a small number of initiators and investors, which at the same time excluded most of the concerned protagonists, such as the owners and tenants of Beirut city centre, from the decision-making (Schmid 2006, 368).

The formation of Solidere generated, therefore, strong resistance; various groups of concerned citizens and professionals did attempt both to protest and to find alternatives to this threatened privatization of the city centre (Martin 1994; Makdisi 1997, 672). They were further spurred on by the level of destruction of what was left of central Beirut. In 1994, reconstruction began in earnest and resulted in some 80% of the land of the BCD being cleared of its buildings, making, of course, the need for extensive reconstruction an absolute necessity (Schmid 2006, 370). A number of different groups protested against Solidere and their plans for the BCD. They included property-owners and former tenants, the mostly Shi'a refugees who were supported by Hezbollah and Amal, artists, writers and academics, and various specialists such as architects and planning professionals, and those concerned with protecting the historic urban environment (Schmid 2006, 373). The protests were against a number of issues: expropriation of property; the clear profit orientation of the project that did not correspond to public interests; the lack of democratic principles and public control; the actual architectural design of much of the plan that included oversized highways and skyscrapers and use of a uniform, globalised architecture; the general division of the centre from the rest of the city, including the creating of Martyrs Square into a highway that would effectively reinforce the division of the civil war; and the destruction of the historic fabric (Schmid 2006, 373).

These objections to the latest plan were generally fought out in the media. On the one hand Hariri and Solidere presented the planned, ultra-modern Beirut as 'the Hong Kong of the Mediterranean' which built on the desire to modernise and rebuild the economy, and provided very attractive images of Beirut as a major international centre of commerce. On the other hand, detractors tended to argue for a 'Paris of the Middle East', linking back to the pre-war image of Beirut, which played on Beirut's multi-confessional image; they linked the expropriation and destruction of Beirut's centre by Solidere as an attempt to erase Beirut's history (Schmid 2006, 375). This well-founded accusation of Solidere's physical erasure of Beirut's history, particularly that of the civil war, is evinced by Hariri himself, at a ceremony commemorating the twenty-fifth anniversary of the start of the war, in 2000, when he declared that not a single building should be kept that would remind people of the civil war as there should be no need to preserve such a painful memory (quoted in Becherer 2005, 18). A sentiment remarkably similar, it is worth noting, to that of Kohl's in relation to the surviving architecture of the Third Reich and GDR in East Berlin after the GDR's demise (see Berlin chapter).

As is evident, protests against Solidere, which even included issues of human rights' abuse (Human Rights Watch 2006), were ultimately futile. Solidere had the greater resources and could fund expensive promotional advertising, and had, Schmid (2006, 375) argues, a significant element of control over the media: while initially protestors of the plan and Solidere were able to draw public attention to the issues via use of newspapers and television, gradually Solidere were able to stifle this by, for example, threatening the withdrawal of advertising if a newspaper or TV station was critical. Added to which Hariri had his own media empire with its ties to various stations and papers, for example the Future Television Network and Radio Orient. Finally in 1996 an audio-visual law was passed that dramatically reduced the number of television stations that could broadcast in Lebanon, causing at least three stations critical of Hariri and the plans for central Beirut to close (Schmid 2006, 376). Consequently the fragmented opposition, with no definite alternative to Solidere to offer, crumbled in the face of the powerful imagery of a new economically successful BCD (Schmid 2006, 376).

In 1998, Schmid carried out a survey to investigate opinion of Solidere, which he broke down into religious communities. It is evident that even amongst the Maronite Christians, there is a strong showing of support for Solidere by 1998. Traditionally, it was the Maronite Christian community who was most concerned for the built heritage, including the archaeology, and were highly vocal critics of Solidere, as exemplified by, for instance Naccache (1998) in his paper 'Beirut's memorycide: hear no evil, see no evil' and Makdisi's (1997) paper 'Laying Claim to Beirut: urban narrative and spatial identity in the age of Solidere'. The master plan that Solidere are working to, however, has had to change and adapt since 1993 to take in some of the criticisms levelled at them in the early 1990s.

The total project area of the BCD is approximately 180 hectares of which almost 60 hectares are reclaimed land and it is divided into ten different sectors, including a Conservation Area that centres on the Place de l'Etoile, that are each dominated by one particular aspect, such as the Hotel Area or the Bourj (Martyrs Square) Axis, but are all of mixed use (Gavin and Maluf 1996, 128). Solidere is responsible for overseeing the rebuilding of the BCD, for infrastructure works and for the redevelopment of a number of key or magnet sites (i.e. their redevelopment would attract other development), such as the Souks site, but not all buildings were expropriated by Solidere nor are they responsible for all the actual rebuilding. Government-owned property and twenty-six public and religious buildings were classified as exempt from the master plan and remained in possession of their owners. Other retained buildings, often ones considered worthy of conservation, could also be retained by their owners who had the option to restore these, though to strict Solidere guidelines not only on the time they had to complete these works but also on how these buildings were to look (Gavin and Maluf 1996, 17). Other private developers are responsible for individual plots, though they too must adhere to strict guidelines laid down in the master plan. The comprehensive nature of the plan, which details everything from new development on the reclaimed land to open spaces and types of trees to be planted, is explained in the glossy *Beirut Reborn* (Gavin and Maluf 1996).

Solidere is a Lebanese company that restricted the sale of its 'B' shares ('A' shares were the shares allocated to those with property claims in the BCD) to Lebanese including expatriates firstly and to Arabs secondly. In contrast to this, and indeed Dar al-Handasah's earlier plans, though perhaps reflecting large Lebanese expatriate communities in Europe and North America, the influences for the present master plan that Solidere works to appear to have been drawn almost exclusively from Europe and North America (Gavin and Maluf 1996; Gavin 1998, 220). Aside from the aim to win back the businesses and international standing it had prior to 1975, the other strong influencing factor has been the Gulf, particularly to draw business from there, and to make Beirut a 'destination' (A. Gavin pers. comm.). In deciding on the form of the master plan, Solidere's planners examined the post-World War II planning and rebuilding of European cities such as Warsaw along with the modernist planning ideals of the 'clean sweep' (Gavin and Maluf 1996, 46). From some European cities it was recognised that people valued what historic buildings survived and, in the case of Warsaw, demanded their rebuilding – partly to restore identity and partly as a result of nostalgia for the pre-war times. The other, somewhat contradictory, tendency in the post-World War II years was towards that of the clean sweep or *tabula rasa*, which was a reaction to the haphazard development, the over-crowding and the slums that had developed in many European, and indeed American, cities in the first half of the twentieth century, as discussed previously. Solidere decided on a master plan that they thought incorporated and balanced both these trends – what they identified as the 'patrimonial' and the 'tabula rasa' trends (Gavin and Maluf 1996, 46). In the preliminary plans, however, the idea was that only buildings within the designated Conservation Area would be conserved, but that outside that area, the emphasis was to be on clearance and redevelopment (Gavin and Maluf 1996, 53).

Solidere themselves consider the rebuilding of the BCD not so much as a post-war rebuilding project but as a regeneration project (Gavin 1998, 217), which perhaps it is in many ways. Central Beirut was extremely badly damaged not only from street fighting, small-arms fire, mortar bombs and air raids, but because there was also the fact that, by 1990, many buildings had been abandoned for some ten to fifteen years. The state of decay and the vegetation that grew up there are evident from photographs taken just after the cessation of hostilities (Trawi n.d. [c.2003]). The massive financial and social disintegration that the ruins of central Beirut represented appeared to be not dissimilar to what had happened to some inner city areas in both Britain and the USA in the 1970s and 1980s as discussed in Chapter 2.

The private-public partnerships that carried out the big regeneration projects of Baltimore and Boston that had started in the 1960s were aimed to create service industries and to attract visitors: those 'bored suburbanites' who would flock to a restored city centre that would provide a quality of life far superior to that of the shopping centre (Hall 2002, 383-4). The Baltimore Inner Harbour redevelopment was one of the main influences for Solidere's redevelopment of Beirut's central district (Gavin and Maluf 1996, 66).

The destruction and rebuilding, and the approach to commemoration, in the BCD reflects the 'amnesty and amnesia' approach of the post-war period as set in place by the Ta'if Accord. With the exception of the multi-period archaeological site slated to become the 'Garden of Forgiveness', the evidence of the war is being hastily eradicated. The rebuilding of the city centre has been comparatively rapid (central London and Berlin were still more ruined than rebuilt a decade after the end of the second world war), though there is still much that needs to be done. The Souks site project was seriously delayed due to planning permission problems after Hariri was replaced as Prime Minister in 1998. Work restarted in May 2005 and it was finally opened in October 2009. Despite Solidere's interest in re-creating the multi-confessional aspect of central Beirut, Martyrs Square appears to be almost the last space to be regenerated (figure 52). There was an international design competition in 2005, which a Greek landscape design team won, though there is little further information available (Solidere 2005c). In the master plan, part of the southern end of Martyrs Square was designated to include an entertainment venue – the 'egg' or 'soap'-shaped cinema, Beirut City Center Building, was to be restored as part of this plan. In October 2006, however, Abu Dhabi Investment House purchased a huge section of the south end of Martyrs Square and ruled out any such venue (Wilson-Goldie 2006). This commercial development is called Beirut Gate.

Figure 52: Martyrs Square 2007 looking south: City Center Building to left of centre; Mohamad Al Amine Mosque with Rafiq Hariri's grave in the white tent to right

III: CONSERVATION AND ARCHAEOLOGY

Conservation and archaeology prior to 1990

The principal origins of interest in the sites and monuments of the Middle East stem from two western orientated aspects. The earlier is the interest in Biblical archaeology and the sites of the 'Holy Land' and the latter is the principally eighteenth-century grand tours to countries around the Mediterranean to visit and learn about the great monuments of Greek and Roman antiquity. The Middle East has drawn pilgrims from Europe from a very early date, and continued to do so despite the defeat of the Crusaders. By the eighteenth century many Western (European and American) Christian pilgrimages took on a more missionary aspect as they believed that conquest and 'modernisation' of the Holy Lands was a kind of spiritual destiny; a belief that continued into the nineteenth century though somewhat re-orientated under the secular belief in material progress (Silberman 1991, 77). This ideological 'restoration from desolation', Silberman (1991, 77) argues, guided the origins and development of European archaeological and historical study in the region. The region was more attractive in historical essence than in its then present reality, and it was this 'glorious' classical and religious past that in the 1850s, western archaeologists began excavating to find evidence of. In the nineteenth and early twentieth centuries this archaeological interest became tied in with the all-encompassing colonial interests of the European powers in the region, as personified in, for example, Gertrude Bell. As Edward Said (2003) argues in *Orientalism*, the contemporary European view of the East, or 'Orient', in the nineteenth and early twentieth centuries, was as the 'other' – an opposite to 'civilised' and 'advanced' Europe.

Consequently, Lebanon has played host to many foreign archaeologists. While these include those such as the German team that worked at Ba'albek between 1898 and 1905, it has been the influence of the French that has been strongest. One of the first people to excavate in Lebanon was the French orientalist and philologist Ernest Renan at Byblos, Tyre and Sidon when Napoleon III sent him to the region in 1860. The French government, via their Foreign Office, provided generous financial support for large, long-term excavations on monumental sites, though they tended not to be nearly as generous when it came to urban excavations (Audouze & Leroi-Gourhan 1981, 173). In Beirut, when the French administration was in the process of redeveloping the city centre in the early 1920s, excavations were carried out that produced evidence of the Roman period. Later, in the 1940s, another French archaeologist, Jean Lauffray, also excavated in central Beirut and also concentrated on the Roman remains discovered around the Place de l'Etoile, drawing up the first hypothetical plan of Roman Beirut (Lauffray 1944-45, plate 1). It has been suggested that the French colonists saw themselves as re-establishing 'Roman imperium' and that by imposing an orthogonal layout on the irregular Arab cityscape, civilisation and progress were wining against the perceived chaos and lawlessness of Arab urbanism (Raymond 1994, 3). To this end it is interesting to note that Ecochard's early career was that of an archaeological surveyor, though in Damascus rather than Beirut (Ghorayeb 1998, 107).

The origins of the practice of archaeology in Lebanon thus have a European, principally French background. This is also the case in the teaching and study of archaeology in the country. Education in Lebanon in general was something dominated by foreigners, principally European or American religious or cultural missions both at secondary and university level (Hourani 1991, 327). In Beirut, for example, there is the Jesuit University of St Joseph, which had French governmental support, and the American University, originally the Syrian Protestant College, that taught in English both set up in the nineteenth century. An archaeological course was also established at the American University in the early 1930s, and then in the 1960s, the St Joseph University began also to offer an archaeological course but it was based on classical studies (Seeden 1993). The only university to teach archaeology through Arabic is at the Lebanese University, but here too this was based on an outdated French history of art programme (Seeden 1993). In France, as elsewhere in Europe, classical archaeology tended to be amalgamated with ancient history and history of art and concerned with monumental architecture (Audouze & Leroi-Gourhan 1981, 173). Classical and prehistoric archaeology did also tend to dominate in Europe, including Britain. As seen previously, medieval archaeology, particularly that in urban centres was not considered nearly as highly until after 1945. In Lebanon, the same tendencies were also apparent, so that while there was some interest in Crusader material, there was little in Islamic or Ottoman material (Davie 1997). This is an element not just of the archaeology of Lebanon, but throughout the Middle East. European interest in classical and biblical archaeology meant that later Islamic and Ottoman periods – effectively anything after the period of the Crusaders – was given little attention (Silberman 1991, 82).

The consequences of the rather Eurocentric bias towards the classical and biblical past, compounded by a tendency of some Levantine Christian groups, principally the Maronite Christians, to identify themselves with elements of this prioritised past, has been a tendency for some Lebanese to view Lebanon's archaeological sites as something not relevant to them except as a source of income – either legally as tourist attractions or illegally from the pilfering of saleable antiquities; the latter was a particular problem during the civil war (Ward 1994, 66; Seeden 1990, 141; Fisk 1991). There is also a Eurocentric/Maronite Christian tendency to consider that the majority of Lebanese suffer from what Ernest Renan described as '*une complète inintelligence de l'antiquité*' (quoted in Sader 2001, 220). At a very basic level, this apparent lack of interest is perhaps contradicted by visitor numbers recorded for the Beirut National Museum and a number of major sites between 1945 and 1966. The Beirut National Museum was opened in its own purpose-built building in the 1930s. As recorded in various volumes of the *Bulletin du Musée de Beyrouth*, in 1945, the museum had *c.*17,700 visitors that year, rising to *c.*18,200 in 1956 and then jumping to *c.*58,500 in 1966, the last year of published figures before 1975. In other words, annual visitors to the museum in Beirut had increased by almost a third between 1956 and 1966. This jump is also seen at other sites, for example visitors to Ba'albek in 1945 were *c.*47,000; by 1956 this annual figure had reached *c.*56,200 and by 1966 it was *c.*145,400. The excavations at Byblos and Tyre also drew increasing numbers of people – in 1956 *c.*18,300 visited Byblos and *c.*2,800 visited Tyre; in 1966 the number of visitors per annum had risen to *c.*100,300 and *c.*26,100 respectively (Anon 1944-45, 120; Anon 1965, 125; Saidah 1967, 180). These figures do not, of course, record who the visitors were or why they visited – were they foreigners or locals? Christians or Muslims? Had they visited for a day out, or because they were simply curious, or because they had a deeper interest in the past? These increases appear, however, to reflect the growth in Lebanon's population, which grew from *c.*1.15 million in 1945 to *c.*2.18 million in 1964 (Diab 1999, 68), suggesting a not insignificant interest by at least some sections of Lebanon's population in the archaeology of their newly independent country.

As in Britain, there was no legal protection of sites and monuments in Lebanon until the late nineteenth century. In 1884 Osman Hamdi Bey, head of the Imperial Museum in Istanbul, encouraged the Ottoman government to pass a law, the *Asar-i Atika Nizamnamesi*, that not only prohibited the export of any antiquities from the empire but also gave the Ottoman government an exclusive legal and cultural claim to antiquities throughout their empire (Makdisi 2002). This facilitated, for example, Hamdi Bey's excavations at and removal of the Royal Necropolis at Sidon to the Imperial Museum in Istanbul along with other artefacts and sculptures such as the large statue of Ashtarte from Ba'albak (Seeden 1993). This law thus provided little real protection as it was more a case of protecting Lebanon's antiquities from getting into rival European hands then for the sake of Lebanon's heritage *per se*.

The next legal attempt at protecting Lebanon's built heritage including archaeology came during the French Mandate period. The legislation for the Mandate of Syria and Lebanon is a document of six pages of which three-quarters of one page is given over to Article 14 that deals specifically with the protection of antiquities and the regulation of archaeology. Article 14 opens with a declaration that the Mandate will within a year draw up a law on antiquities for Syria and Lebanon based on eight provisions the article goes on to list. The first defines 'antiquity' as meaning 'any construction or any product of human activity earlier than the year 1700'. Another provision relevant here is the fourth one, which states that 'any person who maliciously or negligently destroys or damages an antiquity shall be liable to a penalty'. Other provisions detail that authority is required to excavate, that an export licence is needed to remove antiquities from the country, and that any item that is discovered must be handed in to a relevant authority but that the finder is entitled to payment (French Mandate for Syria and the Lebanon 1923, 181).

Article 14 of the Mandate formed the basis for Decree No. 166/L.R. *Règles Générales des Antiquités* that was published in November 1933 (Ministere de Culture 2006). This is a comprehensive piece of legislation relating not just to antiquities in general but also specifically providing for a register of historic buildings, aspects of financial provision, issues of private property, archaeological excavations and the trade in antiquities. It was originally drafted by the French High Commission in Syria and Lebanon but influenced by the then head of the Directorate General of Antiquities (DGA) of Syria and Lebanon, Henri Seyrig. The Directorate had been established in 1929, when Seyrig was appointed. He also established the *Institut Français d'Archéologie de Beyrouth* after World War II, had very advanced thinking for the period in relation to the protection, conservation *in situ* and documentation of sites and monuments (Seeden 1993). The provisions of the Mandate's Article 14 remain, such as all antiquities are property of the state, with the exception of those on property belonging to religious communities, and any discoveries must be reported to a relevant authority within twenty-four hours of being found (Articles 5 and 9 respectively). Article 18 of the 1933 law reiterates that to cause damage or to destroy any antiquity is a crime subject to prosecution. The 1933 law has had subsequent amendments and additions made to it since then but these are comparatively minor and in effect it is this 1933 law that is still in place in Lebanon. Although adequate on paper; it is the lack of enforcement of it, particularly during the war years, that has been the major problem (Seeden 1993).

Figure 53: **Roman remains originally discovered near Place de l'Etoile in 1926-27**

Beirut is, archaeologically and historically, an immensely wealthy city with almost five thousand years of occupation, which also makes it one of the oldest continuously inhabited cities in the world. While the French were redeveloping the centre of Beirut around the Place de l'Étoile in 1926-27, the main discoveries, just to the south of the Mosque al-Omari, were the rows of huge columns that dated to the Roman period and may have been part of a basilica (Jidejian 1997, 85). From these excavations part of a sculptured architrave and five columns were reconstructed not *in situ* but in a small square opposite the National Museum, where they remain today (figure 53). Between 1941 and 1947, the French archaeologist Jean Lauffray also carried out large scale excavations in and around the Place de l'Etoile. He drew up a hypothetical map of Roman Beirut and it was his work that, up to the early 1990s, remained the main source of information about Roman Beirut (Will 1992, 222; Sader 1998, 23-24; 27).

In the 1960s more Roman columns were unearthed but this time left *in situ* in the centre of Place de l'Étoile. As their bases were well below ground level they stood in a pit with only the upper part at the modern-day street level. In the process of reconstruction in the 1990s they were either reburied or removed and the Miguel Abed Clock, designed by the architect Mardiros Altounian in 1934 who also designed the Parliament Building in 1931, was put back in place. The Roman Baths below the Serail were also uncovered at this time, and conserved for display (Will 1992, 222).

It was not, however, just Roman archaeology that came to light in central Beirut. Also discovered in 1926, during the construction of a new building to the north of Martyrs Square, was an Egyptian sphinx later identified as being of Amenenhat IV, the last pharaoh of the Twelfth Dynasty and dating to 1798-1789 BC (Ward 1994, 66). Instead of this important find halting the construction work, it was sold, only to surface again two years later in the British Museum where some detective work tracked its provenance (Ward 1994, 67; 68). In 1954, in the same vicinity, a developer called in some archaeologists as a cave had been found during digging for a new building. This cave contained four tombs, two of the Middle Bronze age and two of the Late Bronze age (Chéhab 1955, 50).

Archaeological work in the centre of Beirut was also carried out between 1975 and 1990, when cessation of hostilities allowed. In 1977, some excavations were carried out in the vicinity of the Greek Catholic Cathedral of St Elie and the Greek Orthodox Cathedral of St George by the DGA in an attempt to locate the Roman law school, but these were unsuccessful (Will 1992, 224). In the early 1980s, a start was made on a comprehensive survey of downtown Beirut as it was hoped that, because many buildings had been destroyed, excavations to discover Beirut's pre-Roman settlement could be carried out, but a renewal of fighting meant the project had to be abandoned before it had hardly begun (Ward 1994, 70).

Conservation and archaeology from 1990

Considerable damage was done to Lebanon's built heritage during fifteen years of war. By 1977, central Beirut was already badly damaged and deserted, so most buildings were not repaired or maintained but left to the ravages of the weather, further conflict-related destruction, or demolition by unscrupulous developers. All of the historic buildings of central Beirut suffered damage, including the Grand Serail, the Military Hospital and the Ottoman Clock Tower, the Municipality building on Rue Weygand and other French Mandate buildings of the Place de l'Etoile, many religious buildings including the Mosque Al Omari, originally the twelfth-century Crusader cathedral of St John (figure 54), and its neighbour Mosque Emir Mansour Assaf; Mosque Majidiye; the Ottoman Amir Munzer mosque, the cathedrals of the Greek Orthodox St George, Greek Catholic St Elie and Maronite St George. All of these have since been restored, though an extra storey was added to the Grand Serail, and are fully functioning; the Ottoman era Military Hospital now houses the CDR. The National Museum (outside the BCD), sitting at one of the main checkpoints of the Green Line, suffered extreme damage; it re-opened to the public in November 1997 after extensive refurbishment both of the building and of its surviving contents. With the exception of the short film that shows the rediscovery of the hidden artefacts and their rehabilitation, no evidence of the damage caused by the war was preserved (Tahan 2006, 5).

Figure 54: Mosque Al Omari

Of St Martyrs Square's numerous cinemas, only the Opera was restored, though as a music megastore. Beirut's more modern architecture, that of the 1950s and 1960s which helped to construct an identity for a young post-colonial republic (el-Dahdah 1998, 73), has been almost entirely disregarded. A rare survivor is the City Center Building, designed by the Lebanese architect Joseph Philippe Karam and built in 1965 on the west side of Martyrs Square. It is one of central Beirut's most iconic buildings though it remains a shell since the Civil War. Until recently it was planned to renovate it into a cultural entertainment centre (of which there are none as yet in the BCD), and has been used as such despite its ruined appearance. Its future, however, is again threatened, as mentioned previously, by the development plans of Abu Dhabi Investment House as they have declared the retention of the building as 'non-viable' (Wilson Goldie 2006).

As noted previously, the law in place in 1990 to protect Lebanon's cultural heritage was the 1933 Law of Antiquities. Although it was hardly designed to deal with modern developer-led urban archaeology, it could provide an adequate level of protection for Lebanon's built heritage if and when it was fully applied and respected. Specific articles of the law could and were applied to protect Beirut's archaeology. Ortali-Tarazi (2001-02, 355), then of the DGA, mentions five articles which are of particular relevance. Article 56 states that excavations may not take place without State authorisation as represented by the DGA, and article 59 states that there must be a contract between the DGA and the excavator. Article 18, in particular, stresses that it is forbidden to destroy or damage in any way either standing remains or portable antiquities. Article 26 relates to the registering of antiquities as historic monuments, stating that this can only be done by ministerial decree based on the advice of the DGA, and lastly Article 19, possibly one of the more crucial laws in the case of Beirut's archaeology, of which the first part states:

Les plans relatifs à l'expansion des villes et à leur embellissement ne peuvent être décidés, que suite à l'approbation du Directeur du Service des Antiquités. Un ingénieur du service des antiquités contribue à établir ces plans (Ministere de Culture 2006).

This effectively means that plans to expand or develop urban centres cannot be approved without the approval of the DGA, and that an engineer from the DGA must be involved with these plans. Both Articles 18 and 19 gave the DGA, in theory, full power to protect the urban archaeology, even if developer-led large-scale urban excavations had been virtually unknown in 1933, and they would have been effective even on the scale required by Beirut's post-war development if the DGA had had sufficient trained personnel to implement them (A. Seif pers. comm.). The DGA was seriously under-resourced and understaffed – its immediate post-war qualified personnel was precisely four (Sader 2001, 224), and there was a dearth of Lebanese archaeologists trained in urban excavation. Furthermore, the DGA were dealing not just with Beirut's archaeology but that of the entire country combined with other issues such as the serious damage done to the National Museum (Asmar 1996, 7; Sader 1998, 37; Seeden 2000, 178).

The 1991 Dar al-Handasah plan was considered entirely unsuitable, not least due to the outcry against the level of destruction of the surviving urban fabric. A revised plan was drawn up, but between 1993 and 1994 this master plan was reputably changed six times in response to public concerns (Hamdan 1994). The number of buildings to be retained had to be revised upwards by over 50% to a total of 291 (Gavin 1998, 222). The vast majority of these buildings are, however, within the area designated as the Conservation Area, which is centred on the Place de l'Etoile and the streets of Foch and Allenby. Outside of this area, the emphasis was to be on clearance and rebuilding (Gavin and Maluf 1996, 53). The method of conservation applied to virtually all the buildings consists of retaining and repairing the façades while completely modernising the interiors. While this has been lauded as generating a new building type: the renovated office building consisting of a historical façade and a modern interior (Saliba 2003, 11), this is not really conservation in the holistic sense of the word but façade-retention. As Jad Thabet (1998) argues in relation to the al-Sarayeh (City Hall), retaining facades simply hides a new construction that usually has no relationship at all to the building's historical configuration. The interiors of the majority of buildings in the BCD were, however, severely damaged and in many cases it was just the shell of the building that survived. Furthermore, retention of the façades is better than retaining nothing (arguments about pastiche, the importance of new architecture etc. aside). It is argued that Solidere's over-arching control of the BCD assured that these façades were saved rather than demolished by individual developers, as may have happened because, according to Thabet (1998), architectural heritage is of little importance in Lebanese society and culture. A great deal of attention has been paid to the Conservation area and its elegant predominantly French Mandate period buildings, as demonstrated in Robert Saliba's (2003) book, *Beirut City Center Recovery: the Foch-Allenby and Etoile Conservation Area*. The conservation of so many French Mandate and Ottoman buildings has led to the claim that Beirut is the first Arab city to come to terms with its colonial heritage (Saliba 2003, 13). There is a claim by Shi'as, however, that the Maronites and Sunnis enjoyed the protection of France and the Ottoman Empire respectively (Klaushofer 2007, 88), so perhaps this colonial heritage is considered more benignly than may otherwise be supposed, bearing in mind that Beirut is traditionally considered a Sunni city, and the two leading political positions are held by a Maronite Christian and a Sunni. The foreword of Saliba's (2003) *Beirut City Center Recovery* is by the chairman of Solidere, Nasser Chammaa, who, however, provides what is perhaps the ultimate reasoning behind the Conservation Area, and also for conserving archaeological sites within the BCD, which is to attract visitors, tourist-related services and new residents to the area (Chammaa in Saliba 2003, 9).

From archaeological investigation prior to 1990, it was realised that Beirut sat on significant archaeological deposits, though the actual extent and depth could only be guessed at. In 1992, Dr Lelia Badre of the Museum of the American University of Beirut (AUB) invited Dr John Schofield of the Museum of London to give a lecture at the AUB Museum. He was asked for his opinion about the likely archaeological requirements in relation to the redevelopment of central Beirut. He held discussions with not only the principal archaeologists in Beirut, but with architects that would deal with the historic architecture, and he also met Henry Eddé of Dar al Handasah, Ghassan Tahir of OGER Liban and Fadl Chalak of the CDR. As a consequence of this visit, Schofield produced a report detailing his recommendations for the management of Beirut's archaeology (Schofield 1992). His report is a short but comprehensive document detailing the stages the archaeological project should go through and highlighting the likely complexity of the project ahead. To emphasise the latter point, he draws comparisons between the City of London and central Beirut. The intramural City of London is 133.5 hectares; the Museum of London's archaeological service for the City was established in 1974 and was, by 1992, employing over 200 professional archaeologists, was 75% funded by private developers and had a turnover of £3.9 million. Such a unit to deal with Beirut's archaeology, he suggested, must be of similar scale (Schofield 1992, 10). He was later invited by Professor Helga Seedan to give a three-week seminar at AUB on current urban archaeological practices, which was attended not just by students by archaeologists already working in Beirut (H.Seeden pers. comm.).

In 1991, the Lebanese government had called in UNESCO for advice regarding the cultural heritage. In that same year, UNESCO representatives held discussions with the CDR, and an agreement was reached to establish a programme of co-operation regarding the archaeology and historic monuments of central Beirut. By September 1993, when Schofield visited Beirut again, this time as a consultant for UNESCO, archaeological work had already begun, principally the digging of test pits including on sites to the north of St George Maronite Cathedral by a Lebanese University team, directed by Muntaha Saghieh; at the north end of Martyrs Square by IFAPO, directed by M.P. Lenoble; and behind the Rivoli Theatre, also the north end of Martyrs Square, by the AUB Museum, directed by Leila Badre. These sites were to become the Zone des Eglises site, the Petit Serail site, and the Tell site respectively. The report to UNESCO highlighted several issues. One seems to be the overall lack of co-ordination or harmonisation between sites and their directors, added to which there was already a certain amount of intra-archaeological rivalry/resentment developing, as exemplified by a letter to the newspaper *An-Nahar* complaining that some Lebanese archaeology professors were being excluded from the project, which did not help relations with Solidere (Schofield 1994, 6; 12). Schofield did, at least, manage to introduce an overall numbering system for the excavations (the BEY site numbering). Another problem was that while the Beirut UNESCO office seem to have been reasonably helpful, UNESCO generally seems to have been over-bureaucratic and essentially ineffective,

> 'The work of all the archaeologists in Beirut and especially of the UNESCO consultants was held back and made difficult by certain inefficiencies in the working arrangements within UNESCO [due to] lack of easy communication between Paris and Beirut, and virtually no forward planning' (Schofield 1994, 13-14).

In November 1993, a document entitled *Réhabilitation de la Direction Générale des Antiquités et Soutien à la reconstruction du Centre-Ville ed Beyrouth* (LEB/92/008), was signed by the Lebanese government, the UN Development Programme (UNDP) and UNESCO. The DGA was to oversee the excavations of the city centre, while UNESCO, via an International Scientific Committee, would advise. Finances for the excavations, for the first year at least, were to come from, principally, the Hariri Foundation (US$1 million) and the UNDP (US$300,000) (UN 1993). There was, however, no further provision for finances beyond the first year. Due to the large scale of the work ahead, the Minister for Culture and Higher Education, Michel Eddé, then put out a call for international assistance with the archaeological project. Consequently teams from fifteen different institutions, from Lebanon and from Europe, worked on at least 133 excavations in the BCD area (Ortali-Tarazi 2001-02, 356). Many of the excavations initially doubled as training excavations, for example the AUB/Leverhulme excavations of the Souks (Perring *et al* 1996) and the Place Debbas excavations run by a team from the Universities of Frieburg and Berlin (Heinz and Bartl 1997).

In 1994, the government issued a decree to complement the 1933 Law of Antiquities. In the *General Planning Regulations of Beirut Central District and its Sectors*, article 4 relates to archaeological excavations (Curvers and Stuart 2004, 250-251). These stipulate that the BCD excavations will take place in two phases: a programme of borehole excavations during the second half of 1993, and then an extensive programme in the BCD Sub-sector Rb. These excavations will be required to take place over two years, 1994 and 1995. This was to ensure the infrastructure works in that sector would start at the beginning of 1996, and that any archaeological discoveries could be integrated intohe reconstruction projects of that sector (Curvers and Stuart 2004, 250). The second part of Article 4 stated that the supervision of the excavations would be carried out by the DGA according to four principles. These required archaeologists to provide details in advance of their work programme such as its aims, cost, timing, and methods of financing. If any major discovery was made, archaeologists had to inform the Planning Authorities, the Real Estate Company and the relevant developers in writing, and work with these organisations to find the best way of integrating such discoveries into the BCD reconstruction projects. It was further stressed that archaeological work was to be programmed to not delay the reconstruction works, and that the archaeologists' work would be coordinated by a committee incorporating representatives of the General Directorate of Planning, the DGA, the CDR and Solidere, and would be chaired by the General Director of Planning.

Once the funding from the Hariri foundation and UNDP ran out, Solidere took over the funding of most of the archaeological work, though funding also came from sponsoring institutions such as the Leverhulme Trust and the University of Amsterdam. Compared to Dar al-Handasah/Solidere's carefully worked out and overall plan for the BCD, there was never any such overall plan for the archaeology, even after agreements had been reached to allow for excavation. Everything was handled on a site-by-site basis. One of the huge problems concerning the archaeological projects and Solidere was, as mentioned above, that the initial plan made no provision for the former, and although it was modified in 1994, it was still extremely difficult to make any further changes to integrate any *in situ* preservation (Ortali-Tarazi 2001-02, 356).

Once the infrastructure works were nearing completion in 1996, private developers could begin to redevelop individual plots. Archaeology was still seen by many as merely something likely to cause delay and expense, and sites did sometimes disappear overnight or when no one was around supervising machine clearance. Attempts were made to establish a set of procedures for developers, some of the details being worked out thanks to an interested and sympathetic developer becoming involved when part of the north track of the Cardo Maximus was uncovered in the basement of the building he was working on (BEY 087, Curvers and Stuart 1998-99, 28). The various Islamic religious authorities were never too keen on archaeological remains under their mosques. In one instance, the recording of archaeological layers discovered during the renovation of the Mosque Dabbaghiye was effectively prevented by representatives of Dar Fatwa (Curvers and Stuart 1998-99, 17). A similar problem arose during the building of Hariri's mosque on the west side of Martyrs Square. The site was excavated as BEY 142 by Muntaha Saghieh and Ibrahim Kouwatli, and remains of the Roman east-west colonnaded street were found.

There are very mixed opinions on Solidere's provision for the archaeological work. If Solidere is to be believed, then the archaeology, and certainly any sites they considered worth saving, once it became clear that they would have to deal with it, were all rapidly incorporated into its plans; areas were to be made available for archaeological exploration and what they termed a strategic approach was to be adopted to ensure that every site would be evaluated before redevelopment so that no 'significant' archaeology be destroyed (Gavin and Maluf 1996, 28). Indeed, some of the Solidere team were nominally interested, principally Jean-Paul Lebas, then Deputy General Manager, who was supportive from an early stage (H. Seeden pers. comm.). A number of Solidere staff were taken to Jorvik in York to show what could be done with archaeological finds in terms of developing a tourist attraction, which also generated some enthusiasm. Solidere also appointed their own in-house archaeologist, Dr Hans Curvers.

On the other hand, it is suggested that Solidere only took over financing the archaeological work because not to would risk major public-relations issues and further delay (Sader 2001, 225). It should be remembered at this point that Solidere were beholden to their shareholders, and like all developers, they could suffer serious financial consequences if targets were not met. Others will argue that the level of destruction of Beirut's physical heritage was such that it was 'memorycide' (Naccache 1998). Another major issue were the often insurmountable disagreements that arose between the DGA and Solidere on occasion. Solidere appears to have over-ridden the DGA when it suited them, on occasion seeming to interpret the law to suit themselves (for example BEY 072; Curvers and Stuart 1998-99, 15). They were, however, in an infinitely stronger position than the politically weak and seriously under-resourced DGA so that although the DGA naturally reacted against some of Solidere's decisions, it tended to be in a way that came across as inept – on occasion causing the temporary halting of work or making decisions that did not necessarily make a great deal of sense at the time – which means they often failed to change Solidere's course of action. There have been complaints that Solidere often did not allow sufficient resources, in terms of finance or time, for some excavations, despite the fact that it was in Solidere's interest that the archaeological work be completed on schedule. On the other hand, there were complaints that the archaeologists often overran their timetables and then needed extensions (Curvers and Stuart 2004, 251). There was also the problems inherent in having no overall plan for the archaeological work, nor a great deal of cooperation between sites and teams (Perring 1999, 15). There was even times when archaeologists appeared to conspire against each other (for example BEY 130 was to be investigated by Curvers but was apparently disputed by Badre as she believed it to be part of her BEY 003 site; Curvers and Stuart 1998-99, 20).

All these problems were often heavily influenced and made more complicated by political and religious issues. The issues of archaeology and conservation were often used as political weaponry by those who were anti-Solidere and anti-Hariri. Of course it depended on the site as to who was interested in having it saved for whatever reasons, often nothing to do with archaeological conservation and everything to do with wanting to stop the development. Often they assumed that the archaeologists were totally against any redevelopment that would destroy the archaeology and thus assumed that the archaeologists were automatic allies against Solidere; they were then disappointed when support from archaeologists was not automatically forthcoming (Seeden 2000, 181). The most vocal group was, it seems, the Maronite Christians. Consequently anything even rumoured to be 'Phoenician' and in danger of destruction caused instant protest, as experienced with the discovery of a pre-Hellenistic cemetery on site BEY 045 (R. Thorpe, pers. comm.). BEY 045 was subsequently destroyed due to non-adherence to the agreement as to how the site was to be dismantled made by UNESCO, Solidere, the DGA and the site's developers, Prime Estates (R. Thorpe, pers. comm.; figures 55-56), but on more than one occasion the 'Phoenician card' was played in order to ensure sites were conserved, as will be detailed below. It should be noted, however, that factions usually cared for what they perceived to be their own heritage while not caring for anyone else's, as demonstrated by attitudes towards the Mamluk ribat, also detailed later. There is little notion of any commonality of the past, and if anything there seems to be increasing religious divisions of society, hence the division of cultural heritage by a 'this is mine, that is yours' attitude (J. Farchakh Bajjaly, pers. comm.). Thus public support for archaeology and conservation was and remains a double-edged sword and often greatly complicated matters. Furthermore, public reaction to the archaeology was very mixed. Some suggested that the archaeological discoveries created a type of public space that was exciting and challenging (Kabbani 1998, 257), while others have argued that it was the archaeological excavations were the final episode in a systematic erasure of modern Beirut (el-Khoury 1998, 260), and so it goes on.

It is clearly evident that it was only the sheer tenacity of the archaeologists involved that ensured that any archaeology was done at all, and that such an amount of work was done in what were often very demanding circumstances. The acknowledgements at the end of the report of site BEY 007 give some indication of this, mentioning that the excavations were carried out under extremely onerous physical, contractual and financial conditions, that required several of the team to work unpaid and for everyone to work from dawn to dusk in order to get the site completed within the time, personnel and financial requirements issued by Solidere. Work even continued during the April 1996 Israeli offensive, stopping only briefly when a member of the team narrowly missed being hit by a ricocheting bullet from nearby anti-aircraft fire (Thorpe 1998-99a, 53).

Figure 55: BEY 045 going

Figure 56: BEY 045 gone

Whatever assessment is made about Solidere's treatment of the archaeological layers prior to and during excavation and their infrastructure rebuilding, they have, it would seem, given substantial thought to the plans for the integration and signage of the sites to be conserved. Having been encouraged to view the archaeology positively from the point of cultural tourism and providing Beirut with an historical identity other Middle Eastern cities such as Dubai do not have, they have extensive plans for the surviving archaeological sites. Initially these plans were for a single archaeological park in the Zone des Eglises to where surviving archaeological remains would be taken and reconstructed. This idea, announced by Chamaa on the BBC World Service, implied no other conservation of archaeological sites *in situ* (Schofield 1994, 3). This idea was, understandably, argued against and dropped (J. Schofield pers. comm.).

One of the main aims of the master plan was to reconstruct or reinstate the public utilities, streets and open spaces of central Beirut; in fact over thirty parks and public spaces were planned (Gavin and Maluf 1996, 13; Gavin 1998, 231). One of these areas is a new square, the Khan Antoun Bey Square, planned for just north of the Souks development. This square will be the starting point for the heritage trails planned for the BCD that are aimed to pass on the message of 'city memory' via the different layers of the city's past (Gavin 1998, 232). These walks, associated with different periods of the city's history, include the Old Shoreline Walk which will be a linear park tracing the line of the pre-war waterfront and Promenade des Francais; the Ottoman Wall Walk that will run along the Ottoman sea wall and cut through the New Financial District; and the Archaeology Trail (Gavin and Maluf 1996, 87). The last is to be a circuit through the BCD linking all the 'heritage events', which include landmarks, historic buildings, archaeology parks and their museums and 'integrated archaeological features' and shall offer visitors 'displayed and narrated evidence of 5,000 years of history, integrated within the fabric of the modern city' (Gavin 1998, 232). The development of heritage trails is, in theory, a good idea as it allows for the individual sites to be integrated into a greater whole, i.e. that of the history of the central Beirut and to be connected in some form instead of them being isolated monuments. One of the starting points of the archaeological trail will be the new museum at the Tell site, which will also hopefully mean that people will be able to make connections between the physical remains of the city outside with the artefacts and displays inside.

They also have put some thought into the signage. Fabrizio Fuccelli who was the Project Manager of the Solidere's Heritage Project, designed a series of different sign types for historic buildings and for archaeological sites. These signs are to be of Pyrolave, a glazed volcanic stone from Toulouse that has been used for, amongst others, the French Metro signs. It is particularly hard wearing and will allow for, for example, the reproduction of photographs. These signs will have various information depending on what is required. For the archaeological sites there are several types of signs planned: one that will include the walking map, old photographs and historic maps; others that will include a plan of the excavation, photographs of the site immediately after excavation – particularly relevant for those sites that were reburied or partly reburied again. It is aimed to include a short story or anecdote as well. The texts are to be done by May Davies for the historic buildings and Rula Zein for the archaeological sites. It is understood that people are not going to want to stand around reading a great lengthy sign and so supplementary information will be provided in an accompanying leaflet available in different languages. The signs are to be trilingual – in English, French and Arabic. The idea for the heritage trails and the signage are based partly on what was done in Athens in preparation for the Olympics (F. Fuccelli, pers. comm.). In Spring of 2007, however, the Heritage Trail project was postponed due to the political situation.

IV: THE SITES

Ten examples of sites conserved for display will be discussed here. These are the Roman Baths below the hill of the Grand Serail; the Roman remains under the former Banco di Roma; the so-called Phoenician quarter, the Byzantine shops and mosaics, the medieval ditch and the Mamluk shrine of the Souks site; the Ottoman seawalls just to the north of the Souks site; the Tell site, the Hellenistic Quarter on the site of the Petit Serail on Martyrs Square and the Zone des Eglises, or, as it is known, the Garden of Forgiveness, to the west of Martyrs Square. Both the Phoenician Quarter and the Tell site required a ministerial decree to preserve them.

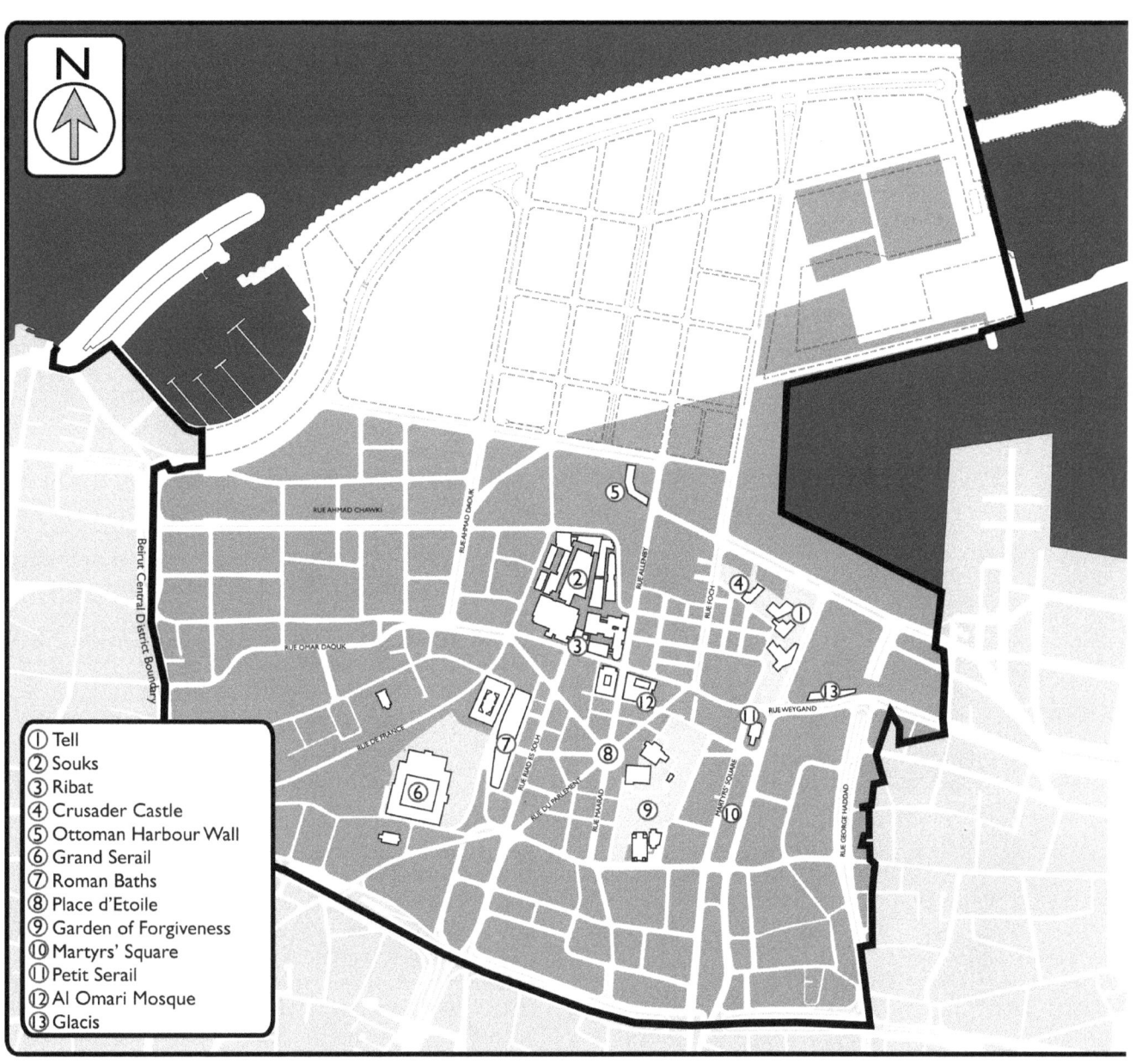

Figure 57: Central Beirut: sites mentioned in the text

The sites of the Tell, Garden of Forgiveness and Martyrs Square were still waiting to be conserved in 2009, though a fence has, at least, gone up around the Petit Serail site. The Phoenician Quarter and the Ottoman seawalls, reburied to preserve them until conservation works could begin, and the medieval ditch could not be viewed due to building works. The reconstruction is very much an ongoing process, and consequently the conservation for display of most of the archaeological sites has been left to last, primarily because it is considered by Solidere as part of the landscaping work (though recent political events have also caused some delay). While this is understandable, it means that the sites that are exposed have been left without any protection or apparent maintenance for years. This is much the same way the Corporation of London viewed the archaeological sites to be conserved as part of the Barbican development in the 1950s (see London chapter), and the way the Stadtschloss remains have been left (see Berlin chapter).

The Roman Baths

The Roman Baths are set into a hill below the Grand Serail, which slopes down towards the back of the buildings that face onto Bank Street (figure 58). The site was initially excavated and conserved sometime before the 1970s. Excavations in the vicinity in the post-war period revealed extra features including reservoirs, both rock-cut and constructed, and remnants of a heating system and a smaller room with marble slabs. The initial reasons for this excavation had been in advance of a possible under-ground car park, but Solidere changed its plans in order to integrate these remains into the 'Roman Baths Garden Project' (BEY 117; Curvers and Stuart 1998-99, 18).

Figure 58: Roman Baths

The site consists of several components. There are the conserved archaeological remains themselves to the south of the area and to the north there is a public garden that has been designed to resemble ancient and Mediterranean gardens, which has been planted with some of the herbs used to produce essential oils, fragrances and medicines in antiquity, and still are (Solidere 2005a). While the archaeological site is itself inaccessible to the public, it is easy to see all the features from the surrounding area.

The Roman Baths site is detailed on Solidere's website under the 'Squares and Gardens' section. The whole area of the site is designed to serve, on a day-to-day basis, as somewhere for people to meet and sit outside, and on occasion as an open-air venue for events such as concerts. The site is indeed a pleasant place to be – away from the traffic and with plenty of places to sit – and is clearly a popular meeting place, especially for young people. The site provides a completed example of the type of work that Solidere is considering for the Garden of Forgiveness, the Ottoman sea walls and, to some extent, the Tell site. What is clearly evident is that Solidere has regarded the archaeological remains of this site in terms of landscape features that have provided a theme for this particular public space.

The Arcaded Building

In the early 1990s, an Italian team from the *Centro Ricerche Archeologiche e Scavi di Torino* carried out archaeological investigations on the Place de l'Etoile (Centro Richerce 2006). The excavations under the former Banco di Roma, adjacent to the Parliament building, revealed the remains of an arcaded building that may be part of the Roman forum or basilica (BEY 009, Marquis and Ortali-Tarazi 1996). It was agreed with the government that these columns should be placed back *in situ* (Comité Scientifique International 1996, 20; Ortali-Tarazi 1998-99, 10). At a cost of $135,000 an Italian team from the Centro Scavi numbered and carefully removed the building remains to be stored with the DGA.

In November 2006, work began to reinstate the Roman arches *in situ* in the basement and the work was completed in 2007 (*An-Nahar* 10th April 2007). The arches are behind glass but at their original level, and with information panels. The conservation work cost some $90,000, paid for by the Italian government and carried out by an Italian team led by Fedora Filippi.

The Souks

The Souks excavations were one of the first excavations to start, and were the most extensive, in the BCD (Perring *et al* 2006). Although the Souks were a major component of central Beirut, as they tend to be in Middle Eastern cities, they were badly damaged due to fighting and general deterioration. Some of them were demolished during periods of calm between 1975 and 1990, as mentioned above, but the bulk of them were completely demolished in the early 1990s. Whether it was really necessary to completely remove such a historically characteristic part of Beirut is a moot point. In a report of 1992, the Souks were noted to be a 'special case', and the report suggested that the decision to demolish so much should be reconsidered as there appeared to be several buildings worth conserving, and it also queried putting in an underground car-park that would have serious implications for archaeological strata (Schofield 1992, 9-10). The general thought was, however, that the souks were in such a bad state of repair, the majority being poor quality buildings, that there was little else that could be done, added to which Solidere had already identified the Souks redevelopment as a major magnet project for the area. The blanket demolition did, however, allow for extensive archaeological investigations.

A colossal plan for the entire Souks site was developed by Spanish architect Rafael Moneo (1998) based on a master plan by Jad Tabet, which included integrating the archaeological discoveries into the design. Excavations were required not least because the redevelopment includes four storeys of underground car-parking (Moneo 1998, 263). Numerous excavations were carried out in this area, and it was decided to conserve four sites: the Phoenician quarter, the Byzantine mosaics, the Mamluk shrine and the medieval ditch. The excavations on the Souks site were given restricted time because it had been planned to develop the site first. Due however to a problem over planning permission that arose after Rafiq Hariri's departure from government, the redevelopment came to a standstill and only restarted in May 2005 (figure 59). The landscaping of the new Souks was done by French space and landscaping consultant Olivier Vidal, who was responsible for incorporating the Mamluk shrine, Byzantine era shops, the medieval city wall remains, late Phoenico-Persian settlement and other artefacts and mosaics (Solidere 2006). As mentioned the Souks are now open.

Figure 59: Souks 2005 looking northeast

The Phoenician Quarter

The so-called Phoenician quarter was discovered in excavations in 1994 of the north-east sector of the Souks site, BEY 010. The excavations produced evidence from the Iron Age (Persian period, 550 - 333 BC) up to the Ottoman period (Sayegh 1996, 235). The Iron Age layers, in Sector D of the site, consisted of the well-preserved remains of six buildings that were orientated on an east-west axis and with interiors that were divided into a number of varying-sized spaces. These buildings were identified as a rare Iron Age residential quarter dated to the 5th-4th centuries BC (Sayegh 1996, 240; 269).

As a consequence of its dating, this Iron Age residential quarter was quickly promoted as being a Phoenico-Persian or simply a Phoenician quarter. Initially, however, its conservation *in situ* was by no means certain. A section of the site was accidentally removed by bulldozers (Karam n.d.), which drew UNESCO's condemnation (Comité Scientifique International 1996, 20). The site became the centre of a great deal of publicity (Sader 1997, 161), and, as with the Tell site, the Phoenician element was a strong motivating force for many, to the extent there was a 'sit-in' (a favourite way of protesting in Beirut) to demand its conservation. The UNESCO International Scientific Committee recommended that, owing to its uniqueness in Beirut's archaeological heritage and because it was a Phoenician site, it should be conserved *in situ* (Comité Scientifique International 1996, 20) and a ministerial decree was issued to ensure this (Ortali-Tarazi 2001-02, 357). It was subsequently reburied in sand until it can be conserved for display. The plans are to incorporate it within the ground floor.

The Byzantine Shops and Mosaics

Excavations were carried out in the southern area of the Souks area, on BEY 006, beginning in June 1994. In an area along Rue Weygand, to the west of what had been Souk Tawileh, a large portico with mosaic paving dating to the Byzantine period (c.330-660 AD) was uncovered. Behind this portico, which dated to the second century AD, was discovered a row of at least eleven shops dating to c.525-550 AD (Perring *et al* 2006, 19). Each of these shops was numbered, from east to west, in the mosaic in front of each doorway. These numbers were written in the Greek alphabet but running right to left as in Arabic. The mosaic lettering began with the letter 'A' and was preserved up to the letter 'E' (the fifth shop), where the site reached the limit of the excavation. Outside the excavation area the mosaic was still evident over some sixty square metres but there it was destroyed during unsupervised machine clearance by the developers (Perring *et al* 1996, 193, 195). The discovering of the mosaic paved portico and numbered shops of a Byzantine souk is considered to be some of the most impressive mosaic records from a single urban site (Seeden 2000, 175). A proposal for their reintegration and display in the new Souks development was submitted to the DGA, Solidere and UNESCO in 1995 (Perring *et al* 1996, 195). Owing to the complicated nature of the evidence, it was suggested that computer-aided displays and reconstructions would probably be necessary. The surviving walls and floors were lifted and numbered so that they could be reconstructed, and it was suggested that each shop could then explore a separate theme, such as fullery and laundry, perfumery, or glass and tableware. Owing to the fragile nature of the original mosaics, a decision has been made to put instead a carefully designed copy of the mosaics in situ. The original mosaics remain unconserved sitting in storage in Saida.

The Medieval Ditch

Medieval Beirut was walled with some seven gates. There may have been some sections of the wall surviving after the war, as Schofield (1992, 8) suggests and as was the case in London and Berlin, pieces may have been incorporated into standing buildings or boundary walls. There is also a mention to what may have been part of the medieval wall being destroyed in the immediate post-war years (Fisk 2001, 665), though no above-ground remains of a medieval town wall was observed prior to the souks' demolition (H. Curvers. pers. comm.). Nothing survives today, except in place names such as Bab Idris. The line of this wall was known to run along the western edge of the souks, so excavations were planned for this part of the Souks site also. Excavations revealed evidence of the ditch or fosse that accompanied this wall, though no evidence remained of the wall itself (Mongne 1996, 288). Excavations carried out in the north-west of the Souks area, bordered by what was Tarablus Street, Souk Jamil and Patriarch Hoayek Street, revealed evidence of a glacis of eleventh century AD date and a ditch cut into the bedrock. Along the top of the bedrock-cut ditch were blocks laid to continue the steep slope of the ditch. These blocks were mortared and covered, in places, with a lime plaster (Curvers and Stuart 1996, 232). The ditch was abandoned during Ottoman times, though when exactly is unclear (Mongne 1996, 289).

As with the Phoenician quarter, it has been decided to retain this ditch for display within the commercial zone of the new souks. This was initially proposed by Solidere and was supported by the International Scientific Committee who considered it important to conserve the medieval ditch as an important topographical indicator of the extent of medieval Beirut (Comité Scientifique International 1996, 21). What exactly is to be done with it in terms of its display is as yet unclear. It will find itself one floor down in the underground car park, which is never a good space to display archaeological sites, as is evident from, for example, the West Gate and small section of medieval wall conserved *in situ* in London Wall underground car park (see London chapter). Originally it was marked out as a 'city wall and archaeology garden' (Gavin and Maluf 1996, 86). Then there were plans for there to be a café, but this has since been considered unfeasible, so the creation of a small museum around it was suggested, but by mid 2007 there were still no evident plans for the site (H. Curvers, pers. comm.).

The Mamluk Ribat

At the southern side of BEY 006 of the Souks site, just north of Rue Weygand stands Beirut's only surviving late Mamluk monument, the ribat of Ibn 'Iraq al-Dimashqi (figure 60). The ribat was built in 1517 by the Sufi Ibn 'Iraq al-Dimashqi and was part of a larger complex, the extent of which is unknown, that became a private *madrasa* or *zawiya* where Islamic law and theology were taught (Seeden 1995, 12). This ribat had effectively disappeared from view due to the old souks and buildings all around it and was only rediscovered in the process of post-war clearance. The story of its survival seems to be that when a bulldozer driver attempted to demolish it, he suffered from temporary paralyses and then the same happened to a second driver. It subsequently became a popular shrine and the decision was made to conserve it. It was initially considered a Shia shrine – Ibn 'Iraq suggesting a holy man from Iraq. Its presence in the BCD made it immensely important for the local Shia population (Becherer 2005, 27). This was not exactly popular amongst Beirut's dominant Sunnis so they conducted their own research, establishing that he was a devout Sunni Muslim from Syria, and promptly attached the 'al-Dimashqi' to the name. The sacredness of the site, something apparently somewhat alien to the more secular Sunni sect was explained by declaring that Ibn 'Iraq al-Dimashqi was a Sufi, and the site was not a *mazar* – a place of residence but a *zawiya* – a place of religious instruction. The *zawiya* was then closed off with barbed wire and a sign was duly affixed to the most visible side of the ribat giving the 'correct' genealogy (Bercherer 2005, 27).

Figure 60: Souks site: Mamluk Ribat, 2004

The immediate area around the ribat was excavated as it was likely that this area would produce evidence of the little-studied Islamic period settlement in Beirut (Perring *et al* 1996, 176). Remains of houses and gardens and a glass workshop were uncovered, dating to the Fatimid/Crusader period, and subsequent investigations uncovered Hellenistic and Roman remains (Perring *et al* 2006, 17).

The ribat has been conserved *in situ* and a new plaza, 'Ibn Iraq Square', has been constructed around it, though the ribat is overshadowed by new surrounding buildings. It is to be part of the 'Jewellers Block' – the south-east corner of the Souks site that will comprise entirely of jewellers shops and offices – designed by Kevin Dash and Rafik Khoury (Solidere 2006). Now that the Souks have been completed, the ribat has been conserved and finds itself part of the fashionable and upmarket new shopping complex.

The Ottoman Harbour Wall

In an area to the north of the Souks development, excavations were carried out in 1996 in the area of the old Ottoman harbour (BEY 007; Thorpe 1998-99a). There were four successive sea walls dating from possibly the Classical period to the Ottoman period, of which the fourth and last, dating to the Ottoman period, was the most impressive. Approximately seventy metres of the harbour wall survived, running mostly north-west but turning west and disappearing under the boundary of the excavation. This surviving wall was up to 1.8 metres thick and had a maximum height of 3.35m. It was constructed of limestone blocks on lower courses of sandstone blocks backed with randomly coursed sandstone rubble set in a red sandy mortar and with iron ties consolidating the outer face. Two mooring rings survived in the outer face (Thorpe 1998-99a, 38). The preservation and extent of the harbour wall was such that Solidere decided to redesign their plans for the area in order to conserve it (Thorpe 1998-99a, 32). It is to become the focus of the Ottoman Wall Walk that will go along the wall's surface through the new Financial District (Gavin and Maluf 1996, 89). The design for this Marine Walk has been done by Gustafson and Porter (see Garden of Forgiveness).

The Ancient Tell and Glacis

Figure 61: Tell site looking north-northwest

The position of the ancient tell was partly guessed at due to discoveries made in the vicinity since the 1920s that included, as mentioned previously, the sphinx of Amenenhat IV, and some Bronze Age burials discovered in 1954 (Ward 1994, 66; Chéhab 1955, 50). The raised ground had been a Muslim burial ground until the end of the nineteenth century, when it was removed by the Ottomans The north-west corner was taken up with a crusader castle and some later Ottoman buildings. The crusader castle was mostly destroyed in the process of building a new port between 1870 and 1900 (Finkbeiner and Sader 1997, 119). It seems that archaeologists working during the period of the French Mandate were aware that this may be the area of Beirut's earlier settlements but it was not investigated nor protected and in the 1950s, the Rivoli Theatre, the Byblos warehouse and other high-rise buildings were built in the area (Sader 1998, 29, 30).

Excavations began on the site in 1993. Remains uncovered from at least four excavations have been preserved as part of the multi-period 'Ancient Tell' site (figure 61). These remains include a Middle Bronze Age glacis and monumental gate, followed by successive glacis or ramparts and an Iron Age settlement (BEY 003; Badre 1997, 28; 68). To the north west of these finds was the remains of a crusader castle, the foundations for which had cut through the earliest of the settlement evidence on the site, dating to the Early Bronze Age (Badre 1997, 14). To the south of BEY 003 were the excavations of BEY 020 and 013 (Finkbeiner and Sader 1997; Karam 1997). The remains conserved from these as part of the Tell Site include a massive Late Bronze Age – Iron Age glacis, which was still more than five metres high in places (Jablonka 1997, 124). This glacis carried on to east and west, coming up in BEY 013, along with the foundations of some circular towers of Hellenistic date (Karam 1997, 113; figure 62).

Figure 62: Hellenistic tower foundations to east of Tell site

The decision to conserve the Tell site was made by ministerial decree in October 1996 by the then Minister for Culture and Higher Education, Michel Eddé (Badre 1997, 92). The fact that the finds on the Tell site were labelled and presented in the media as 'Phoenician' was instrumental in the conservation decision even though settlement on the site began at an earlier stage (H. Sader, pers. comm.). Some work to conserve the site for display was carried out after the excavations and a sign identifying the various remains was put up. A seventy-five metre stretch of the Iron Age glacis with its access stairway has been restored but a mere 40cm away from the base of the glacis has been built a ten metre high cement retaining wall for the major traffic artery of Rue Cadmus – Rue Wegand (Sader 2004, 228).

The site is awaiting full conservation, and for the moment it is unprotected and overgrown. Initially Solidere had planned to put a road through this area to continue down to the harbour area but the ministerial decree prevented this. The plan is to design a city museum that will incorporate the Tell in some fashion; suggestions have also been made to connect it under the road to the site of the Petit Serail foundations and Hellenistic remains to be conserved on Martys Square (see below). How this is to be done is, as yet, undecided (H. Curvers pers. comm.).

In relation to the north-west portion of the Tell Site, which includes the remains of the crusader castle (figure 63), a landscape scheme for a plaza, 'Citadel Square' has been presented by Machado and Silvetti, a design consultancy based in Boston, USA (Machado and Silvetti 2007). On their website it is described as follows:

> 'The solution includes objectifying the promontory in order to celebrate it as the origins of the city. This strategy is achieved through a number of interventions; creating water features on either side of the rock to evoke both the ancient harbor as well as the medieval moat; the strategic removal of dirt to reveal critical elements of the ruins such as the Ottoman barrack floor; the creation of a 'secret garden' in the area where the promontory had been removed over the ages, thus serving as a visual continuation of what once was; and, finally, specially designed retaining walls that are temporary in nature but heavy in appearance that allow visitors vistas of both the city and the archeological park from on high' (Machado and Silvetti 2007).

Figure 63: Citadel Square

The Petit Serail Site

Excavations in the northern half of Martyrs Square on the site of the Petit Serail produced evidence of the Iron Age, Byzantine and medieval periods, but importantly an extensive habitation area of Hellenistic date was uncovered (figure 64) (Aubert and Neury 1999, 29). These Hellenistic remains, surrounded by Ottoman arches from the basement of the Petit Serail, were in a well-preserved state and included features such as doorways that gave an indication of the relationship between rooms and between the buildings and the street. They also provide evidence of the only Levantine town to date with continued occupation between the fourth and first century BC (Aubert and Neury 1999, 29).

Figure 64: Petit Serail site, Martyrs Square

The excavator suggested to the DGA that these remains should be conserved for display, and they suggested that these recommendations be made to the International Scientific Committee of UNESCO. UNESCO agreed with these proposals but the site was in fact due to be part of a six-storey underground car park planned for Martyrs Square. Consequently three options were put forward: to conserve the site in the open air surrounded by the Ottoman arches; to conserve the site within the car park – it would be on level two – but this would cause the destruction of the Ottoman arches; and the third was to dismantle the site and reconstruct it somewhere else (Aubert and Neury 1999, 30). The open air option was by far the better option but it still necessitated the dismantling of the Hellenistic remains so that they could be re-assembled at a later date when other surrounding work was completed. The structures were duly carefully recorded and labelled, and removed to an empty site just to the north in front of the Tell site in 1997, where they remain, and there is still an overgrown hole in Martyrs Square with the Ottoman arches still *in situ*. Plans to conserve this site are linked to the whole redevelopment of Martyrs Square and the conservation of the Tell site. In 2005 there was a design competition for Martyrs Square, held by Solidere (2005c), which included the Petit Serail site. A Greek landscape design team were successful and are presently trying to solve the conservation issues of the site *vis a vis* the construction of the proposed underground car park (H. Curvers, pers. comm.).

The Zone des Eglises or 'Garden of Forgiveness' or Hadiqat as-Samah

An area that covers just over a hectare between Martyrs Square and Place de l'Etoile, was excavated between 1993 and 2000 (figure 65) (Saghieh-Beydoun *et al* 1998-99; Curvers and Stuart 1998-99, 18). In the northern corner (BEY 113) part of a large room with a floor of marble slabs was uncovered, which has been suggested as possibly being part of the famous Roman Law School (Curvers and Stuart 1998-99, 18; Curvers 2005). Over the rest of the area (BEY 004), Hellenistic, Roman, Byzantine and medieval remains were uncovered (Saghieh-Beydoun *et al* 1998-99, 95). The Hellenistic period included a roadway lined with housing and workshops. The Roman finds included evidence of a colonnaded north-south roadway, identified as the Cardo Maximus, and settlements (Saghieh-Beydoun *et al* 1998-99, 95; Solidere 2005b). There have been complaints about this particular archaeological site including about the standard of the archaeological work; and that Solidere provided extensive resources for the site even though it had been designated an archaeological park and was under no threat from development, meaning that such resources could have been better used on more urgent sites.

Figure 65: Garden of Forgiveness in 2007 looking northeast (white tent in background is covering Hariri's grave)

The notion of a 'garden of forgiveness' came from an idea put forward by Alexandra Asseily, which Solidere agreed to, that suggested the creation of a space for people to gain inspiration and strength, and for introspection and reflexion, which would be based on a design making use of flowing water and Lebanon's flora, and which could encourage peace and healing (Asseily in Solidere 2005b).

The design for the garden was the result of an international competition that was won by Kathryn Gustafson of the London and US-based landscape designers Gustafson Porter The area is to be divided into five main areas: from north to south are the Northern garden and terraces; the plaza and visitor centre; the central Decumanus area with its Hellenistic remains and Roman settlement; and the Cardo Maximus area that runs along the western side of the site. The area is also to be planted up with various trees and shrubs. This design was commended by the Royal Institute of British Architects' Urban Space by Design competition in 2005. It was also an exhibit at the Museum of Modern Art (MoMA) in New York as part of an exhibition called 'Groundswell' that aimed to highlight landscape projects that played a key role in revitalising urban spaces (MoMA 2005). In the press release MoMA linked the Garden of Forgiveness with another park, Christophe Girot's Invalidenpark in former East Berlin (1992–97)[6] as urban spaces that addressed emotionally charged issues of past civil unrest while transcending cultural differences (MoMA 2005).

Not everyone, however, is entirely happy with the idea of either a 'garden of forgiveness' or using archaeological remains in such a fashion (Wilson-Goldie 2005; Mobassaleh 2000). Firstly the term 'forgiveness' is perhaps not the most appropriate as it is unclear who is to do the forgiving and who is to be forgiven and, what's more, given the accepted social amnesia, what is to be forgiven (Wilson-Goldie 2005). It has also been suggested that this park has been made to absorb all the remembering of the Civil War in central Beirut when in reality most of this 'remembrance' is only to be found in the name of it (Sarkis 2005, 285). The Topography of Terror it most certainly is not, but it must be remembered that it took Berlin almost forty years before it was recognised that the past had to be acknowledged rather than buried; this is something that shall be returned to in the general discussion chapter.

In terms of the archaeological remains, there is a general tendency in Lebanon, as in Europe, to view historic masonry remains as the '*patrimoine*' that should not really be disturbed, and consequently there was some disquiet among local archaeologists about the use of an archaeological site in this fashion (J. Schofield pers. comm.). The jury that decided on the winning design, one of six short-listed contestants that came from, amongst others Mexico and Japan/USA, was a panel of eight, five Lebanese including Solidere's chairman, Nasser Chammaa, the architect, Pierre Khoury, and Alexandra Asseily, and three others including one archaeologist, John Schofield (Solidere 2000). The Gustafson Porter design was considered much more sympathetic to the archaeological remains than the other entries (J. Schofield pers. comm.). There appears, however, to have been little consultation with the DGA over the site, and damage has been done to the archaeology, for example a medieval wall was demolished and a Byzantine mosaic removed when building a cement retaining wall at the southern end of the site (A. Seif, pers. comm.). Furthermore, the design will include amongst other added features the planting of trees throughout the garden (Gustafson Porter 2000;

---

[6] Girot redesigned Invalidenpark and included a sculptured fountain arrangement called the 'Sinking Wall' to commemorate both Gnadenkirche that was torn down in 1967 and also the Berlin Wall that used to cross this area (Senate Department 2007).

2005). While carefully selected and planted trees and plants may not create problems and may even help to reduce overheating of and the effects of wind and pollutants on archaeological remains, the root systems of trees planted over archaeology can cause severe damage (Caneva *et al* 2006, 168; 166), which does not seem to have been realised by the contestants (J. Schofield pers. comm.).

The DGA did commission S. Roskams and H. Hurst, two British archaeologists, to put together an alternative design for the garden that took into account a more comprehensive understanding of the archaeological remains (Hurst and Roskams 2000), but it seems unlikely that this will be influential in the long term. As with the Roman Baths, the conservation of the extensive archaeological remains of the area are to be seen first and foremost as a landscape project rather than a conservation project. It is believed that the cost of the garden will be about US$30 million, but it is hoped a trust fund via sponsors can be set up to fund this (A. Gavin, pers. comm.; H. Curvers pers. comm.). Although it was originally scheduled to be open to the public in 2007, the political situation then caused plans to be put back. Work on the western part of the garden did apparently start in 2005. Since then BEY 113 has been covered and the Cardo site has been temporarily covered to allow for the construction of the western retaining wall. Nothing more has happened with the site to date.

V: Discussion

The reconstruction of the BCD was based on a master plan designed by Dar al-Handasah. They initially made little provision for either conservation of the surviving historic urban fabric or for archaeological investigation in central Beirut. Changes were subsequently forced on this master plan by public and professional outcry at the level of proposed destruction. The lack of initial provision for the built heritage, and indeed the subsequent rather superficial approach to it, may be for several other reasons, from the complex to the more prosaic. There is an academic, albeit general, argument that may be relevant: developing countries, it has been suggested, have, not surprisingly, a principal urge to modernise and build anew, which also often includes getting rid of colonial heritage. At the same time, however, they have often been slow to appreciate all that the historic landscape of a city represents in terms of links with the past, and the physical manifestation and development of the social and cultural traditions that give the present-day city its meaning and character (Steinberg 1996, 495). This is complemented by the argument that one of the legacies of the Mandates, both British and French, in the Middle East is that of 'creative destruction', and that their imposing of their order on some Middle Eastern cities, for instance in the building of a new town that inevitably housed the wealthy and drew people away from the old town, caused a certain separation between past and present (Daher 2005, 290). The more prosaic argument is based on an assumption that, as Lebanon was consumed by civil war for fifteen years, it must, in theory, be well behind external developments in the fields of urban redevelopment and planning, and in such things as protection of the historic urban environment. Dar al-Handasah was established in Beirut in 1956, it has since, however, become a multi-national business taking over a number of North American companies in the 1980s, and working in North America, the Far East, Africa and the Middle East (Dar 2007). That such a company would not be up to date with international trends and standards is, therefore, inconceivable.

Solidere came to recognise, to some extent, both the social importance of the built heritage, as seen in their reference to post-war European cities such as Warsaw, though juxtaposed by reference to the modernist tendencies of the 'clean sweep' (Gavin and Maluf 1996, 46), and the cultural heritage value in terms of providing Beirut with a marketable historic identity and in attracting tourists. This is most evident in the Conservation Area. Some of the aspects that affect urban development, conservation and archaeology generally are very much in evidence in the BCD. Solidere works to very stringent temporal and financial frameworks, as does urban development in general, and they have considerable obligation to their shareholders (particularly those who lost their property in return for controlling A-shares). Solidere appears to have been supportive of the archaeology when it suited them, less so when it did not, and despite their interest in displaying archaeological sites, they appear to have little understanding or appreciation for the academic reasons and values of archaeology.

In relation to archaeological work, plans were subsequently made for initial trial trenching, the full excavation of key sites, such as the Tell site, and salvage excavation of a number of other sites. From 1994, Solidere agreed to fund most of the archaeological work, though funding also came from various other, mostly international, academic and research institutions. The archaeological work was affected by a number of problems: the DGA were under-resourced and lacked power in the face of Solidere's politically-supported remit; there were over a dozen different organisations running excavations with little overall harmonisation and co-operation between them; it seems there was rarely sufficient temporal and financial resources for the archaeological work, and much of it was done amid heated discussions, disagreements and misunderstandings; and politically/religiously motivated public and media with their often negative or misconstrued interests. The divisions of the civil war are still evident in Lebanon, and, appear to be getting worse (J. Farchakh Bajjaly, pers. comm.), aided and abetted by outside/foreign influences. The built heritage, particularly the archaeology in the BCD since redevelopment began in the early 1990s has been caught up in these divisions, as evident in the sometimes extreme reactions to even just rumours about sites, for example BEY 045 (R. Thorpe pers. comm.). 'Phoenician' and classical archaeology still seem to be the favoured periods. In the case of the Phoenician, or more correctly, Iron Age, material, this has been supported by what appears to be two opposing factions. The Maronite community tend to argue that they are descended from the Phoenicians, which is contentious (Salibi 1988, 173). On the other hand the legendary image of the Phoenicians as educated, successful entrepreneurial sea-goers and traders is very much the image that the government wants to promote for Lebanon, especially Beirut. Therefore the interest in Phoenician sites is greatest and comes from two different often conflicting angles, sometimes to the detriment of archaeology from other periods (Cumberpatch 1995-96, 161).

Solidere, as mentioned above, has been able to appreciate the cultural-heritage attraction and aesthetic values of the sites that are to be conserved for display. Their plans for the heritage trail and signage are to be commended, though since 2005, a number of the sites have had their conservation work postponed due to political instability, and work on the Heritage Trail was stopped for apparently similar reasons in 2007, though the rebuilding has continued regardless, as is evident from the Souks site. The Heritage Trail, assuming it is eventually put in place, may make the archaeology relevant by ensuring physical as well as intellectual access. It is a way of dealing with the conserved-for-display archaeological sites in an overall framework, integrating them into the history of the city and linking them up with other historic evidence and museums. This means that, unusually, they will not just be individual and disparate sites left in isolation, and it should also mean that people can more easily grasp the wider picture of Beirut's long history. The sites that have been proposed for conservation for display represent most of the main periods of Beirut's history – the Bronze Age, Iron Age/Phoenician, Hellenistic, Roman, Byzantine, Medieval and the Ottoman periods. Of these sites, two were the result of ministerial decrees – the Phoenician quarter and the Tell site; three because archaeologists and the International Scientific Community promoted them – the Hellenistic quarter, the Byzantine shops and mosaics, and the medieval ditch; two because Solidere decided on them – the extension to the Roman Baths and the Ottoman sea walls; and one, the Mamluk ribat, because some sections of the public wanted it saved. The values considered most highly are aesthetic, though with consideration to what people may learn from them. The Phoenician sites demonstrate a certain politicisation of the archaeology, both from the point of view of being considered to represent Maronite heritage, whose power and numbers have dwindled during and in the aftermath of the civil war, and as being historic evidence of the type of image that Beirut wants to promote. The Garden of Forgiveness is aimed at having heavy symbolic values but, other than the name, it is unclear whether it will actually serve the purpose the landscape design is aiming at. In theory, however, it is good to have such a multi-period site conserved for display. Providing the archaeological features are fully respected in terms of explaining the relationships between the different elements and in terms of landscaping, and if they are maintained properly, the garden should at least provide an interesting space in the centre of the city.

As for remembering Lebanon's civil war, it is evidently too early to be commemorating the 1975-1990 war with any self-reflective or acknowledging commemorative type monument, and there may never be one. In Ireland for example there is no general monument commemorating the 1922-23 Civil War, only a small number of plaques dotted about the country remembering individuals who died, as it is still generally considered a too divisive an issue. In Lebanon, it appears to be too soon to attempt such advanced notions as forgiveness, when remembering, acknowledging and accepting need to come first. Lebanese artists are beginning to consider the legacy of the war – as demonstrated in an exhibition of 2006 entitled 'Out of Beirut' held in the Modern Art gallery in Oxford. This exhibition showcased work from contemporary Lebanese artists, including film-makers and writers and dealt with such difficult areas as those who were kidnapped and disappeared. The catalogue of the exhibition is available in Beirut. Having said that, a new sign was erected in 2009 on the edge of Martyrs Square saying that a new memorial to honour the victims of the civil war is to be built, and, over a photograph of war-torn buildings, says 'Remember'. This suggests it will be in addition to the Garden of Forgiveness. Whether the 'Garden of Forgiveness' is an appropriate concept is a moot point, particularly given Lebanon's continuing instability. Nonetheless, it would seem that there will be free access to it and to the other archaeological sites conserved for display, and perhaps they could in some way be used, as has been attempted with some archaeological monuments in Northern Ireland (Hamlin 2000), to generate cross-community interest and sense of commonality.

Of the three case studies of this research, it is Beirut that would most definitely be better served by an entire book of its own. The political and social issues surrounding the archaeology and the conservation, Solidere's and the government's roles, and the whole urban context of Beirut, are extremely complicated, very sensitive and a situation that is in a perpetual state of flux. In that sense it represents the socio-political situation throughout much of the Middle East today.

CAROLINE A. SANDES

CHAPTER SIX

DISCUSSION

I. INTRODUCTION

The preservation of archaeological sites in cities is not a new phenomenon. Even the conservation of smaller sites and fragments, those with which this research is primarily concerned, is not a new practice, as demonstrated in the City of London by, for example, the remains of extra-mural Roman and medieval towers preserved in the basement of the former General Post Office (now Merril Lynch) and in Cripplegate in the early twentieth century. Since the end of World War II, however, the number of sites conserved for display in urban contexts has grown – in the case of the City of London many such sites conserved for display and present today were in fact conserved in the post-war period up to the 1960s. The damage inflicted by World War II on urban centres led to, in the cases of Britain and Germany, the start of urban archaeology in living cities as a process of urban redevelopment, as demonstrated in the chapters on London and Berlin. Since then, archaeological investigation has increasingly become an intrinsic part of the urban redevelopment process, particularly in the developed world. As explained in Chapter Two, there is now a tendency to preserve *in situ* by reburying, rather than preserve by record via excavation, and to conserve sites for display within the buildings being developed on the site, rather than keeping the site free of development. Furthermore, while since the 1960s there have been many advances in the theories of archaeological practice, many of these developments in urban archaeological practice have taken place with little directly relevant theoretical discussion. Moreover, theories of conservation that have been developed are for historic buildings and by extension large-scale archaeological monuments. As is discussed in this chapter, the consequences are that the practice of the conservation of smaller and more fragmentary/less readily identifiable urban archaeological sites has fallen into the shadows in terms of academic and theoretical archaeological and conservationist debate, resulting in a lack of development of a specific valuing system, to an ad hoc, site-by-site approach to decision-making about such sites, and to conserving such sites without any long-term consideration or management. While this ad hoc site-by-site approach is feasible for large-scale urban sites and for rural sites and monuments where their values are more evident or the land-use pressure may be less, it is rapidly becoming untenable for the more fragmentary sites within the increasingly crowded and fast-changing urban environment of the majority of the world's cities today.

II. VALUES OF URBAN CONSERVED FOR DISPLAY ARCHAEOLOGICAL SITES

As discussed in Chapter Two, values, or rather the questions and discussion of what to conserve, why and for whom, are still something relatively underdeveloped when compared to the practical aspects of conservation (Mason and Avrami 2002, 15, 19). Feilden (2003, 3, 6), however, has identified three groupings of values of historic buildings, which are emotional, cultural and use. Many of Feilden's values apply to the smaller types of archaeological sites that are of concern here. These include emotional values such as identity and continuity, and cultural values such as documentary, historic, archaeological, aesthetic, landscape and scientific. But the problem is that while many of these values are easily recognisable in a large archaeological monument such as the Acropolis, Athens, or in an historic building such as the Charlottenburg Palace, Berlin, it takes a certain amount of educated interest or a professional eye to look at some of the sites detailed here in order to ascertain any value at all. Furthermore, and not surprisingly, the 'use' value of such sites is even more difficult to appreciate and consequently it would seem that any use value, other than its assumed demonstration of cultural values, is rarely considered.

It is, therefore, necessary to examine and redefine these values with the more fragmentary archaeological sites and ruins in mind, in order that a more directly relevant set of reasoning and system of valuing may be identified and bought to bear on decisions about their conservation, presentation and management. This requires attempting to answer the 'why?' and 'who for?' questions, as these form the basis of the valuing. In examining the sites of the case studies for this research, it is apparent that each site was conserved for one or more of five essential reasons:

1. academic;
2. commemorative;
3. active public interest;
4. political; and
5. landscape design (attraction).

Academic reasons include archaeological or historical values such as scientific, physical evidence, historical representation, education, age and scarcity: in London, St Alphage's Tower is a rare survival of standing medieval church architecture in the City; in Berlin, the Grand Hotel Esplanade was, by 1989, the only surviving historic building of the Potsdamer Platz; in Beirut the Ancient Tell site is some of the earliest evidence of Beirut's settlement. Commemorative reasons are based on values of remembering or dealing with a difficult or terrible event or aspect of the past. These sites include the war-ruined church of St Dunstan-in-the-East, London, the Topography of Terror, Berlin, and the Garden of Forgiveness, Beirut. These two sets of reasons, academic and commemorative, are the bases of two principal sets of values; virtually all the sites detailed in this research fall into one or the other category with sites such as the Berlin Wall and the Garden of Forgiveness belonging equally to both.

The remaining three reasons are not mutually exclusive and are most usually to be found in addition to one or other of the first two: in Berlin, for example, it was active public interest that caused the Kaiser-Wilhelm Gedächtniskirche ruins to be saved for their commemorative value. In Beirut, there was a 'sit-in' to demand that the so-called Phoenician Quarter be conserved, partly for its perceived academic value. Active public interest may be closely linked to political reasons, as is certainly the case in the last example and as examined in the Beirut Chapter. Political reasons mainly include values of identity and/or continuity, as demonstrated in the willingness to maintain sections of the City Wall in the Barbican Estate, London, but they may also result in the destruction of a site because it is deemed 'politically negative', as seen with some buildings in Berlin. Political reasons and valuing are examined later in the section on the post-war city. Lastly, there are landscape design or attraction reasons. This is when a site is conserved also to provide a focus for an open space or because it is can also be seen as a form of 'urban heritage art'. It is a reasoning most evident in sites such as the ruined church sites in London and in sites such as the Roman Baths in Beirut. 'Attraction' value is the one most easily recognised by urban development professions and is further examined in Section III below.

As mentioned above, however, the primary reasons are academic and/or commemorative, with one or more of the other three in addition. It is for one of these two reasons that sites are conserved – in other words this is the 'why'. This also identifies 'what' is being conserved: the sites that this research is primarily concerned with loosely divide into two sub-groups:
1. archaeological sites; and
2. commemorative ruins.

As a site may belong to both groups, it is a question of which set of values is seen as dominant, and that ultimately depends on who is doing the valuing. The question of who places what value on which sites is discussed later in this section, but firstly, the question of 'who?'

Values and those who are doing the valuing are intrinsically bound, so the questions of 'what' is being conserved and 'why' should not be separated from 'who for'. Indeed, the division between 'who' and 'who for' is a false dichotomy between 'the decision-makers' and 'the public', since the former may also be included in the latter when, for example, visiting such a site during their free time. A major issue is, therefore, properly identifying 'the public'. The public interest in the conservation of urban archaeological sites and ruins has been noted, but campaigns over the saving of sites also simultaneously demonstrate who has not wanted the sites in question conserved. In the case of the Temple of Mithras, London, a considerable number of interested members of the public wanted the site conserved but the archaeologists and the developers were against it; in the case of the remains of the Gestapo Headquarters that are the basis of the Topography of Terror exhibition, Berlin, the archaeologists and a considerable number of the interested public wanted the site conserved but the West German government were against it. In the case of the Phoenician Quarter, Beirut, archaeologists, interested members of the public and the government wanted the site conserved but the developers did not. It is evident, therefore, that different groups of people with different sets of reasons and values are involved and therefore interaction and compromise are required before a site is either conserved or destroyed. These different groups are generally considered 'stakeholders', but it is possible to identify them more specifically. Based on the reasoning and values established above, four main groups of public or stakeholders may be identified, along with a fifth group that should at least be noted:

1. cultural built heritage professionals – archaeologists, site conservation specialists and others who work with the cultural built heritage as an intrinsic part of their profession;
2. development professionals – those people and organisations involved in the business of urban development, such as developers and architects, who have to deal with archaeology and historic buildings in the course of their work;
3. politicos – those in positions of political power or those who have some political concern with having a site either conserved or demolished in order to support their cause;
4. the interested public – those who are interested in or concerned for archaeological sites and historic buildings but for personal rather than directly professional reasons; and
5. the uninterested public – the significant number of people who have no interest or conscious involvement with in the cultural built heritage, nor consider it relevant to their daily lives.

These groups may be easily further subdivided and may also intertwine, for example educators and tour guides could easily fit into both or either of the cultural built heritage professionals and interested public groups, depending on their level of involvement. Furthermore, not all these groups may be involved altogether at the same time in influencing the decision-making about whether or not a site is to be conserved. In many cases the decision is made between the first two groups – i.e. those directly involved with the site concerned. This may be successful, as demonstrated with the city wall at Coopers Row, London, or it may be a disaster, as demonstrated by the Grand Hotel Esplanade, Berlin. The involvement of the politically-concerned may or may not help – in the case of the Tell Site in Beirut, a ministerial decree and using 'the Phoenician card' ensured the site's survival, but in the case of BEY 045, political pressure appears to have actively contributed to the site's destruction (R. Thorpe pers. comm.). As examined in the Beirut Chapter, in Lebanon there is a very fine line, if one at all, between the politically-concerned and some sections of the interested public. The involvement of the interested public can, therefore, also have a negative as well as a positive effect on any decision.

What is evident from these groups is that when they influence the decision-making they are simultaneously representing the 'who' and the 'who for' in the fundamental questions of 'who is doing the valuing?' and 'who is the site being conserved for?': each group may consider 'the common good' as their reason but it seems more likely that each group to a greater or lesser extent is arguing for the conservation of a site for their own particular reasons and values and therefore for themselves. This is not necessarily a bad thing; it depends on the effect of the dominant set of values on the actual conservation and display of the site in question, as shall be seen.

The next question is, then, what are the actual values that each group give to urban archaeological sites and ruins? The development professionals and the politicos shall be examined in Sections III and IV respectively, so firstly the built heritage professionals and interested public. As has been discussed above, the principal reason for conserving a site is either academic or commemorative, and sometimes both. The academic reasons are, for the most part, based on the values that the professionals would consider such a site to contain – scientific, physical evidence, historical representation, education, age and scarcity. These are in reality the most enduring of the values and equate to what Riegl (1903 [1996], 70) considered to be the historical value, and what Mason and Avrami (2002, 16) consider to be the objective values of a site. It is for these academic values that the majority of the sites considered in this research are conserved for.

In relation to commemorative reasons, the value of such sites is not so much in themselves but the events and, sometimes, the people, they are connected to, most often the event in question has caused the site's ruination. In the case of London's ruined church sites, which tend also to have a strong landscape design reasoning behind their conservation, the value of such sites is strongly connected to aesthetic values, where 'aesthetic' means relating to perception by the senses, rather than its more limited modern meaning of relating only to appearance. In other words, the value of a commemorative site is in its ability to generate some sort of emotion or to stir the imagination of the visitor; the idea is that the visitor should remember and contemplate what has happened on the site. It is the interested public that appear to be most vocal in having such sites conserved. In London, the idea of using bomb-ruined churches as war memorials was first put forward by a collection of writers, art historians and others in a letter to *The Times* in 1944, and in West Berlin it was members of the public who wanted the Kaiser-Wilhelm Gedächtniskirche and the foundations of the Gestapo Headquarters retained. The interested public are, however, the most multifarious group, ranging from those who have a vague or passing interest to the highly knowledgeable and actively concerned. It may also include those who are interested but for negative reasons – those who actively want a site to be destroyed – something which often concerns sites with commemorative value: not everyone wants to remember, as is clearly seen in arguments about conserving sections of the Berlin Wall. It is also an issue often strongly tied to political reasons, as will be discussed later in Section IV.

The interested public often, however, recognises some of the academic values detailed above, and often campaigns to save a site that they recognise these types of values in. This is evident in the campaigns to save some of the sites in Beirut, though these did combine with strong political reasons – i.e. as a way of stopping Solidere's work or as a way of a particular section of society promoting their own historical identity, principally the Maronite Christian use of 'Phoenician' sites. The most obvious example of the public campaigning to save a site for ostensibly academic rather than commemorative or political values is the Temple of Mithras, but this is worth closer examination.

The Temple of Mithras in London in the 1950s generated massive public interest. The archaeologists – Professor Grimes and the Ancient Monuments Board – were very interested in excavating and recording it but placed little value on conserving it since it would cost a great deal of money that would be better spent on other sites. The owners and developers of the Bucklersbury House site had no interest in conserving it – it would take up valuable space and would be very difficult to engineer. The public furore over the site was such that it had the potential to disrupt what was then the most expensive development in central London, and consequently the government became involved. The reason that the Temple of Mithras was finally conserved was because the developers offered to pay to have the surviving masonry of the temple dismantled, stored and then later reconstructed so that they could continue developing the site, and it seems that this decision was made before other options were fully thought out. In reality the only group who wanted the site conserved was the interested public, who queued day after day to visit the remains. Why were they interested? Was it because of genuine interest in evidence of London's Roman past; the imagination stirred by the presence of a pagan Roman Temple; the high level of coverage given to it by the media; or was it just a diversion from the effects of rationing and ruins that London was still suffering from in the aftermath of World War II? Or was it, as Lyon (2007) has argued, about the public protesting against the 'dehumanization of City space' as the blitzed City was rebuilt to fill its new role as a financial centre, and against the domination of archaeologists in decisions about what was considered worth conserving and what was not (Lyons 2007, 18; 19)? What is certain is that the publicity over the site did not generate any significant increase in donations from the public for London's beleaguered archaeological sites. Added to which, interest died off quite quickly once the decision to save the temple remains was made. Arguably this suggests that its value was seen at the time as an intriguing diversion both for the media and the wider public. But, the Ministry of Works continued to receive occasional communication from the public over the eight years it took before the temple was reconstructed, which, on the other hand, indicates very genuine interest amongst at least some members of the public in having the site conserved for display. A similar scenario was played out during the campaign to save the Rose Theatre in the 1980s in London. Once the decision to save the site was made, the majority of the interested public, including a prominent contingent from the acting community, disappeared, but there remains a small active and dedicated group, the Rose Theatre Trust, who continue to work towards getting the site properly conserved.

The interested public is then, in reality, a rather nebulous grouping clearly composed of a variety of different sub-groups that come and go depending on their own reasons and values and what they wish to achieve by either conserving a site or having it removed (or perhaps by just being involved in the campaign to save the site). In this sense, it is important to identify which values are the more long-term and objective and which are the more short-term and subjective.

As mentioned above, the most durable and objective values are academic values – the values of a site as scientific, physical evidence, historical representation, education, age and scarcity are unlikely to change over time, excepting the effects of new discoveries and, of course, how well the site is maintained. Commemorative values are, arguably, more mid-term and as the temporal distance grows between what is being commemorated and the present day, the commemorative value gradually has less and less meaning. This is a cause of concern for sites such as Auschwitz and Oradour-sur-Glane and other very many sites throughout the world that commemorate ghastly atrocities that under no circumstances should be forgotten. But this is as much a matter of how and what history is taught, and the levels of sensitivity and intelligence visitors bring to the sites in question, as how such sites are presented and managed. What is worth noting is that sites conserved for commemorative values quite often also have academic values that will prevail or will increase over time. The surviving sections of the Berlin Wall is such an example. These still have commemorative value for those who lived with the division of the country, and for families and friends of those killed as a consequence of that division. As time passes its value will lie in the academic values of historical representation, physical evidence, age and, indeed, scarcity, as understood by those who argued in favour of conserving the Berlin Wall from the beginning (see Berlin Chapter).

The presence of other, non-academic, values and the ability for values to mutate over time are factors that should be considered in the conservation and long-term management of sites. They are also factors that may be judiciously used to argue for the conservation of a site – for example highlighting shorter term but perhaps more publicly- or developer-appreciated commemorative or landscape design values – that may ensure that in the long-term the academic values of such a site are conserved also. These other values will now be considered within the wider urban context and then the context of the post-war city.

III. Conservation of Archaeological Sites in the Modern Urban Context

The urban redevelopment professionals – principally urban planners and designers, architects, property speculators and developers have been loosely grouped together as the development professionals. They are not, understandably, in the business of conserving the historic urban landscape but to make a profit by developing urban property. That the majority of urban redevelopment professionals has little empathy with the cultural built heritage, and that archaeology in many cases tends to be tolerated rather than actively understood is a perpetual aspect of urban redevelopment, as is evident from the case studies. Since before World War II until about the 1970s, one of the main driving forces behind urban redevelopment was modernism. As discussed in Chapter Two and the subsequent case studies, this resulted in very specific ideas about how cities should be planned and subsequently function. Modernism involved a certain belief in the ability to create an ideal urban world for the future and so generally demanded a break from the past – old cities merely represented slum-ridden, polluted, congested, socially-discontented chaos and, with the exception of the occasional historical building of outstanding importance, modernist planners and developers did not generally place conservation on their list of priorities. This was most clearly seen in post-war West Berlin, where large numbers of historic buildings were swept away. It is an attitude that prevailed throughout the Western world well into the 1970s and 1980s, despite both a recognition by the early 1970s that modernism had run its course, and a change of public attitude towards being in favour of conservation and of protecting the historic urban landscape, including archaeological sites, from annihilation.

The social changes of the 1960s and the increasing evidence that the utopian ideals of modernist urban planning and architecture, once translated into practice, were in fact causing greater social problems than they were solving, led to a socio-cultural change that is generally identified as postmodernism. Two of the fundamental driving forces behind both modernist and postmodernist urban redevelopment are capitalism and the concept of creative destruction. This effectively requires the constant redevelopment and turnover of property in some way – either by demolishing a building that is no longer profitable in order to build a new one, or by buying and selling. While the modernist urban planner aimed at creating a better, long-term urban environment for working and living, the private sector postmodernist urban designer aims primarily at the smaller-scale, shorter term with the emphasis being purely on profit-making and even, some would argue, on creating the post-justice city where some of the wider social (i.e. unprofitable) concerns can be completely disregarded (Cuthbert 2003, 5).

What is obvious from this brief if very simplified summary of the driving forces of urban redevelopment is that the conservation of fragmentary archaeological sites and ruins that have no direct financial value is the antithesis of urban redevelopment. Under modernist redevelopment, complete removal of the past was the ideal, but with postmodernism came an acceptance by urban redevelopment professions that people need both visual variety and historic reference points in their urban environments (Morris 1981, 261; Ossowksi in Jankowski 1990, 84). The problem is that this has translated into a superficial use of the past and the physical remains of it without any appreciation or deeper understanding of it. The past is viewed as a resource, as Jencks (1992, 23) argues, to be either consulted or plundered. This is most obviously seen in the way a new development is superficially rooted into the locality by the use of local historic names, for example the modernist building behind St Alphage's Tower is called St Alphage's House, and a brand new development on Cannon Street, London, not far from the Temple of Mithras, has been named The Walbrook, being developed by Minerva Plc. This use of local historic names is also seen in the Sony Center, Potsdamer Platz, with its Café Josty and Esplanade Residence. Other ways are by drawing attention to even the most superficial of links between the past and the present, exemplified in the banner Solidere had, at one time, along the front of the new Souks development in Beirut, 'Perfume through the millennia', based on archaeological discoveries of excavations of the old souks. There is also the age-old practice of copying historic architectural detail, which at best can be quite imaginative but at worst is merely pastiche.

Nonetheless, it is fair to say that most urban redevelopment professionals are still quite prepared to demolish historic buildings or remove archaeological strata unrecorded if there is no law, or no enforcement of that law, to protect them. This remains a perpetual problem worldwide, as is highlighted by the many charters and official documentation issued by organisations such as UNESCO over the decades since World War II, and as demonstrated by, for example, the initial Dar al-Handasah plans for Beirut. Furthermore, Solidere's approach to the built heritage, including archaeological sites, in their redevelopment of the BCD seems one based primarily on appearance or 'attraction' value. In other words, archaeological sites are valued for their landscape design value. This is not a new concept; it is based on the aesthetic value found in commemorative ruins and can be traced back to the appreciation of ruins of the Picturesque tradition. In the case of London's ruined churches, and the section of City wall of St Alphage's Churchyard, there was a strong element of landscape design value in the decision to conserve these sites. Each fulfilled the modernist requirement of green space; in fact each of these sites, and even St Alphage's Tower, are primarily considered by the Corporation, who is responsible for them, not as monuments but first and foremost as gardens. In Berlin both the Klosterkirche ruins and the sections of medieval town wall are surrounded by green space. In Beirut, the Roman Baths for example, are detailed on Solidere's website under 'Squares and Gardens' (Solidere 2006).

In reality, however, landscape design value of a site is not actually a value in its own right, in the sense that it is not intrinsic to a site as its academic values may be, but one that can be created. It is a value that can complement academic and/or commemorative values. Crucially, it is the value that urban development professionals seem to recognise most readily, and it is what can make a site attractive to visitors. For sites conserved within buildings, this landscape design value becomes a question of 'interior design' or museum display, depending on whether the site finds itself in, for example, the foyer of a building, or it is in its own space in a basement. While it is tempting to see the academic values of a site as the foremost priority with landscape design values being inconsequential, landscape design values are vital for ensuring a site is an asset not an eyesore, and as such are discussed later when considering the display of sites.

As mentioned above, landscape design value is, as demonstrated by examples from the case studies, the value most appreciated by the development professionals. This in itself is not necessarily a problem, but it is when it is the only value appreciated. This tends to be accompanied by a complete lack of understanding of the academic reasoning for conserving sites *in situ*, a problem so glaringly highlighted when Solidere's Chairman first announced the idea of creating a park into which to move any interesting archaeological building discoveries, equating them at best with artefacts, at worst animals for a zoo.

The lack of appreciation for archaeological sites other than for their landscape design value is a result of a number of factors. Archaeological strata are unpredictable – it is never quite clear what may be uncovered in the process of an excavation, nor if something is going to turn up that may merit conserving. Unpredictability creates risk; risk is the nightmare of all urban redevelopment with its inevitably tight financial and temporal constraints and its emphasis on maximum profit. Developers have, however, begun to realise that the most sensible policy is to deal with the archaeology as soon as possible, rather than wait with misplaced hope that they can get out of it at a later date, and the rise in the number of commercial archaeological consultancies that will handle archaeology for developers is testament to this, as indeed is the growing number of companies who employ their own in-house team of heritage professionals. There is also a growing understanding that rather than run the risk of a massive public upset, such as that over the Temple of Mithras and over Dar al-Handasah's initial plans, archaeology can be put to good public relations use.

What appears to be a problem is the lack of understanding on the part of developers about why decisions are made to conserve a site *in situ*, which results in sites being shut away in basements, or in entirely insensitive contexts, as in the case of St Alphage's Tower; 'conserved' in an inappropriate way, as with the Grand Hotel Esplanade, or being left for months or years with not even temporary protection or maintenance until the development is ready to proceed, as is happening in Beirut with the Tell and the Petit Serail sites and in Berlin with the Stadtschloss site. This lack of understanding and its results are a direct consequence of the fact that no clear criteria have been developed as to why something should be conserved for display, and how it should be managed over the long term. An argument is usually put forward on a site-by-site basis, or a law enforces it. This can be a disaster, leading to some sites being conserved without good reason while others are destroyed, as is evident from the case studies. The questions of planner Huw Mosley discussed in Chapter Two, come to mind: 'Do you really know what you are saving – and is it really that important?' (Moseley n.d. [1998], 50). Urban developers do, of course, have ways of destroying sites while ostensibly fulfilling the requirements to conserve them – as evidently seen in the conservation of the Grand Hotel Esplanade and of St Alphage's Tower. Perhaps a third question should then be added to Mosley's two, which would be, 'and can you explain to a non-archaeologist why it is important?'

In the period after World War II, most of the sites conserved in London were conserved in the open air as this was considered the preferable context for them. In recent years, however, there is a growing tendency to conserve sites within the buildings that are built to occupy the site, as demonstrated at the previously mentioned APPEAR conference in Brussels in 2005. This, of course, has the advantage of being able to conserve the site without rendering the entire property unprofitable. There is, however, the unanswered, question of how to reconcile such sites conserved inside with the greater urban context outside. Once conserved inside, usually in a basement, while for all intents and purposes still *in situ*, they become something of an artefact – part of what Kalliopi Fouseki calls an 'in situ museum' (K. Fouseki pers. comm.). This has the advantage of being able to develop their display considerably, added to which one gets some sense of how, for example, the city has grown vertically. Furthermore, it is easier to protect a site and its display inside, both from the weather and from various problems that plague outside sites – litter, graffiti, weeds and damaged or decayed signage – but unfortunately sites conserved within private property are often not readily open to the public. The West Gate of the Roman fort, London, is opened once a month when a tour is made from the nearby Museum of London. This is an excellent tour and is generally well-attended, and means the visitor has the added benefit of being able to ask questions about the site. There are many such sites around the City that are not easily accessible to the public, for example the remains of a chapel of the Holy Trinity Priory at Aldgate (Schofield and Lea 2005).

The modern urban context is then a context of perpetual change of which development is an intrinsic part and, whether during modernist urban planning or postmodernist urban design, is primarily driven by creative destruction and capitalism. Attempting to conserve an archaeological site within such an environment has been and continues to be something of an idealistic battle. Nonetheless it is an important battle if cities, home to 3.3 billion people, half of the world's population (UNFPA 2007, 1), are to retain physical evidence of their historic roots and identity. Consequently the reasons and values of archaeological sites need to be clear and definite, and of demonstrable value beyond archaeologists and other built heritage professionals. The key to this is not only imaginative signage and proper maintenance but long-term management that includes the protection of academic values while appreciating, incorporating and monitoring the wider values as they change. Landscape design values are one such value, but political values are particularly volatile as shall now be discussed.

IV. CONSERVATION AND THE POST-WAR CITY

Sultan Barakat, Director of the Post-War Recovery and Development Unit, York, has examined some of the issues of cultural heritage in post-war reconstruction (Barakat 2006; 2007). He has argued that in terms of the cultural heritage in general there has been an absence of an overall vision for dealing with it within post-war rebuilding both generally and specifically, resulting in only piecemeal approaches. He has also explained that it should not be assumed that a shared vision of the importance and need for the recovery of the cultural heritage existed, but that it needed to be established and built upon. Two of the most important needs of people in post-war recovery is to reconfirm a sense of identity and to regain control over one's life (Barakat 2005, 11). He stressed that the recovery of cultural heritage is not confined to physical rebuilding but is also dependent on economic and social recovery, and that the issues of belief and religion have to be addressed. He also highlighted that the active participation of the local communities is crucial, and that ultimately what is needed is time to establish alliances and partnerships (Barakat 2006). It is a truism to say that archaeology is as affected by politics as much as virtually everything else is. That politics, often complicated by religion – the two being indistinguishable in countries such as Lebanon – further affects how archaeological and historical sites and monuments are regarded. While during wartime these effects are intensified, it seems apparent that the danger to the cultural built heritage and archaeology within urban areas is just as great, if not more so, in the immediate post-war period, as demonstrated by the level of destruction in West Berlin and Beirut.

It is evident from the case studies that very little if any consideration was given to conservation and archaeological matters in the initial rebuilding plans; as Barakat (2007, 26) mentioned, this continues to be the case today. There are several reasons for this – the first is circumstantial. Cities that have experienced prolonged and/or very heavy bombardment and street fighting are inevitably in very poor shape, both due to the inevitably extensive physical damage done and due to unavoidable neglect. Heavy bombing causes severe structural damage; buildings may be burnt out or flooded; broken windows, doors and damaged roofs and walls mean no protection from either looters or the weather. The priority is to get the city to function again in some way, including responding to the numerous urgent requirements for housing and shelter. Inevitably there are limited resources for this process, and it may take many months for aid packages to be agreed upon and actually implemented. Consequently, protecting or stabilising any but the very important damaged historic buildings and monuments is hardly a priority.

As also noted in the case studies, war damage also generates opportunities for profitable redevelopment in its aftermath. In Beirut, it was recognised at an early stage by Rafiq Hariri that the reconstruction of central Beirut could be a highly profitably enterprise. In the immediate post-war period, planning and antiquity laws are often difficult if not impossible to enforce when the state apparatus is not fully functioning, and when most people are focussed on rebuilding their lives. During this period, it is comparatively easy for buildings to be demolished and areas cleared of 'ruins' without too much interference, and to build without any prior archaeological investigation. This is evident in Beirut both during the war and immediately afterwards.

Of course, in terms of a city's archaeological strata, the clearance of buildings in the post-war period can open up a unique opportunity for excavation and research. One of the problems of the immediate post-war period is that archaeologists are rarely involved in any of the early stages of post-war reconstruction planning. While it was understandable in post-World War II London and Berlin, it was unfortunate in the case of Beirut. Archaeologists were involved but not, it would seem with the actual planning and not until about 1992. This has meant that excavations and any sites that may need conserving have to be incorporated into pre-existing plans that have little temporal space for them and no room for anything unpredicted. In other words, to ensure that the archaeology is dealt with as thoroughly as possible, there needs to be an overall, long-term comprehensive plan that is thought out well in advance of work actually starting, and it is crucial that it be done in tandem with the redevelopment plans. After all, as is evident from London, Berlin and Beirut, post-war rebuilding was being planned while the wars in question were still very much being fought. Furthermore, post-war urban rebuilding takes significant amounts of time, usually decades. Much of central London and central Berlin had many ruined buildings still in evidence by the late 1950s-early 1960s. Even in the BCD, parts of which Solidere have rebuilt remarkably quickly, still retains significant portions that have yet to be redeveloped, most obviously around Martyrs Square. On this basis, there is time for thorough archaeological investigation provided that the priorities be identified and the schedule and resources are planned in properly from the beginning and over the long-term. A crucial responsibility for archaeologists is that the academic importance, and indeed relevance of the resulting knowledge of the city's past, based on archaeological research, be explained in such a way as to establish a greater general level of appreciation of it by the urban planning and development professions beyond it as a tourist attraction and a landscape feature.

The other major issue of the post-war period for the built heritage is politics itself. This is most clearly evident in Berlin in the destruction after World War II, of, for example the historic buildings that had been the Gestapo Headquarters in West Berlin, and of the Stadtschloss in East Berlin. It is also clearly evident in the comments by Chancellor Kohl about demolishing surviving Third Reich and GDR buildings in Berlin, and in Prime Minister Hariri's comments, referred to earlier, about ridding Beirut of any physical evidence of the civil war.

This danger to historic buildings considered by the ruling power to be tainted or 'politically negative' is acute. 'Politically negative' or tainted buildings and monuments are those that have become associated with the vanquished regime or losing side, regardless of their architectural merit, previous histories, or any other positive aspect or value. In the case of Berlin, it was anything to do with Hitler, the Nazis and the Third Reich, and after the end of the Cold War it was anything to do with the GDR. In Beirut's Central District, there has been a tendency to cover up or get rid of physical evidence of the civil war. In Iraq there is concern about how to keep some of the Saddam Hussein-era buildings and monuments, many of which have already been damaged (Crawford 2007).

The issue is this: to destroy built heritage because it is considered politically negative tends to be an unfortunate aspect of a short-term reactionary political mood. It does nothing to help heal or solve the issues that these buildings are purported to represent. In the long run, the removal of such buildings will leave something of a gap in the city's historical make-up and may also mean the loss of significant historical architecture and monuments because of a single phase of their often multi-phase histories. The removal of the historical buildings, including the eighteenth century Prinz-Albrecht-Palais renovated in c.1830 by one of Germany's most historically famous architects, K.F. Schinkel, solely because it had been requisitioned for use by Hitler's Security Services is one such example. The importance of retaining historical architecture or of maintaining a city's physical identity is clearly articulated by the sociologist, Stanislaw Ossowksi, regarding Warsaw after World War II,

> 'If the Warsaw community is to be reborn... if its core is to be constituted by former Varsovians, then they have to be given back their old rebuilt Warsaw to some extent, so that they can see in it the same city, though considerably altered, and not a different town on the same spot. One must take into consideration the fact that individual attachment to old forms is a factor of social unity' (quoted in Jankowski 1990, 84).

The opposing argument is, however, the evident need by the survivors of the conflict in question to move on from its traumas and horrors. This was vehemently stressed by Iraqi journalist, Ghaith Abdul Ahad[7], in response to a suggestion that some of Saddam Hussein's monuments be kept; he argued that they should all go, that there should be a fresh start. In the case of Beirut, and indeed any civil war, there is also the need for a society to find

---

[7] Ghaith AbdulAhad, Iraqi journalist for the Guardian at a British Museum/Guardian seminar: Babylon to Baghdad: can the past help build a future for Iraq?. 15th June, 2004.

some way of living together again. The tendency is to 'forget' about the war. As an interim suggestion, judging by changes in society in Britain, in Germany and indeed, very tentatively, in Lebanon, this tendency or inclination to forget continues until, at the very earliest, the generation that was born during or just after the war reaches adulthood – approximately fifteen to twenty years after the end of hostilities. In Britain there was the positive change in attitude towards the built heritage, amongst other socio-cultural changes, in the 1960s, but it was not until 1995 that a project was set up, the Defence of Britain Project, by the Council of British Archaeology, to create a database of all of Britain's twentieth-century sites and monuments of war (CBA website 2002). In Germany, it was not until the 1980s that interest in the Nazi period began to develop, as demonstrated by the interest in seeing the Gestapo Headquarters site commemorated; and the Holocaust Memorial to the Murdered Jews of Europe in central Berlin, first proposed in 1988 was only completed and officially opened in 2005. An exhibition in Oxford in 2006, 'Out of Beirut' showed how contemporary Lebanese artists were beginning to address the issues of Lebanon's civil war, though the concept of a 'Garden of Forgiveness' remains controversial (Wilson-Goldie 2005).

This 'generation gap' is a tentative suggestion but from the point of this research and the issues of post-war conservation, it is suggested that the length of time needed to protect 'politically negative' built heritage from demolition is an absolute minimum of fifteen to twenty years, in other words for the generation not directly involved or with very little personal or first-hand memory of the war in question to reach adulthood. For their parents the war is most usually a case of painful and terrifying, sometimes guilty, personal memories which they have no desire, or perhaps are unable, to talk about, but for the following generation the war in question has often (though certainly not always) started the slow process of becoming 'history'.

There is, then, a crucial role for archaeologists and conservationists in this immediate post-war period in relation to saving the cultural built heritage. In terms of the consideration of time, 'political time' is short-term: the next press conference, the next election, but 'archaeological time' is long. Archaeologists are trained to deal in sites and artefacts that can be thousands of years old; a generation goes unnoticed and even with medieval and later archaeology, it is usually an insignificant timespan. Likewise, conservationists aim to conserve the built heritage for the longest possible time. Consequently, if anybody can see past the comparatively short length of time that a piece of built heritage may remain politically negative, and recognise its long-term historic values, then it should be archaeologists and conservationists. It is worth noting that the person who did the most to argue for the protection of such unsavoury but historically important sites as the remains of Hitler's Bunker was Berlin's municipal archaeologist, Alfred Kernd'l. It is crucial that sites such as these be retained because, as was argued for the keeping of remains of the Berlin Wall (Hassemer in Klausmeier and Schmidt 2004, 8), it is important to keep physical evidence of 'this madness'. One of the crucial roles of archaeologists and conservationists in the immediate post-war period is arguing for and aiming to protect politically negative but historically valuable built heritage, both above and below ground.

The other aspect of post-war politics and its ability to affect the cultural heritage, specifically archaeology, is seen most obviously in Beirut. Some will argue that the civil war never really ended, it is now just fought out in different arenas (Klaushofer 2007). These arenas included, most notably here, the archaeology discovered in central Beirut with, for example, Christian Maronites laying claim to sites considered to be Phoenician; the competing Shi'a and Sunni claims to the Mamluk ribat, and a variety of people who were anti-Solidere attempting to use the archaeology to stop the development. This can have significant, often negative consequences for archaeological sites, their destruction or their conservation, as demonstrated by BEY 045 and the Phoenician Quarter respectively. These again are subjective, short to medium term values and should be weighed up accordingly when it comes to decisions about whether to conserve a site or not.

There is also a role for conserved archaeological sites to play in the post-war city, as commemorative ruins and as a way of helping to bridge division. London, Berlin and Beirut all have sites that are considered as commemorative ruins. In London, it is ruined churches. This is an appropriate use of them as it continues some of their original functions such as a place of reflection and commemoration. Secondly, the sanctity and air of the sublime that an historic church tends already to be imbued with may be maintained to some extent by this use. A bomb-damaged historic church, therefore, tends to emphasise the tragedy rather than the horror of war. Elsewhere war ruined churches have been conserved to emphasise horror, notably that which is part of the ruins of the village of Oradour-sur-Glane, south-west France, where the SS massacred the village's population in 1944.

In Berlin, the Topography of Terror is a very specific commemorative ruin. Its aim is to force the visitor to confront and to remember a particularly grim piece of history. Having the physical remains of the Gestapo Headquarters on display *in situ* in central Berlin makes them very hard to ignore while at the same time they are ruins. Ruins suggest decay and something no longer active in the present – this simultaneously allows the visitor, and hopefully any surviving victims, at least some comfort in the fact that this particular phase of horror is safely within the realm of history.

In Beirut, however, ruined churches cannot be used as commemorative ruins as religion plays such a culturally and politically-significant role. The principal religious buildings damaged during the war have all been completely restored. Nor was there one identifiable 'enemy' with its corresponding physical evidence, as in

Berlin. Instead, a commemorative garden that is based upon a large area of archaeological remains has been proposed. The use of such multi-period archaeological remains as part of a garden of forgiveness, or perhaps a garden of reconciliation, is an excellent idea. Commemorating civil war is particularly difficult. In fact, even presenting cultural heritage to a divided community is a challenge. The latter is something that has been worked on in Northern Ireland where some archaeological sites can simultaneously represent positive and negative aspects of history depending on which community one is from. Conserving and presenting such archaeological sites in a positive light for both communities but without hiding any problematic history has been quite a challenge (Hamlin 2000). This has been done by presenting the sites in such a way as to stimulate curiosity in the site itself, how it developed, how it was used, and so forth. The major key to success seems, however, to be in involving the local communities, including using local artists or writers, in the presentation of the sites and by helping to develop a sense of these sites being places belonging to all where everyone may come. In other words, with the right presentation and information, archaeological sites and monuments may be used to emphasise a common past and to highlight positive aspects of that past, while at the same time providing a place where more negative aspects of the local history can be learnt about and accepted or at least better understood. Proper conservation, emphasis and presentation of the remains in the proposed garden in Beirut could then provide a much-needed positive environment for something such as a garden of forgiveness, and go someway to developing the concept of a common past. The need for a common past is crucial for the cohesion of any multifaceted society, but one in desperate need of promotion in Lebanon, now more so than ever.

Another factor worth mentioning is the very excavation of archaeological sites in the post-war city are an indirect consequence of the destruction of war is, in fact, one of the few positive results of that destruction. The conservation of such sites, particularly in complicated post-war situations such as that of Beirut, could promote this positive aspect as representing something of the phoenix of knowledge from the ashes of war.

V. Presentation and Use of Fragmentary Archaeological Sites

In 1964, a member of the public wrote to the City Engineer of London City Corporation to say how pleased he was that 'pieces of the past' such as St Alphage's Tower, had been conserved, and that he was sure that many others would agree, but he went on to express surprise that, after all the trouble of doing so, that there was no sign giving any information about the site (CoL 1964). St Alphage's was duly given a sign, though with little of the information that the letter-writer suggested, such as a sketch of the complete church or people associated with it. A number of issues regarding St Alphage's conservation and display reflect a prevailing attitude to the conservation and maintenance of many urban archaeological sites worldwide. It currently stands in a very forlorn state, complete with flaking stone work due to air pollution and other clearly visible structural and fabric problems; vegetation growing from it; completely insensitive surroundings, and an antique sign that hangs in the place it is least likely to be seen. The patch of garden between it and London Wall road is the only part of the site that appears to receive any regular maintenance.

The site was conserved, rightly so, for academic reasons, and also on principle to avoid setting a precedent where the Corporation, having given an undertaking to conserve the site, could then get away with reneging on that undertaking. This could be interpreted as a political reason as it would not have done to have the Corporation over-ride the authority of a government ministry, the Ancient Monuments Board being part of the Ministry of Works. Despite the evident interest of the public, however, no other values of the site appear to have been considered – certainly no public interest nor landscape design values were identified or taken into consideration in its display. It was, for all intents and purposes and in an oxymoronic fashion that is all too common, conserved and abandoned. This undermines the academic values it was conserved for, as the site becomes to resemble less an archaeological monument and more some derelict masonry, but what is more it renders the site useless: it is not obviously demonstrating any cultural value; it will not attract visitors nor generate any interest in them, nor inform those who may recognise that it might be more than derelict masonry; it will not add anything to its surroundings; and it will not support any argument made to a developer as to why such sites should be conserved for display.

What appears to be the problem is archaeology and conservation professionals will conserve a site for its academic values, and tend to assume that the public will automatically appreciate these. Some elements of the interested public will indeed appreciate these values but in general these smaller sites are much more difficult to comprehend without clear and imaginative signage, and even more so if they are decaying and have become a receptacle for litter, graffiti and weeds. There is also a tendency amongst the professionals to dismiss or consider less relevant the non or less academic reasons why the public may want a site conserved or the values that the public may place on a site, as demonstrated by the Temple of Mithras. More obviously, this appears to translate into how a site is displayed. This is seen when, for example, a site is conserved within an almost clinical context that usually involves a sea of gravel, railings to keep one away and a jargon-heavy sign but with little thought given to its long-term display and presentation, hence the subsequent out-of-date or lost sign, the litter, and general air of neglect that these sites often then exhibit. This clinical context is seen in London, not so much in the post-war period but since the late 1970s with sites such as the Bishop of Winchester's Palace and the

Postern Tower, and in Berlin with, for example, the section of Customs Wall.

Sites conserved more with the public in mind are some of the sites conserved within parks, and commemorative ruins. As discussed above, these are concerned more with aesthetic values and they tend to be much more attractive sites. Their aim is, after all, to attract and to stimulate people – as demonstrated by London's ruined churches and, to a different degree, Berlin's Topography of Terror. Sites valued for their landscape and inherent attraction tend also to be better provided for, as seen in Beirut where there are plans to landscape them, provide them with signage and to incorporate them into a heritage trail. The over-dominance of aesthetic and/or landscape values over academic values can, however and as with the reverse, be detrimental to the essence of the site. The plans for the Garden of Forgiveness in Beirut, while very comprehensive and indeed attractive, appear to overwhelm the archaeological remains and any message they may carry in their own right. What is important, then, is that there be a balance between academic, aesthetic and landscape values.

Aesthetic and landscape values tend to be the more attractive to the greater number of people, so in order to encourage people to stop at a site long enough to read the sign and thus begin to appreciate the academic values, there needs to be some aspect of the site that triggers interest and the imagination. A way to do this is to provide a use for such sites. The successful conserved for display sites tend to be such sites that have this secondary value. In London, the stretch of City Wall of St Alphage's Churchyard was designed to also be part of small park – this site is attractive and a pleasant place to sit. The stretch of City Wall at Coopers Row is an excellent example of a site with a use – it provides an attractive and unique backdrop for a café, which at one time the café was advertising. The Klosterkirche ruins in Berlin are used for cultural events such as open air sculpture exhibitions; the Roman Baths, Beirut, have a garden at one end and an adjoining space for open-air concerts. The other way to use such sites is to incorporate them via signage and/or a walking route, into the wider context of the historic city. This simultaneously allows people to get a more overall picture of what the original context of the site in question was and, hopefully, stimulate them into visiting other sites or even a museum. This was the idea behind the London Wall Walk of the 1980s (Chapman *et al* 1985), but much of the signage has since fallen into disrepair. Solidere's plans for the sites in Beirut are to incorporate them into trails, and Berlin has made some attempts to do this via the Senate Department for Urban Development website.

An another important aspect of such sites is that they are, by the very fact of them being *in situ*, authentic historical markers or signs. This is also an aspect that may be put to good use, but rarely is: these smaller sites are infinitely more accessible and available to people than larger sites. For one thing, if they are conserved outside, they merely require that people pause for a moment to read the sign, and many people do. In this way many people who may never contemplate visiting an archaeological site or a museum, who may not be able to afford the often high costs of visiting larger sites, or indeed be prepared or able to travel to visit a larger site, have easy access to a small physical piece of the past. To a lesser extent this may also be the case for sites conserved within buildings, so long as they are identified and readily accessible. The crucial aspect is that sites be well maintained and managed over the long term, and have interesting, accurate, informative, and intellectually-accessible signage that is up-to-date and includes where more information may be had, for instance details of a relevant website, publication and/or museum.

VI. CONCLUSION

There are several aspects that have become clear in the course of this research. In relation to the post-war situation, the whole process of how a country recovers is a comparatively new area of research (Barakat 2005, 10). The inclusion of cultural heritage within this process is evidently still in its infancy, and it is crucial that archaeologists and conservationists become involved at the earliest possible stages of post-conflict urban redevelopment planning to ensure that provision is made for archaeological research and conservation. The destruction caused by war, or indeed any major destructive disaster, offers a unique opportunity to gather extensive knowledge and evidence about a city's past but time and again this opportunity has not been fully exploited due to archaeological concerns not being included from an early stage of the post-war planning, and because the importance the role of archaeology and conservation in post-conflict recovery is not generally appreciated. Archaeological research and the sensitive conservation and display of key sites can help to re-establish identity, continuity and local pride, to foster understanding and a sense of a common past, or to provide sites where the past can be more accurately articulated and hopefully understood, and thus can actively help the healing process, as demonstrated in Northern Ireland (Hamlin 2000), as being increasingly recognised (Stanley-Price 2007). Archaeologists and conservationists can also help to protect politically negative but historically important sites and buildings that, in the long-term, will carry important academic values such as historical representation and evidence but may also help people to come to terms or to commemorate various aspects of the war in question when they are ready to do so.

Archaeologists and conservationists cannot, however, hope to be fully included within urban redevelopment plans, particularly those for post-war rebuilding, if they do not have clear agenda and a set of fully explicable and broadly applicable values, particularly when it comes to decisions about whether to conserve a site or not. Development and the practice of urban archaeology and of the conservation of archaeological sites for display, and the attitudes towards the cultural built heritage are all very much tied in with current urban redevelopment practice and with socio-political trends, as exemplified by modernism and postmodernism. A dichotomy, however, exists between urban development and conservation of archaeological sites for display in that the latter is the antithesis of the former. It is evident that the many international documents in relation to the importance and need to protect the cultural built heritage, including archaeological sites, are making little impact on the development professions as a whole, and there remains little understanding or appreciation for the built heritage generally and archaeological sites specifically amongst them. Furthermore, while there have been many advances in the theory and practice of archaeology and conservation, there has been little development in the theory of the conservation of fragmentary archaeological sites within the urban landscape. As a result approaches to such sites have generally been decided upon based on site-by-site considerations with inadvertent assumptions about, or a lack of appreciation for, public interest. There has, therefore, been little development of specific values or considerations of use or management, often resulting in sites being conserved in an unsuitable fashion or left unprotected, not properly displayed, and not being properly maintained. At worst this renders them an eyesore and makes their reasoning for conservation unintelligible.

In relation to conservation theory and to Mason and Avrami's (2002, 15, 19) questions as to 'what' and 'why' sites are conserved, added to which is 'who for', answers can now be provided for fragmentary urban archaeological sites:
- *What* is being conserved are:
    1. archaeological sites, and/or
    2. commemorative ruins;
- *Why* they are being conserved is primarily for:
    1. academic and/or
    2. commemorative reasons, based primarily on:
        I. academic and/or
        II. aesthetic values, but also often due to:
            iii. active public interest, and/or
            iv. political values and/or
            v. landscape design (attraction) values.
- *Who* is making the decisions and who these sites are being conserved for are, arguably, non-divisible in that all are members of 'the public'. Therefore, five basic groups of the public or stakeholders can be identified:
    1. cultural built heritage professionals;
    2. development professionals;
    3. politicos;
    4. the interested public; and
    5. the uninterested public.

With the exception of the last group, all these groups tend to become involved or influence, to greater or lesser extents, the making of a decision about whether to conserve a site or not. Sometimes this influence may be indirect, for example a developer may agree to conserve a site to avoid bad publicity. All these groups tend to argue for or agree to the conservation of sites based on their own values, which are not mutually exclusive and may double up: built heritage professionals will argue for a site to be conserved based on academic values; development professionals may agree to such action based on landscape design and attraction value; the politically-concerned and the interested public will have a potentially myriad variety of values but primarily based on socio-political themes such as identity and continuity, general interest that is short, medium or long-term, academic values such as historical representation and education, and/or on commemorative and aesthetic values.

The real issue then is whose values are dominant, and this is inevitably reflected in the display of the site. Those sites that are consciously designed to attract the public are generally more successful, in that they are better presented and maintained and are, consequently, more attractive sites. These are sites that while having academic values, have had other values identified about them – generally commemorative but also landscape design values, which are the values that tend to have wider appeal. The worst or least appealing sites tend to be those conserved solely for academic values. Consequently when deciding to conserve a site for display, it is crucial that the interested public, particularly local interested public, be of primary concern. These are the stakeholders who will benefit most from the site and/or live with the site in their midst. Consequently the site must be made intellectually and physically accessible firstly to them (as opposed to the built heritage professionals). Correspondingly, while a site should be conserved *primarily* for its long-term academic values, unless it is a site that is extremely special and rare, a site should not be conserved *only* for academic values. There is rarely need to conserve minor archaeological sites for display for purely academic reasons and values. As with Reigl's 'scrap of paper' ([1903] 1996, 70; see Chapter Two), the vast majority of archaeological information and evidence to be found in such fragmentary urban archaeological sites will almost always be found in major sites. Furthermore, methods of recording such as sampling, survey and photography are highly developed at this stage, and as discussed in Chapter Two, complete excavation and preservation by record is a much more effective and holistic way of understanding a site. Therefore, unless a site has academic *and* other publicly-relevant values, then such a site should not be conserved for display.

Such academic and publicly-relevant values also translate into use values. These use values include providing a city with easily accessible historic signs or markers that are evidence of city's history and historic identity and as a way of identifying the city's broader historic context. Furthermore, they can be used to provide cultural heritage tourist attractions, particularly if incorporated into or used to establish green spaces and heritage trails. These small sites often generate a sense of discovery when they are tracked down and can provide an alternative way of visiting and discovering the city in question. What is crucial is that sites be intellectually and physically accessible, that they have relevant signage and be well-maintained and managed over the long-term. In such a way, these sites may help to foster interest amongst people with no former interest (i.e. the uninterested public) and help generate some interest among local people in the history of their locality. The last aspect is particularly important. Much attention and resources are given worldwide to sites and monuments considered to be of national and international significance. While this is understandable, this can also have the side-effect of isolating people from their own heritage, not least due to the large entrance fees that these sites must normally charge and that such sites seem aimed exclusively at tourists (it would, for example, be interesting to know how many residents of the borough of Tower Hamlets, much of which is deprived, have visited the Tower of London?). Furthermore, not every place has its own nationally important site, but they will often have sites that are of local importance and it is these sites that are an everyday feature of local life. Consequently, more attention could usefully be given to sites of local interest, such as the fragmentary archaeological remains and ruins conserved in urban contexts, as a means of providing a step to encouraging interest in archaeology generally and making the past more accessible both physically and intellectually. This may also have the added benefit of fostering a sense of relevance and connection to such sites, and help to develop in the local population a sense of responsibility towards them.

To conclude then, fragmentary archaeological sites conserved for display in the urban context should only be conserved for display if:
1. their academic values may be combined with other recognisable public values;
2. they can be conserved *in situ*;
3. that provision will be assured for their long-term management including maintenance of the site and its signage; and
4. they are intellectually and physically accessible.

In terms of future research, surveying of city residents and visitors – for example the residents of the Barbican Estate, London – to discover what they think of the presence of historic remains and if they value them is an obvious next step. Similarly, surveying the urban development professions to ascertain what they know of archaeology, how they rate it and what could be done to foster greater understanding, is another step that could be taken.

In relation to existing sites, many need to have proper management plans put in place to end the unfortunately characteristic but easily solved problems of weeds, litter and missing or damaged signage. The conservation of historic buildings, urban archaeology and the conservation of fragmentary archaeological sites for display are deeply embedded within in the modern urban context, identified with having or being made to carry many values. It is important that the positive values be identified, promoted and properly appreciated not just for the sites concerned but for archaeology as a whole. Furthermore, the city is place of constant and rapid change and growth; these small sites have a crucial role to play as historic reference points amid such perpetual change.

The public, non-academic, values are summed up by a lady in Coventry who commented, on pausing to ask me what I was doing as I was contemplating a site identified only as 'the medieval ruin' outside a 1970s building, 'Ah', she said, 'they make you slow your pace'.

REFERENCES
Primary Sources

Corporation of London, 1954. Minutes of the Improvements and Town Planning Committee Meetings Vol 57. Held at the London Metropolitan Archives.

Corporation of London, 1959. Minutes of the Improvements and Town Planning Committee Meetings Vol 62. Held at the London Metropolitan Archives.

Corporation of London, 1964. Engineer's Departmental Files: St Alphage, London Wall (1956 -1964). Held at the London Metropolitan Archives.

Inland Revenue 1940 IR 37:148: St Alphage's File between 1940 and June 1962. Held at the National Archives, Kew.

Minister of Works 1940 Work 14: 1087: Ancient Monuments, London Wall, Tower Hill section extending 75 yards N from Trinity Place File date 25/5/1940. Held at the National Archives, Kew.

Minister of Works 1949 Work 14:1088: Ancient Monuments London Wall (sites of nos 19-20, Tower Hill, Stepney, London): Acquisition. File date: 5/11/49. Held at the National Archives, Kew.

Ministry of Works 1954. Work 14: 2588: Ancient Monuments: City of London (Area 4): Compulsory Purchase Order, including St Alphage, London Wall, and Tower of St Alban, Wood St: Legal arrangements. File Date: 3/8/54; closed 4/3/63. Held at the National Archives, Kew.

Minister of Works 1954 Work 14:2592: Ancient Monuments: Temple of Mithras, London. Excavations. File date 24/9/54. Held at the National Archives, Kew.

Ministry of Works 1932 Work 14: 3120: Ancient Monuments Inspectorate: London Wall, Wakefield Garden. File date: 9/5/32. Held at the National Archives, Kew.

Ministry of Works 1941 Work 14: 1235: Ancient Monuments: London Wall: various portions from Falcon Square to just beyond Cripplegate, revealed by air raid damage. File opened 11/3/41. Held at the National Archives, Kew.

Ministry of Works 1941 Work 14: 1804: Ancient Monuments: London Wall sites of nos. 22 and 23 Tower Hill, Stepney File opened 14/1/1941; closed 16/3/1965. Held at the National Archives, Kew.

Ministry of Works 1947 Work 14: 2034: Ministry of Works: Ancient Monuments London: Excavation of Reconstruction Sites in London and papers relating to Roman and Medieval Excavation Council. File opened 1947; closed 1958. Held at the National Archives, Kew.

Ministry of Works 1951 Work 14: 2043: Ancient Monuments: London Wall: section bounding St Alphege Churchyard: Works. File date: 13/3/51. Held at the National Archives, Kew.

Ministry of Works 1951 Work 14: 2042: Ancient Monuments: London Wall: section adjoining the south side of Falcon Square: Works and Preservation; includes papers on Plaisters Hall, Barbican. File date 2/11/1951. Held at the National Archives, Kew.

Ministry of Works 1952 Work 14: 2044: Ancient Monuments: London Wall, section bounding Cripplegate Churchyard, and southwards to and include Route 11 (including Bastions 12, 13 and 14, and West Gate of Fort). Barbican Redevelopment - London Wall File date 29/1/52. Held at the National Archives, Kew.

Ministry of Works 1952 Work 14:2041: Ancient Monuments: London Wall, section extending 75 yards north from Trinity Place: Works. File date: 22/12/52. Held at the National Archives, Kew.

Ministry of Works 1959 Work 14: 1721: Ancient Monuments: King Edward VII Building, GPO, London EC: Roman Wall: Works File date 2/6/59. Held at the National Archives, Kew.

Secondary Sources

Abercrombie, P., 1959. *Town and Country Planning*. First edition 1933. Oxford: Oxford University Press.

Akers, D.S., 1996. *Urban Conservation - Legislation and Practice in the Federal Republic of Germany: a comparative report*. Oxford: Oxford Brookes University.

Ancient Monuments Act, 1931. [21 & 22 Geo. 5. Ch. 16.] London: HMSO.

Anon, 1944-45. Chronique. *Bulletin du Musée de Beyrouth* 7: 109-120.

Anon, 1965. Chronique. *Bulletin du Musée de Beyrouth* 18: 111-128.

APPEAR, 2005. *Urban Pasts and Urban Futures: bringing urban archaeology to life, enhancing urban archaeological remains. Proceedings of the international and interdisciplinary symposium, Brussels 4th-5th October, 2005*. http://www.in-situ.be/D28_en.pdf; last accessed 3/06/07.

APPEAR 2007. In Situ. *www.in-situ.be*. Date accessed 1/06/07.

Appleyard, D. (ed.), 1979. *The Conservation of European Cities*. Cambridge, Massachusetts and London: MIT Press.

Ashurst, J., 2007. Introduction - continuity and truth. In J. Ashurst (ed.), *Conservation of Ruins*. xxv-xxix. Oxford: Butterworth-Heinemann.

Ashworth, G.J. and Tunbridge, J.E., 1990. *The Touristic-Historic City*. London and New York: Belhaven Press.

Ashworth, W.A., 1959. *The Genesis of British Town Planning*. London: Routledge and Kegan Paul Ltd.

Asmar, C., 1996. Les fouilles du Centre-Ville de Beyrouth. *BAAL (Bulletin d'Archéologie et d'Architecture Libanaises)* 1: 7-13.

Aubert, C. and Neury, P., 1999. Une methode de

conservation au centre ville: le quartier Hellénistique. *National Museum News* 9: 29-33.

Audouze, F. and Leroi-Gourhan, A., 1981. France: a continental insularity. *World Archaeology* 13 (2): 170-189.

Avrami, E., Mason, R., and de la Torre, M., 2000. Report on research. In E. Avrami, R. Mason, M. de la Torre (eds) *Values and Heritage Conservation: research report*. Los Angeles: The Getty Conservation Institute, 3-11.

Badre, L., 1997. BEY 003 Preliminary Report: excavations of the American University of Beirut Museum 1993-1996. *BAAL (Bulletin d'Archéologie et d'Architecture Libanaises)* 2: 6-94.

Baker, F., 1990. The Problems of Conservation in a Unifying Berlin Archaeological. *Review from Cambridge* 9(1), 167-169.

Baker, F., 1993. The Berlin Wall: production, preservation and consumption of a 20th-century monument. *Antiquity* 67, 709-33.

Balfour, A., 1990. *Berlin: the politics of order 1737 - 1989*. New York: Rizzoli International Publications, Inc.

Barakat, S. (ed), 2005. *After the Conflict: reconstruction and development in the aftermath of war*. London & New York: I.B. Tauris.

Barakat, S. 2006. Post-conflict reconstruction and recovery of cultural heritage. Paper presented at the Archaeology in Conflict Conference, CAA, Institute of Archaeology, November 2006.

Barakat, S. 2007. Postwar reconstruction and the recovery of cultural heritage: critical lessons from the last fifteen years. In N. Stanley-Price (ed.), 2007. *Cultural Heritage in Postwar Recovery*. 26-39. Rome: ICCROM Conservation Studies 6.

Barley, M.W., 1977. Preface. In M.W. Barley (ed.) *European Towns: their archaeology and early history*. vii-x. London: Academic Press.

Baugher, S., and DiZerega Wall, D., 1997. Ancient and modern united: archaeological exhibitions in urban plazas. In J. H. Jameson Jr, (ed.), *Presenting Archaeology to the Public: digging for truths*. 114-129. Walnut Creek, California., U.S.A: AltaMira Press.

BBC News Online, 2006. http://news.bbc.co.uk/go/em/fr/-/1/hi/world/europe/5061280.stm. Date accessed 09/06/06.

BBC Radio 4, 2006. *Stadium of Spooks*. Radio programme aired 5/6/06; 8pm.

Becherer, R., 2005. A matter of life and debt; the untold costs of Rariq Hariri's new Beirut. *The Journal of Architecture* 10 (1): 1-42.

Berducou, M., 1996. Introduction to Archaeological Conservation. In N. Stanley-Price, M. Kirby Talley Jr, A. Mellucco Vaccaro (eds), *Historical and Philosophical Issues in the Conservation of Cultural Heritage*. 248-259 Los Angeles: The Getty Conservation Institute.

Berlin.de 2006. http://www.berlin.de/tourismus/sehenswuerdigkeiten.en/00140.html. Date accessed 26/06/2006.

Beyhum, N., 1992. The crisis of urban culture: the three reconstruction plans for Beirut. *The Beirut Review* 4: http://www.lcps-lebanon.org/pub/breview/br4/index.html. Date accessed 06/04/07.

Biddle, M., and Hudson, D. with Heighway, C., 1973. *The Future of London's Past*. London: Rescue Publications 4.

Burg, A., 1995. *Downtown Berlin: building the metropolitan mix*. Berlin, Basel, Boston: Birkhäuser Verlag.

Caneva, G., Ceschin, S. and De Marco, G., 2006. Mapping the risk of damage from tree roots for the conservation of archeological sites: the case of the Domus Aurea, Rome. *Conservation and Management of Archaeological Sites* 7: 163-170.

Casson, H., Colvin, B., and Groag, J., 1945. *Bombed Churches as War Memorials*. London: The Architectural Press.

Centro Richerche Archeologiche e Scavi di Torino 2006. Beirut – the arcades of the Banco di Roma. http://www.centroscavitorino.it/en/progetti/libano/beirut.html. Date accessed 3/07/07.

Champion, T., 1996. Protecting the monuments: archaeological legislation from the 1882 Act to PPG16. 38-56. In M. Hunter (ed.), 1996. *Preserving the Past: the rise of heritage in modern Britain*. Stroud: Alan Sutton Publishing Ltd.

Chapman, H, Hall, J and Marsh, G, 1985. *The London Wall Walk*. London Museum of London.

Chéhab, M. 1955. Chronique. *Bulletin du Musée de Beyrouth* 12, 47-58.

Clark, K., 2001. *Informed Conservation: understanding historic buildings and their landscapes for conservation*. London: English Heritage.

Clark, K., 2004. Between a rock and a hard decision: the role of archaeology in the conservation planning process. In T. Nixon (ed.), *Preserving Archaeological Remains in situ? Proceedings of the 2nd conference 12-14th September 2001*. 202-208. London: Museum of London Archaeological Service.

Clarke, H. B., 1999. The experience of Dublin and its satellite townships. In E P Dennison (ed.) *Conservation and Change in Historic Towns: research directions for the future*. York: CBA Research Report 122 145-157.

Clarke, P.W., 2003. The economic currency of architectural aesthetics. In A.R. Cuthbert (ed.), *Designing Cities: critical readings in urban design*. 28-44. Oxford: Blackwell Publishing.

Clay Large, D., 2002. *Berlin: a modern history*. London: Penguin. First UK edition 2001.

Cleere, H., n.d. [1998]. Closing remarks. In M. Corfield et al (eds) *Preserving Archaeological Remains in Situ: proceedings of the conference of 1st-3rd April 1996*. 187-189. London: Museum of London Archaeology Service.

Coblenz, W., 2000. Archaeology under Communist control: the German Democratic Republic, 1945-1990. In H. Härke (ed.), *Archaeology, Ideology and Society: the German experience.* 304-338 Frankfurt am Main: Peter Lang GmbH.

Collins, M., 1994. Land-use planning since 1947. In J. Simmie, *Planning London.* 90-140. London: UCL Press Ltd.

Comité Scientifique International, 1996. Rapport du Comité Scientifique International, Beyrouth 27 novembre - 3 décembre 1995. *BAAL (Bulletin d'Archéologie et d'Architecture Libanaises)* 1: 14-22.

Copeland, T., 2004. Presenting archaeology to the public: constructing insights on-site. In N. Merriman (ed.), *Public Archaeology.* 132-144. London and New York: Routledge.

Corfield, M., Hinton, P., Nixon, T., and Pollard, M. (eds), n.d. [1998]. *Preserving Archaeological Remains in Situ: proceedings of the conference of 1st-3rd April 1996.* London: Museum of London Archaeology Service.

Cosgrove, D.E., 1994. Should we take it all so seriously? Culture, conservation, and meaning in the contemporary world. In W E Krumbein, P Brimblecombe, D E Cosgrove, and S Staniforth (eds), *Durability and Change: the science, responsibility, and cost of sustaining cultural heritage.* 259-266. Chicester: John Wiley and Sons Ltd.

Council for British Archaeology, 1953. *The Preservation of Buildings of Historic Interest: a note on the Town and County Planning Act 1947.* London: Council for British Archaeology.

Council for British Archaeology, 1954. *Memorandum on the Ancient Monuments Acts.* Second edition London: Council for British Archaeology.

Council for British Archaeology, 2002. A review of the Defence of Britain Project http://www.britarch.ac.uk/projects/DOB/review/index.html. Date accessed 28/07/07.

Council of Europe 1992. *European Convention on the Protection of the Archaeological Heritage (the Valletta Charter).* http://conventions.coe.int/Treaty/en/Treaties/Html/143.htm. Date accessed 4/03/07.

Crawford, H. 2007. Saddam Hussein and the heritage of Iraq. Paper presented at the 8th Cambridge Heritage Seminar: Revisioning the Nation: cultural heritage and the politics of disaster, Cambridge University, May 2007.

Cruickshank, D. and Vincent, D., 2003. *Under Fire: people, places and treasure in Afghanistan, Iraq and Israel.* London: BBC Books.

Cumberpatch, C. G., 1995-96. Archaeology in the Beirut Central District: some notes and observations. *Berytus* 42: 157-171.

Cumberpatch, C.G., 1998. Approaches to the archaeology of Beirut *National Museum News* Spring, 18-21.

Curvers, H., 2005. The Archaeology. http://www.solidere.workwebsite.net/garden. Date accessed 01/02/07.

Curvers, H.H. and Stuart, B., 1996. BEY 008: The 1994 Results. *BAAL (Bulletin d'Archéologie et d'Architecture Libanaises)* 1:228-234.

Curvers, H.H. and Stuart, B., 1998-99. The BCD Archaeology Project 1996-1999. *BAAL (Bulletin d'Archéologie et d'Architecture Libanaises)* 3: 13-30.

Curvers, H.H. and Stuart, B., 2004. Beirut Central District Archaeology Project 1994-2003. In C. Doumet-Serhal, A.Rabate and A.Resek (eds.), *Decade: a decade of archaeology and history in the Lebanon.* 248-260.

Cuthbert, A.R. (ed.), 2003. *Designing Cities: critical readings in urban design.* Oxford: Blackwell Publishing.

Daher, R.F., 2005. Urban Regeneration/Heritage Tourism Endeavours: the case of Salt, Jordan 'local actors, international donors, and the State'. *International Journal of Heritage Studies* 11 (4): 289-308.

Dar al-Handasah, 2007. www.dargroup.com. Date accessed 10/02/07.

Davie, May, 1997. Le patrimonie architectural et urbain au libain: pour qui, pourquoi, comment faire? Enjeux et identités dans la genèse du patrimoine libanais. http://almashriq.hiof.no/lebanon/900/902/MAY-Davie/patrimoine.html. Date accessed 01/02/07.

Dennison, E. P. (ed.), 1999. *Conservation and Change in Historic Towns: research directions for the future.* York: CBA Research Report 122.

Der Förderverein Klosterruine e.V., 2007. www.klosterruine-berlin.de/liste.htm. Last accessed 11th June 2007.

Diab, H., 1999. *Beirut: Reviving Lebanon's Past.* Westport, USA: Praeger Publishers.

Diefendorf, J.M. (ed.), 1990. Introduction: new perspectives on a rebuilt Europe. *Rebuilding Europe's Bombed Cities.* 1-15. London: Macmillan Press Ltd.

Diefendorf, J.M., 1993. *In the Wake of War: the reconstruction of German cities after World War II.* New York and Oxford: OUP.

Dieters, L., 1979. Historic Monuments and the Preservation of Monuments in the German Democratic Republic *Journal of the Society of Architectural Historians* 38 (2), 142-147.

Dolukhanov, P. M., 1996. Archaeology and nationalism in totalitarian and post-totalitarian Russia. In J.A. Atkinson, I. Banks and J. O' Sullivan (eds), *Nationalism and Archaeology: Scottish Archaeological Forum.* 200-213. Glasgow: Cruithne Press.

Eade, J., 2000. *Placing London: from imperial capital to global city.* New York and Oxford: Berghahn Books.

Earl, J., 1996. London government: a record of custodianship. In M. Hunter (ed.), *Preserving the Past: the rise of heritage in modern Britain.* 56-76. Stroud: Alan Sutton Publishing Ltd.

el-Dahdah, F., 1998. On Solidere's Motto, "Beirut: Ancient City of the Future". In P. Rowe and H.

Sarkis (eds), *Projecting Beirut: episodes in the construction and reconstruction of a modern city.* 68-77 Munich, London, New York: Prestal.

el-Khoury, R., 1998. Beirut sublime. In P. Rowe and H. Sarkis (eds), *Projecting Beirut: episodes in the construction and reconstruction of a modern city.* 260-262. Munich, London, New York: Prestal.

Esher, L., 1981. *A Broken Wave: the rebuilding of England 1940-1980.* London: Allen Lane.

Fehring, G. P., 1991. *The Archaeology of Medieval Germany.* London and New York: Routledge.

Feilden, B., 2003. *Conservation of Historic Buildings.* First edition 1992. Oxford: Architectural Press.

Fenwick, J., 2007. Tara and the M3 Twice-Tolled Motorway. http://www.nuigalway.ie/archaeology/Tara_M3.html. Date accessed 28/07/07.

Finkbeiner, U. and Sader, H., 1997. BEY 020 preliminary report of the excavations 1995. *BAAL (Bulletin d'Archéologie et d'Architecture Libanaises)* 2: 114-166.

Fisk, R., 1991. The Biggest Supermarket in Lebanon: a journalist investigates the plundering of Lebanon's heritage. *Berytus* 39: 243-252.

Fisk, R., 2001. *Pity the Nation: Lebanon at war.* Oxford: Oxford University Press. First edition 1990.

Folorunso, C. A., 2000. Third World development and the threat to resource conservation: the case of Africa. In F. P. McManamon, and A. Hatton (eds), *Cultural Resource Management in Contemporary Society: perspectives on managing and presenting the past.* 31-39. London and New York: Routledge.

Forshaw, J.H. and Abercrombie, P., 1943. *The County of London Plan 1943.* London: Macmillan and Co. Ltd.

Forty, F.J., 1955. *London Wall by St Alphage's Churchyard: exposure and presentation of Roman and Medieval work on the town wall of London.* The Guildhall Miscellany No. 5.

Frauenkirche Dresden, 2006. http://www.frauenkirche-dresden.org/. Date accessed: 25/07/2006.

French Mandate for Syria and the Lebanon 1923. Supplement: Official Documents. *American Journal of International Law* 17 (3): 177-182.

Gavin, A., 1998. Heart of Beirut: making the Master Plan for the renewal of the Central District. In P. Rowe and H. Sarkis (eds), *Projecting Beirut: episodes in the construction and reconstruction of a modern city.* 217-233. Munich, London, New York: Prestal.

Gavin, A. and Maluf, R., 1996. *Beirut Reborn: the restoration and development of the Central District.* London: Academy Editions.

Gerrard, C., 2003. *Medieval Archaeology: understanding traditions and contemporary approaches.* London and New York: Routledge.

Ghorayeb, M., 1998. The work and influence of Michel Ecochard in Lebanon. In P. Rowe and H. Sarkis (eds), *Projecting Beirut: episodes in the construction and reconstruction of a modern city.* 106-121. Munich, London, New York: Prestal.

Gold, J.R., 1997. *The Experience of Modernism: modern architects and the future city 1928-1953.* London: E. & F.N. Spon.

Gottwaldt, A., 1994. A Philosophy of Display. In R. Shorland-Ball (ed.), *Common Roots - Separate Branches: railway history and preservation.* 210-214. London: Science Museum for the National Railway Museum, York.

Green, H.J.M., 1976. Excavations of the Palace Defences and Abbey Precinct Wall at Abington Street, Westminster, 1963. *Journal of the British Archaeological Association* 129, 59-76.

Grimes, W.F., 1968. *The Excavation of Roman and Medieval London.* London: Routledge & Kegan Paul.

Gringmuth-Dallmer, E., 1993. Archaeology in the former German Democratic Republic since 1989. *Antiquity* 67, 135-42.

Gustafson Porter, 2000. Hadiqat as Samah, Beirut. http://www.gustafson-porter.com/intro.html. Date accessed 26/01/07.

Gustafson Porter, 2005. Urban Space by Design: Proposal for Hadiqat as-Samah. http://www.riba.org/go/RIBA/About/RIBALondon_4835.html. Date accessed 25/01/07.

Gutierrez, J.J.G. 1999. Building Homes, Building Politics: Berlin's post-war urban development and ideology. *Central Europe Review: politics, society and culture in Central and Eastern Europe* 1, 21.

Haas, W., 1999. The presentation of research in and under existing buildings. *Conservation and Management of Archaeological Sites* 3, 69-82.

Habermas, J., 1998. 1989 in the shadow of 1945: on the normality of a future Berlin Republic. *A Berlin Republic: Writings on Germany.* 161-181. Cambridge: Polity Press. First German edition Frankfurt a Main Suhrkamp Verlag 1995.

Hain, S., 2001. Struggle for the inner city – a plan becomes a declaration of war. In W J V Neill and H-U Schwedler (eds) *Urban Planning and Cultural Inclusion: lessons learnt from Belfast and Berlin.* 57-68. Basingstoke: Palgrave Macmillan.

Hall, P., 2002. *Cities of Tomorrow: an intellectual history of urban planning and design in the twentieth century.* Oxford: Blackwell Publishing. First edition 1988; this edition third.

Hamdan, K., 1994. Smart patches, shame about the coat. *New Internationalist* 258. http://live.newint.org/issue258/smart.htm; accessed 01/12/06.

Hamlin, A., 2000. Archaeological heritage management in Northern Ireland: challenges and solutions. In F.P. McManamon and A. Hatton (eds), *Cultural Resource Management in Contemporary Society: perspectives on managing and presenting the past.* 66-75. London and New York: Routledge.

Hanssen, J., 1998. 'Your Beirut is on my desk'

Ottomanizing Beirut under Sultan Abdülhamid II (1876-1909). In P. Rowe and H. Sarkis (eds), *Projecting Beirut: episodes in the construction and reconstruction of a modern city.* 41-67. Munich, London, New York: Prestal.

Härke, H., 1991. All quiet on the Western Front? Paradigms, methods and approaches in West German archaeology. In I. Hodder (ed.), *Archaeological Theory in Europe: the last three decades.* 187-222. London and New York: Routledge.

Härke, H. (ed.), 2002. The German Experience. In H. Härke (ed.), *Archaeology, Ideology and Society: the German experience.* 12-39. Frankfurt am Main: Peter Lang. First edition 2000; this edition second.

Harvey, D., 1990. *The Condition of Postmodernity.* Oxford: Blackwell Publishers Ltd.

Hasegawa, J., 1992. *Replanning the Blitzed City Centre: a comparative study of Bristol, Coventry and Southampton 1941-1950.* Buckingham & Philadelphia: Open University Press.

Haynes, I., Sheldon, H. and Hannigan, L. (eds), 2000. *London Under Ground: the archaeology of a city.* Oxford: Oxbow Publishers.

Hebbert, M., 1998. *London: more by fortune than design.* Chichester: John Wiley & Sons.

Heighway, C.M., 1972. *The Erosion of History: archaeology and planning in towns.* London: Council for British Archaeology.

Heinz, M. and Bartl, K., 1997. BEY 024: "Place Debbas": Preliminary report. *BAAL (Bulletin d'Archéologie et d'Architecture Libanaises)* 2: 236-257.

Herrmann, J., 1977. Research into the Early History of the Town in the Territory of the German Democratic Republic. In M.W. Barley (ed.) *European Towns: their archaeology and early history.* 243-259. London: Academic Press

Hobsbawn, E., 1994. *Age of Extremes: the short twentieth century 1914-1991.* London: Michael Joseph.

Hodder, I., 1991. Archaeological theory in contemporary European societies: the emergence of competing traditions. In I. Hodder (ed.), *Archaeological Theory in Europe: the last three decades.* 1-24. London and New York: Routledge.

Hodder, I., 1999. *The Archaeological Process: an introduction.* Oxford: Blackwell Publishers Ltd.

Holden, C.H. and Holford, W.G., 1951. *The City of London: a record of destruction and survival.* London: Architectural Press.

Hourani, A., 1991. *A History of the Arab Peoples.* London: Faber and Faber.

Hughes, R. et al, 2004. Design and decision on five development sites in London: Governor's House, Millennium Footbridge, Alder Castle, Plantation Place and Park Lane, Croydon. In T. Nixon (ed.), *Preserving Archaeological Remains in situ? Proceedings of the 2nd conference 12-14th September 2001.* 97-136 London: Museum of London Archaeological Service.

Human Rights Watch 2006. http://www.hrw.org/worldreport/Ps.htm. Date accessed 30/11/06.

Hunter, M. (ed.), 1996. Introduction: the fitful rise of British preservation, 1-16. In M. Hunter (ed.) *Preserving the Past: the rise of heritage in modern Britain.* Stroud: Alan Sutton Publishing Ltd.

Hurst, H. and Roskams, S., 2000. Archaeological Consultancy Report on Beirut Central District, sites BEY 004 and 113. Unpublished report for the Directeur Général d'Antiquités, Repubilqe du Liban.

ICOMOS, 1987. *Charter for the Conservation of Historic Towns and Urban Areas (Washington Charter).* http://www.international.icomos.org/towns_e.htm. Date accessed: 1/02/06.

ICOMOS, 1990. *Charter for the Protection and Management of the Archaeological Heritage.* http://www.international.icomos.org/e_archae.htm. Date accessed 24/11/05.

ICOMOS 1994. *Nara Document on Authenticity* Japan. http://www.encore-edu.org/encore/documents/Nara.html. Date accessed: 11/02/03.

ICOMOS Australia 1996. *Charter for the Conservation of Places of Cultural Significance (the Burra Charter).* http://www.gdrc.org/heritage/icomos-au.htm. Date accessed: 17/04/04.

ICOMOS 1999. *International Cultural Tourism Charter: Managing Tourism at Places of Heritage Significance.* http://www.international.icomos.org/charters/tourism_e.htm. Date accessed 29/11/05.

ICOMOS, 2001. Germany. http://www.international.icomos.org/risk/2001/germ2001.htm. Date accessed 01/07/06.

ICOMOS/ICAHM 2000. The *Charter of Krakow: principles for conservation and restoration of built heritage.* http://www.ruraleurope.org/pdf/KRAKOW.pdf. Date accessed: 18/03/03.

Inam, A., 2002. Meaningful urban design: teleological/catalytic/relevant. *Journal of Urban Design* 7 (1), 35-58.

Jablonka, P. 1997. Stratigraphy and Architecture. In U. Finkbeiner and H. Sader, BEY 020 preliminary report of the excavations 1995. *BAAL (Bulletin d'Archéologie et d'Architecture Libanaises)* 2: 124-134.

Jameson, F., 1992. *Postmodernism or, The Cultural Logic of Late Capitalism.* London and New York: Verso.

Jameson Jr, J. H. (ed.), 1997. *Presenting Archaeology to the Public: digging for truths.* Walnut Creek, California., U.S.A: AltaMira Press.

Jankowski, S., 1990. Warsaw: destruction, secret town planning, 1939-44, and postwar reconstruction. In J.M. Diefendorf (ed.), *Rebuilding Europe's Bombed Cities.* 77-93. London: Macmillan Press Ltd.

Jencks, C., 1992. The postmodern agenda. In C. Jencks (ed.), *The Post-Modern Reader.* 10-39. London:

Academy Editions.

Jidejian, N., 1997. *Beirut Through the Ages.* Beirut: Librairie Orientale.

Johnson, M., 1999. *Archaeological Theory: an introduction* Oxford: Blackwell Publishers.

Johnson-Marshall, P., 1966. *Rebuilding Cities.* Edinburgh: Edinburgh University Press.

Jokilehto, J., 1999. *A History of Architectural Conservation.* Oxford: Butterworth-Heinemann.

Jokilehto, J., 2007. Conservation concepts. In J. Ashurst (ed.), *Conservation of Ruins.* 1-9 London: Butterworth-Heinemann.

Jones, B., 1984. *Past Imperfect: the story of Rescue Archaeology.* London: Heinemann.

Kabbani, O.R., 1998. Public Space as Infrastructure: the case of the postwar reconstruction of Beirut. In P. Rowe and H. Sarkis (eds), *Projecting Beirut: episodes in the construction and reconstruction of a modern city.* 240-259. Munich, London, New York: Prestal.

Karam, N., 1997. BEY 013 Rapport préliminaire. *BAAL (Bulletin d'Archéologie et d'Architecture Libanaises)* 2:95-113.

Karam, N., n.d. Archaeology in Beirut: endangered identity. http://www.opuslibani.org.lb/Lebanon/dos001.html. Date accessed 22/01/07.

Khalaf, S. 2006. *Heart of Beirut: reclaiming the Bourj.* London: Saqi Books.

Klaushofer, A., 2007. *Paradise Divided: a portrait of Lebanon.* Oxford: Signal Books.

Klausmeier, A. and Schmidt, L., 2004. *Wall Remnants - Wall Traces: the comprehensive guide to the Berlin Wall.* Berlin and Bonn: Westkreuz-Verlag

Knox, P.L., 2003. The design professions and the built environment in a postmodern epoch. *In A.R. Cuthbert (ed.), Designing Cities: critical readings in urban design.* 357-361. Oxford: Blackwell Publishing.

Kohl, P.L. and Fawcett, C., 1995. *Nationalism, Politics and the Practice of Archaeology.* Cambridge: Cambridge University Press.

Koshar, R., 1998. *Germany's Transient Pasts: preservation and national memory in the twentieth century.* North Carolina: University of North Carolina Press.

Koshar, R., 2000. *From Monuments to Traces: artifacts of German memory 1870-1990.* Los Angeles & London: University of California Press.

Krumbein, W. E., Brimblecombe, P., Cosgrove, D. E. and Staniforth, S. (eds), 1994. *Durability and Change: the science, responsibility, and cost of sustaining cultural heritage.* Chicester: John Wiley and Sons.

Ladd, B., 1998. *The Ghosts of Berlin: confronting German history in the urban landscape.* Chicago and London: University of Chicago. First edition 1997.

Ladd, B., 2004. *The Companion Guide to Berlin.* Suffolk: Boydell and Brewer.

Ladd, B., 2005. Double Restoration: rebuilding Berlin after 1945. In L.J. Vale and T.J. Campanella (eds), *The Resilient City: how modern cities recover from disaster.* 117-134. Oxford: Oxford University Press.

Larkham, P.J., 1996. *Conservation and The City.* London and New York: Routledge.

Lauffray, J., 1944-45. Forums et monuments de Béryte. *Bulletin du Musée de Beyrouth* 7: 13-80.

Layton, R., Stone, P.G. and Thomas, J. (eds), 2001. *Destruction and Conservation of Cultural Property.* London and New York: Routledge.

Legal and General 2006. Legal & General launches Walbrook Square. http://www.legalandgeneralgroup.com/media-centre/press-releases/2006/q2/2006-05-19.html. Date accessed 09/09/06.

Lobbedey, U., 1977. Northern Germany. In M.W. Barley (ed.), *European Towns: their archaeology and early history.* 127-157. London: Academic Press.

Lyon, J., 2007. The Temple of Mithras: changing heritage values in the City of London 1954-2006. *Conservation and Management of Archaeological Sites* 9 (1): 5-37.

Machado and Silvetti 2007. Citadel Square. http://www.machado-silvetti.com/projects/citadel_square/index.php. Date accessed 07/07/07.

Makdisi, S., 1997. Laying Claim to Beirut: urban narrative and spatial identity in the age of Solidere. *Critical Inquiry* 23 (3): 660-705.

Makdisi, U., 2002. Ottoman Orientalism. *American Historical Review* 107 (3) www.historycooperative.org/journals/ahr/107.3/ah0302000768.html. Date accessed 10/01/07.

Manhart, C., 2006. *Post-Conflict Strategies for Safeguarding Cultural Heritage* (lecture given at UCL on 12th January 2006).

Marquis, P. and Ortali-Tarazi, R., 1996. BEY 009: l'immeuble de la Banco di Roma: nouveaux éléments pour l'étude de forum de Béryte. *BAAL (Bulletin d'Archéologie et d'Architecture Libanaises)* 1: 148-175.

Martin, C., 1994. Horizon 2000. *New Internationalist* 258. http://live.newint.org/issue258/smart.htm. Date accessed 01/12/06.

Mason, R. and Avrami, E., 2002. Heritage values and challenges of conservation planning. In J.M. Teutonico and G. Palumbo (eds), *Management Planning for Archaeological Sites: an international workshop organized by the Getty Conservation Institute and Loyola Marymount University 19-22 May 2000, Corinth, Greece.* 13-26. Los Angeles: The Getty Conservation Institute.

McManamon, F. P., and Hatton, A. (eds), 2000. *Cultural Resource Management in Contemporary Society: perspectives on managing and presenting the past.* London: Routledge.

Merriman, N., 2002. Archaeological heritage and interpretation. In B. Cunliffe, W. Davies and C. Renfrew (eds), *Archaeology: the widening debate.* 540-566. Oxford: Oxford University

Press.

Meskell, L. (ed.), 1998. *Archaeology under Fire: nationalism, politics and heritage in the Eastern Mediterranean and Middle East.* London and New York: Routledge.

Meskell, L. (ed.), 1998. Introduction: Archaeology matters. *Archaeology under Fire: nationalism, politics and heritage in the Eastern Mediterranean and Middle East.* 1-12. London and New York: Routledge.

Milne, G., 1995. *Roman London.* London: B.T. Batsford/English Heritage.

Milne, G., 1997. *St Bride's Church London: archaeological research 1952-1960 and 1992-5.* London: English Heritage.

Milne, G., 2002. *Excavations at Medieval Cripplegate, London: archaeology after the Blitz, 1946-68.* London: English Heritage.

Ministere de Culture et L'Enseignement Superieur 2006. Règles Générales des Antiquités: Loi publiée par décret Décret No. 166/L.R. (7 novembre 1933). http://audit2.clio.it/legaldocs/liban/web/1.%20Loi%20N%C2%B0166-1933%20R%C3%A9gles%20g%C3%A9n%C3%A9rales%20des%20Antiquit%C3%A9s.html. Date accessed 10/12/06.

Mobassaleh, Z., 2000. Winning Design Not Applauded By All. *Daily Star,* 21st March, 2000.

MoMA, 2005. Groundswell: Constructing the Contemporary Landscape. Exhibition at the Museum of Modern Art, New York, February 25 - May 16, 2005. http://www.moma.org/about_moma/press/2005/Groundswell_Release.pdf. Date accessed 10/01/07.

Moneo, R., 1998. The Souks of Beirut. In P. Rowe and H. Sarkis (eds), *Projecting Beirut: episodes in the construction and reconstruction of a modern city.* 263-273. Munich, London, New York: Prestal.

Mongne, P., 1996. BEY 008 bis Zone des Souks: degégement du fossé médiéval. *BAAL (Bulletin d'Archéologie et d'Architecture Libanaises)* 1: 270-293.

Morris, C., 1981. Townscape images: a study in meaning. In R. Kain (ed.), *Planning for conservation,* 259-288. London: Mansell.

Moseley, H., nd [1998]. Archaeology and development. In M. Corfield *et al* (eds), *Preserving Archaeological Remains in Situ: proceedings of the conference of 1st-3rd April 1996.* 47-50. London: Museum of London Archaeology Service.

Mumford, L., 1940. *The Culture of Cities.* First edition 1938. London: Secker and Worburg.

Mumford, L., 1961. *The City in History: its origins, its transformations, and its prospects.* London: Secker and Warburg.

Muñoz Viñas, S. 2005. *Contemporary Theory of Conservation.* Oxford: Elsevier Butterworth-Heinemann.

Naccache, A.F.H., 1998. Beirut's memorycide: hear no evil, see no evil. In L. Meskell (ed.), *Archaeology Under Fire: nationalism, politics and heritage in the Eastern Mediterranean and Middle East.* 140-158. London and New York: Routledge.

Nagel, C., 2002. Reconstructing space, re-creating memory: sectarian politics and urban development in post-war Beirut. *Political Geography* 21: 717-725.

Navrud, S. and Ready, R. C. (eds), 2002a. Why value cultural heritage? In S. Navrud and R. C. Ready (eds), *Valuing Cultural Heritage: applying environmental valuation techniques to historic buildings, monuments and artefacts.* 3-9. Cheltenham, UK: Edward Elgar Publishing Ltd.

Navrud, S. and Ready, R. C. (eds), 2002b. Methods for valuing cultural heritage. In S. Navrud and R. C. Ready (eds), *Valuing Cultural Heritage: applying environmental valuation techniques to historic buildings, monuments and artefacts.* 10-27. Cheltenham, UK: Edward Elgar Publishing Ltd.

Neill, W.J., 2004. *Urban Planning and Cultural Identity.* London and New York: Routledge.

Nixon, T., n.d. [1998]. Practically preserved: observations on the impact of construction on urban archaeological deposits. In M. Corfield *et al* (eds), *Preserving Archaeological Remains in Situ: proceedings of the conference of 1st-3rd April 1996.* 39-46. London: Museum of London Archaeology Service.

Nixon, T. (ed.), 2004. *Preserving Archaeological Remains in situ? Proceedings of the 2nd conference 12-14th September 2001.* London: Museum of London Archaeological Service.

O'Dochartaigh, P., 2004. *Germany Since 1945.* Basingstoke: Palgrave Macmillan.

Okamura, K., 2000. Conflict between preservation and development in Japan. In F.P. McManamon and A. Hatton (eds), *Cultural Resource Management in Contemporary Society: perspectives on managing and presenting the past.* 55-65. London and New York: Routledge.

Ortali-Tarazi, R., 1998-99. Fouilles Archéologiques du Centre-ville de Beyrouth 1996-1999. *BAAL (Bulletin d'Archéologie et d'Architecture Libanaises)* 3: 9-12.

Ortali-Tarazi, R., 2001-02. Loi et pratique dans la conservation du patrimoine culturel: le case des fouilles archéologiques dans le centre-ville de Beyrouth. *ARAM Periodical* 13-14: 355-358.

Palumbo, G., 2002. Threats and challenges to the archaeological heritage in the Mediterranean. In J.M. Teutonico and G. Palumbo (eds), *Management Planning for Archaeological Sites: an international workshop organized by the Getty Conservation Institute and Loyola Marymount University 19-22 May 2000, Corinth, Greece.* 3-12. Los Angeles: The Getty Conservation Institute.

Parnell, G., 1993. *The Tower of London.* London: English Heritage.

Paul, J. 1990. Reconstruction of the city centre of Dresden: planning and building during the 1950s. In J.M. Diefendorf (ed.), *Rebuilding Europe's Bombed Cities.* 170-189. London: Macmillan.

Peltz, L., 1999. Aestheticizing the Ancestral City: antiquarianism, topography and the representation of London in the long eighteenth century, 6-28. In D. Arnold (ed.), *The Metropolis and its Image: constructing identities for London, c.1750-1950.* Oxford: Blackwell Publishers.

Perring, D., 1999. Excavations in the Souks area of Beirut: an introduction to the work of the Anglo-Lebanese team and summary report. *Berytus* 43 (1997-98): 9-34.

Perring, D., Seeden, H., Sheehan, P. and Williams, T., 1996. BEY 006, 1994-1995: The Souks Area: interim report of the AUB project. *BAAL (Bulletin d'Archéologie et d'Architecture Libanaises)* 1: 176-206.

Perring, D., Thorpe, R., and Williams, T. 2006. The Beirut Souks Excavations. *Berytus* 48-49 (2004-2005): 8-26.

Planel, P., 1994. Privacy and community through medieval material culture. *In P.G Stone and B.L. Molyneaux (eds), The Presented Past: heritage, museums and education.* 206-215. London and New York: Routledge.

Porter, R., 2000. *London: a social history.* First edition 1994. London: Penguin Books.

Presner, T.S., 2001. Travelling between Delos and Berlin: Heidegger and Celan on the Topography of "What Remains". *The German Quarterly* 24 (4), 417-429.

Pugh-Smith, J., Sermon, R. and Williamson-Taylor, A., 2004. Archaeology and urban regeneration: lessons from Blackfriars multiplex, Gloucester. In T. Nixon (ed.), *Preserving Archaeological Remains in situ? Proceedings of the 2nd conference 12-14th September 2001.* 143-149. London: Museum of London Archaeological Service.

Purdom, C.B., 1946. *How Should We Rebuild London.* First edition 1945. London: J.M. Dent and Sons Ltd.

Raymond, A., 1994. Islamic City, Arab City: Orientalist myths and recent views. *British Journal of Middle Eastern Studies* 21 (1): 3-18.

Reader, J., 2004. *Cities.* London: William Heinemann.

Riegl, A., 1996. The Modern Cult of Monuments: its essence and its development. In N. Stanley-Price, M. Kirby Talley Jr, A. Melucco Vaccaro (eds), *Historical and Philosophical Issues in the Conservation of Cultural Heritage.* 69-83. Los Angeles: The Getty Conservation Institute.

Rowe, P. and Sarkis, H. (eds), 1998. Introduction: projecting Beirut. *Projecting Beirut: episodes in the construction and reconstruction of a modern city.* 9-18. Munich, London, New York: Prestal.

Royal Commission on Historical Monuments, 1928. *An Inventory on the Historical Monuments in London: Volume III: Roman London.* London: RCHM.

Rürup, R., 2003. *Topography of Terror: Gestapo, SS and Reichssicherheitshauptamt on the "Prinz-Albrecht-Terrain": A Documentation.* Berlin: Verlag Willmuth Arenhövel. First English edition 1989; this edition thirteenth.

Rykwert, J., 2000. *The Seduction of Place: the history and future of the city.* Oxford: Oxford University Press.

Rylatt, M., 1977. *City of Coventry: archaeology and development.* Coventry: Coventry Museums.

Sader, H., 1997. Liban: patrimoine en péril. *Travaux et Jours* 60: 159-168.

Sader, H., 1998. Ancient Beirut: urban growth in the light of recent excavations. In P. Rowe and H. Sarkis (eds), *Projecting Beirut: episodes in the construction and reconstruction of a modern city.* 23-38. Munich, London, New York: Prestal.

Sader, H., 2001. Lebanon's Heritage: will the past be part of the future? In A. Neuwirth and P. Pflitsch (eds) *Crisis and Memory in Islamic Societies.* 217-230. Beirut: Ergon Verlag Würzburg in Kommission.

Saghieh-Beydoun, M., 'Allam, M., 'Ala' Eddine, A., Abulhosn, B., 1998-99. BEY 004: the monumental street 'Cardo Maximus' and the replanning of Roman Berytus. *BAAL (Bulletin d'Archéologie et d'Architecture Libanaises)* 3: 95-126.

Said, E., 2003. *Orientalism* London: Penguin. First edition 1978; this fifth edition.

Saidah, R., 1967. Chronique. *Bulletin du Musée de Beyrouth* 20: 155-180.

Salam, A., 1998. The role of government in shaping the built environment. In P. Rowe and H. Sarkis (eds), *Projecting Beirut: episodes in the construction and reconstruction of a modern city.* 122-133. Munich, London, New York: Prestal.

Saliba, R., 2003. *Beirut City Center Recovery: the Foch-Allenby and Etoile Conservationa Area.* Göttingen: Steidl.

Salibi, K., 1988. *A House of Many Mansions: the history of Lebanon reconsidered.* London and New York: I.B. Tauris & Co. Ltd.

Sandercock, L., 1998. The death of modernist planning: radical praxis for a postmodern age. In M. Douglass and J. Friedmann (eds.), *Cities for Citizens: planning and the rise of civil society in a global age.* 163-184. Chichester: John Wiley and Sons Ltd.

Sandes, C.A. 2008. St Alphage's Tower, Cripplegate: monument to tenacity. *London Archaeologist* Autumn 2008 12 (2), 35-39.

Sandes, C.A. forthcoming. 'Null and Void: the Palace of the Republic, Berlin'. In *Studies in Contemporary and Historical Archaeology: Contemporary and Historical Archaeology in Theory: Papers from the 2008 CHAT Conference.* Oxford: British Archaeological

Reports.

Sarkis, H., 1993. Territorial Claims: architecture and post-war attitudes toward the built environment. In S. Khalaf and P.S. Khoury (eds) *Recovering Beirut: urban design and post-war reconstruction.* 101-127. Leiden, New York, Koln: E.J. Brill.

Sarkis, H., 2005. A Vital Void: reconstructions of downtown Beirut. In L.J. Vale and T.J. Campanella (eds.), *The Resilient City: how modern cities recover from disaster.* 281-298. Oxford: Oxford University Press.

Save Tara, 2007. Campaign to Save Tara. www.savetara.com. Date accessed 28/07/07.

Sayegh, H., 1996. BEY 010 les Souks, secteur nord/est. *BAAL (Bulletin d'Archéologie et d'Architecture Libanaises)* 1:235-269.

Schildt, A., 2002. Urban reconstruction and urban development in Germany after 1945. In F. Lenger (ed.), *Towards an Urban Nation: Germany since 1780.* 141-162. Oxford & New York: Berg.

Schimid, H. 2006. Privatized urbanity or a politicized society? Reconstruction in Beirut after the Civil War. *European Planning Studies* 14 (3): 365-381.

Schofield, J., 1992. Recommendations concerning the future management of the archaeology of Beirut. Unpublished report.

Schofield, J., 1994. Report of mission to co-ordinate archaeological work on the centre-ville Beirut Project (17th September – 27th September 1993). UNESCO, unpublished report.

Schofield, J. & Lea, R., 2005. *Holy Trinity Priory, Aldgate, City of London: an archaeological reconstruction and history.* London: Museum of London Archaeology Service.

Schulte-Peevers, A., 2004. *Lonely Planet: Berlin.* Melbourne: Lonely Planet Publications.

Seeden, H., 1990. Search for the missing link: archaeology and the public in Lebanon. In P. Gathercole and D. Lowenthal, (eds), *The Politics of the Past.* 141-159. London: Unwin Hyman.

Seeden, H., 1993. Lebanon's Archaeological Heritage *The Beirut Review* 5, www.lcps-lebanon.org/pub/breview/br5/seedenbr5.html. Date accessed 02/04/05.

Seeden, H., 1995. *Urban Archaeology '94.* Beirut: Solidere (booklet).

Seeden, H., 2000. Lebanon's archaeological heritage on trial in Beirut: what future for Beirut's past? In F.P. McManamon and A. Hatton (eds), *Cultural Resource Management in Contemporary Society: perspectives on managing and presenting the past.* 168-187. London and New York: Routledge.

Senate Department of Urban Development in Berlin http://www.stadtentwicklung.berlin.de/index_en.shtml. Last accessed 3/09/07.

Sennett, R., 1992. *The Conscience of the Eye: the design and social life of cities.* First edition 1990. New York and London: Norton & Company.

Serageldin, M., 2000. Preserving the historic urban fabric in a context of fast-paced change. In E. Avrami, R. Mason, M. de la Torre (eds), *Values and Heritage Conservation: research report.* 51-58. Los Angeles: The Getty Institute.

Sheldon, H. and Haynes, I., 2000. Introduction: Twenty-five years of London archaeology. In I. Haynes, H. Sheldon and L. Hannigan (eds) *London Under Ground: the archaeology of a city.* Oxford: Oxbow Publishers.

Shepherd, J., 1998. *The Temple of Mithras,* London. London: English Heritage.

Silberman, N.A., 1991. Desolation and Restoration: the impact of a Biblical concept on Near Eastern archaeology. *The Biblical Archaeologist* 54 (2): 76-87.

Simmel, G., 1959. The Ruin. In K.H. Wolff (ed.) *Georg Simmel, 1858-1918: a collection of essays with translations and a bibliography.* 259-266. Columbus: Ohio State University Press.

Smith, L., 1994. Heritage management as postprocessual archaeology? *Antiquity* 68, 300-309.

Solidere, 2000. Unpublished brochure: Hadiquat as-Samah (The Garden of Forgiveness): Profiles: Jury and Competitors.

Solidere, 2005a. http://www.solidere.com/thecity/romgard.html. Date accessed 05/02/07.

Solidere, 2005b. http://www.solidere.workwebsite.net/garden/. Date accessed 25/01/07.

Solidere, 2005c. http://www.beirutmartyrssquare.com. Date accessed 01/02/07.

Solidere, 2006. http://www.solidere.com/souks2/BeirutSouks.swf. Date accessed 05/02/07.

Stangl, P., 2006. Restoring Berlin's Unter den Linden: ideology, world view, place and space. *Journal of Historical Geography* 32 (2), 352-376.

Stanley-Price, N.P. (ed.), 1995. *Conservation on Archaeological Excavations.* First edition 1984. Rome: ICCROM.

Stanley-Price, N. (ed.), 2007. *Cultural Heritage in Postwar Recovery.* Rome: ICCROM Conservation Studies 6.

Stanley-Price, N., Kirby Talley Jr, M. and Melucco Vaccaro, A. (eds), 1996. *Historical and Philosophical Issues in the Conservation of Cultural Heritage.* Los Angeles: Getty Conservation Institute.

Starling, N.J., 1985. Reviews: Hermann Behrens: Die Ur- und Frühgeschichtswissenschaft in der DDR von 1945-1980: miterlebte und mitverantwortete Forschungsgeschichte. Arbeiten zur Urgeschichte des Menschen 9. Frankfurt am Main: Verlag Peter Lang, 1984. *Antiquity* 59, 229-230.

Steinberg, F., 1996. Conservation and rehabilitation of urban heritage in developing countries. *Habitat International* 20(3): 463-475.

Stewart, D., 1996. Economic Recovery and Reconstruction in Postwar Beirut. *Geographical*

Review 86 (4): 487-504.

Stimmann, H., 1995. New Berlin Office and Commercial Buildings. In A. Burg, *Downtown Berlin: building the metropolitan mix.* 6-23. Berlin, Basel, Boston: Birkhäuser Verlag.

Strom, E.A., 2001. *Building the New Berlin: the politics of urban development in Germany's capital city.* Lanham, Maryland and Oxford: Lexington Books.

Stubbs, J.H., 1995. Protection and presentation of excavated structures. In N.P. Stanley-Price (ed.), *Conservation on Archaeological Excavations.* 73-90. First edition 1984. Rome: ICCROM.

Tabet, J., 1993. Towards a master plan for post-war Lebanon. In S. Khalaf and P.S. Khoury (eds) *Recovering Beirut: urban design and post-war reconstruction.* 81-100. Leiden, New York, Koln: E.J. Brill.

Tahan, L., 2006. Towards an authentic museum representation: promoting a 'culture of contact' and reconciliation in Lebanese society'. Stanford Archaeology Centre 'Culture of Contact' Conference, February 2006. http://metamedia.stanford.edu:3455/CulturesofContact/135. Date accessed 12/06/07.

Tate Modern 2007. *Global Cities.* Exhibition Catalogue. London: Tate Modern.

Taylor, R., 1997. *Berlin and its Culture: a historical portrait.* New Haven and London: Yale University Press.

Teller, J. and Warnotte, A., 2003. Appear Position Paper 1: The enhancement of archaeological remains in an urban context. *http://www.in-situ.be/contrib_1_en.pdf;* last accessed 3/06/07.

Terry, J., 1905. On the Cripplegate Bastion of London Wall. *Trans London Middlesex Arch Soc* (NS) 1.4, 356-9.

Teutonico, J.M. and Palumbo, G. (eds), 2002. *Management Planning for Archaeological Sites: an international workshop organized by the Getty Conservation Institute and Loyola Marymount University 19-22 May 2000, Corinth, Greece.* Los Angeles: The Getty Conservation Institute.

Thabet, J. 1998. Arab Architectural Heritage: Between Mirrors and Idols. Looking within and beyond the tradition-modernity debate. *Al Jadid*: 4 (25).

Thomas, J., 2004. *Archaeology and Modernity.* London and New York: Routledge.

Thompson, M.V., 1981. *Ruins: their preservation and display.* London: British Museum Publications Ltd.

Thorpe, R., 1998-99a. BEY 007: The Souks Area: preliminary report of the AUB/ACRE Project. *BAAL (Bulletin d'Archéologie et d'Architecture Libanaises)* 3: 31-55.

Thorpe, R., 1998-99b. BEY 045: Preliminary report on the excavations. *BAAL (Bulletin d'Archéologie et d'Architecture Libanaises)* 3: 57-83.

Times, The, 1960. *St. Paul's in War and Peace: 1939-1958.* London: The Times.

Trad, A., 2005. Legacy of Modern Architecture in Beirut, 1950-1975. http://worldviewcities.org/beirut/legacy.html. Date accessed 25/11/06.

Trawi, A., n.d. [c.2003]. *Beirut's Memory.* Beirut: A Print s.a.r.l.

UN General Assembly 1993. Special Programme of Economic Assistance: Assistance for the reconstruction and development of Lebanon (A/48/453; 6th October 1993). http://domino.un.org/UNISPAL.NSF/9a798adbf322aff38525617b006d88d7/a65038c246fd487b85256af5006ec1ee!OpenDocument. Date accessed 16/01/07.

UNESCO, 1956. *Recommendation on International Principles Applicable to Archaeological Excavations.* New Delhi: UNESCO.

UNFPA, 2007. *State of World Population Report* http://www.unfpa.org/swp/2007/presskit/pdf/sowp2007_eng.pdf. Date accessed 03/09/07.

Verdeil, E., 2005. Plans for an unplanned city: Beirut (1950-2000) http://worldviewcities.org/beirut/urban.html. Date accessed 25/11/06.

von Beyme K., 1990. Reconstruction in the German Democratic Republic. In J.M. Diefendorf (ed.), *Rebuilding Europe's Bombed Cities.* 190-208. London: Macmillan.

von Beyme, K., 1991. Architecture and Democracy in the Federal Republic of Germany. *International Political Science Review,* 12 (2): 137-147.

Waller, M., 2004. *London 1945 Life in the Debris of War.* London: John Murray.

Ward, W.A., 1994. Archaeology in Lebanon in the Twentieth Century *The Biblical Archaeologist* 57(2): 66-85.

Will, E., 1992. Nouvelles Archéologiques: vers de nouvelles fouilles à Beyrouth *Syria: revue d'art orientale de d'archéologie* 69: 221-225.

Wilson-Goldie, K., 2005. Laying down roots in Beirut's Garden of Forgiveness. *Daily Star,* November 11, 2005. http://www.dailystar.com.lb/article.asp?article_ID=19954&categ_ID=1&edition_id=1#. Date accessed 11/11/05.

Wilson-Goldie, K., 2006. Wrecking ball awaits Downtown Beirut landmark *Daily Star,* December 12th 2006. http://www.dailystar.com.lb/article.asp?edition_id=1&categ_id=4&article_id=76214. Date accessed 11/12/06.

Wiwjorra, I., 1996. German archaeology and its relation to nationalism and racism. In M. Díaz-Andreu and T. Champion (eds), *Nationalism and archaeology in Europe.* 164-188. London: UCL Press Ltd.

Wolfram, S., 2000. 'Vorsprung durch Technik' or 'Kossinna syndrome'? Archaeological theory and social context in post-war West Germany. In H. Härke (ed.), *Archaeology, Ideology and Society: the German experience.* 180-201. Frankfurt am Main: Peter Lang GmbH.

Woodward, C., 2001. *In Ruins.* London: Chatto and

Windus.

Zancheti, S.M. and Jokilehto, J., 1997. Values and urban conservation planning: some reflections on principles and definitions. *Journal of Architectural Conservation.* 3(1), 37-51.

www.ingramcontent.com/pod-product-compliance
Lightning Source LLC
Chambersburg PA
CBHW041705290426

44108CB00027B/2860